CONCORDIA UNIVERSITY

3 4211 00122

W9-DCU-596

The Student Teacher's Handbook
Third Edition

The Student Teacher's Handbook
Third Edition

Andrew I. Schwebel
The Ohio State University

Bernice L. Schwebel
Douglass College of Rutgers University, Retired

Carol R. Schwebel
Columbus, Ohio, Public School System

Milton Schwebel
Rutgers University

KLINCK MEMORIAL LIBRARY
Concordia University
River Forest, IL 60305-1499

 LAWRENCE ERLBAUM ASSOCIATES, PUBLISHERS
1996 Mahwah, New Jersey

Copyright © 1996 by Lawrence Erlbaum Associates, Inc.
All rights reserved. No part of this book may be repro-
duced in any form, by photostat, microform, retrieval
system, or any other means, without the prior written
permission of the publisher.

Lawrence Erlbaum Associates, Inc., Publishers
10 Industrial Avenue
Mahwah, New Jersey 07430

Library of Congress Cataloging-in-Publication Data

The student teacher's handbook / Andrew Schwebel . . . [et
al.]. — 3rd ed.
          p.   cm.
    Includes bibliographical references (p. 255–259) and
index.
    ISBN 0-8058-2129-5 (cloth : alk. paper). — ISBN
0-8058-2130-9 (pbk. : alk. paper)
    1. Student teaching—Handbooks, manuals, etc.
I. Schwebel, Andrew I.
LB2157.A3S9 1996
370'.7'33—dc20

                                          96-16462
                                          CIP

Books published by Lawrence Erlbaum Associates are printed
on acid-free paper, and their bindings are chosen for strength
and durability.

Printed in the United States of America
10 9 8 7 6 5 4 3 2 1

CONTENTS

Preface

We wrote this third edition because of the changes that have taken place in education, psychology, and our society at large in recent years. These changes are very much related to student teaching and to teaching in general. In updating the book, we were influenced by the helpful recommendations we received from the many college/university supervisors and student teachers who used the last edition.

This edition, like the earlier ones, was written for student teachers. It is designed to be practical and useful, especially during the weeks of student–teaching assignment, but also throughout the early years of teaching.

We are aware that there is no substitute for the instruction, advice, and counsel that student teachers obtain from their college/university supervisor. The personal/professional relationship with one's supervisor cannot be duplicated or replaced by a book. The book can only supplement, and perhaps maximize, the potential of that relationship.

Over the years, student teachers have told us what the student–teaching assignment meant to them: excitement and challenge, concern and anxiety. They shared that information with us in personal conversations, in their written journals, and during discussions in student–teaching seminars. What they shared forms the heart of the book. In essence, they reported to us that they were experiencing the normal and typical human reactions to a brand new undertaking.

This book is about those reactions and how best to cope with them. It is about how to successfully confront the exciting new challenges, and turn the concerns and anxieties into the experience of personal and professional growth. It is also about new ideas concerning classroom management and discipline, cooperative learning, legal issues, special-needs students and mainstreaming, multicultural education and sensitivity to ethnic, gender and racial issues, relating to cooperating teachers, working collaboratively with parents, and other topics.

We wrote this book as experienced professionals sharing ideas with those entering our profession. We visualized the very real challenges student teachers face and the down-to-earth solutions they need.

When possible, we were simple and direct in our analyses and recommendations. But sometimes the problems teachers face are complicated and without easy solutions. This reality is one factor that makes teaching both interesting and challenging.

We took additional steps to make this edition user-friendly. Major topics are highlighted at the beginning of each chapter and critical issues are raised as questions at the end of each chapter. Those additions, and other modifications of the text, make this edition's principles and practices easier for readers to apply.

ACKNOWLEDGMENTS

This book has been a cooperative venture in more than just its multiple authorship. We could not have undertaken it without the benefit of what we learned from our many students over the years. Of special importance are the journals that our student teachers so generously shared with us. We are deeply indebted to them.

We wish to thank Linda Kozusko of the English Department at Rutgers University for her perceptive observations and graphic descriptions of teachers at work, which we incorporated in the book.

We are also indebted to the many educators who generously shared their thoughts with us and, especially, the following three whose constructive advice enabled us to enrich the content of this book immeasurably: Dr. Frances Cagnassola, a teacher in the Newark, New Jersey school system; Professor James Raths, University of Delaware; and Professor Richard Wisniewski, Dean of the College of Education, University of Tennessee.

Collectively, we have benefited over the years from interactions with colleagues in the northeast, the south, the midwest, and the far west of the United States, as well as in Canada, Mexico, Great Britain, India, and other locations.

We have profited enormously from the support of our publisher, Lawrence Erlbaum, his senior associates Judy Amsel and Joe Petrowski, and on a day-to-day basis from Sharon Levy, Promotion Director, Amy Olener, Editorial Assistant, Marcy Pruiksma, Book Production Editor, and Naomi Silverman, Acquisitions Editor.

Finally, our thanks go to family members: Ruth Lubinsky for freeing the authors to complete the first edition by lovingly tending two young children; David Schwebel for typing and indexing the second edition; Sara Schwebel for indexing the third edition; and Dr. Robert Schwebel, another educator, for raising challenging questions that helped keep us close to the grindstone of reality.

Andrew I. Schwebel
Bernice L. Schwebel
Carol R. Schwebel
Milton Schwebel

*We dedicate this book to the memory of Andy,
our beloved co-author.*

PART I

Beginnings

1

Introduction: On Being a Student Teacher

Our aim in this book is to help you make the student-teaching experience a rich and successful one. When deciding what to include from the vast literature on education, teaching, and learning, we examined studies in which student teachers reported their concerns. We also reviewed journal entries of our own student teachers, and we drew on our own experiences as student teachers, teachers, cooperating teachers, and university supervisors.

SOME KEYS TO SUCCESS

Student teachers say they know they are taking on a responsible job. They feel the pressure of having to teach 20 to 30 students in elementary school, 100+ students in middle and high school, to do it well, and especially to do it in the presence of the cooperating teacher and the college/university supervisor. They have to contend with the pressure.

Our experience suggests that the student teacher's comfort on the job is one of the keys to success. By "comfort" we mean that the individual is able to manage the inevitable worries and stresses and to enjoy the challenges of preparing for and teaching the class. We give much attention both to those worries and stresses to help you manage them, and to help you gain maximum learning and fulfillment from your experience.

Other keys to success are planning, preparation, and problem-solving. Still others are understanding and accommodating the diverse students in your classes. We give much attention to those and many other topics.

Among these topics is another of vital importance to the student teacher, namely, relationships. If student teaching had to be characterized by one word, relationships could well be that word. As student teacher, you will be developing relationships with a supervisor, a cooperating teacher, students, and, to a lesser degree, a principal, other teachers, parents, office workers, and custodians. Your success is going to depend on the quality of the relationships you build, especially with your supervisor, cooperating teacher, and students.

THE STUDENT TEACHER AS APPRENTICE

In the field of education, the experience of student teaching is unique. That uniqueness is due in particular to the relationship you form with the cooperating teacher, truly an apprenticeship one. It is the only time in a teaching career that one is an apprentice under the close guidance of an experienced mentor.

For many centuries, beginning during the medieval period of history, young people were trained for work through practical experience. For skilled or professional occupations, learning took place through the relationship between masters and apprentices. The masters were expert in one of the arts, crafts, or trades of their time (a barrister or cobbler, a miller or stone mason), and the apprentices served as assistants for various lengths of time. The apprentices learned by observing the master, by engaging in the activities of the calling, first in small then in larger ways, and finally, under the close scrutiny of the masters, by doing a complete product on their own.

In the process of learning to use the tools and materials of the occupation, the apprentices also acquired the special language of the field, adopted the habits and specialized garments, and absorbed the general mode of thought of fellow craftsmen.

In all, the apprentices became trained (acquired knowledge and skills) and socialized (acquired the language and habits) in preparation for a lifetime's work in the occupation. They also learned to do more than imitate their master: They were free to be creative within their specialty.

The 10, 15, or 20 weeks of your student teaching will have almost exact counterparts to the medieval apprenticeship system. One of its purposes is to help you become socialized into the teaching profession: Through student teaching, you go beyond your textbooks. You observe and you, yourself, experience how real-life teachers behave in class, in schools, and in their relationships with students, other teachers, the principal, and parents.

Also, as the apprentice, you will be working with an experienced teacher. Under his or her scrutiny, you will use the tools and materials of your new trade. Guided by the cooperating teacher, you will move to ever more challenging teaching experiences, first in small ways with individual students and, later, in larger ways with groups of students and with the class as a whole. When this time comes, you will probably find that although the courses and fieldwork that preceded student teaching helped ready you for it, the teaching experience itself caps and gives fullest meaning to all your previous education.

CONCENTRATING ON *YOUR* NEEDS

The weeks of student teaching offer unusual learning opportunities, and you will want to get the maximum possible yield from them. For this reason you should concentrate on yourself during this period—on developing a large variety of skills (e.g., communication, relationship, assessment), and on gaining confidence in leading a class of students.

It may be easier to keep in mind the need to give your professional growth top priority if you remind yourself of your reasons for choosing the teaching profession. Were you attracted by the way of life, by the opportunity to work with children or adolescents, by the time given to reading and study, by the doors it opens to serve other people, or by the work schedule? Recalling your goals will give you a clearer perspective on your priorities.

The long hours involved in your commitment during student teaching may interfere with your personal life. If so, remind yourself of the limited time frame and the satisfaction you will have when the training is over. If you have a spouse or a dating partner who expresses concern about your restricted time schedule, explain that the student-teaching assignment is short in duration yet great in its long-term career significance.

Concerns

It is perfectly understandable that you should have some concerns. The student teacher's position is a demanding one: A novice, still a student, enters a new setting to use newly acquired skills under the watchful eye of experienced professionals. It is not easy, yet most students meet the challenge successfully.

Furthermore, teaching is a high-pressure occupation. At the elementary level, teachers share 6 hours a day, 5 days a week, 40 weeks a year with some 20 to 30 children. At the middle school or junior high school level, teachers contend with more students, who are facing major transitions: rapidly maturing minds and bodies, greater social assertiveness (they speak up more), and the rainbow of emotions expressed by individuals in the throes of peer pressure.

At the high school level, teachers experience continual turnover of students during the course of the day. That means getting acquainted with 100 or more adolescents, all of whom are going through the personal and social changes of pre-adulthood. It also means managing a sizeable number of classes of young people who are at the peak of activity and energy. Some of them will be intellectually curious and excited by what their teachers offer. Others may be unwilling students, simply waiting for the chance to legally end their formal schooling. Still others, although willing students, are drained by the pressure of after-school jobs they hold to help their families financially, or to earn money for cars, clothes, and entertainment.

As if that were not enough to make teaching a high-pressured career, during a typical school year a teacher could be confronted with problems that ordinarily are in the province of psychologists, psychiatrists, counselors, social workers, hearing and speech specialists, and the juvenile division of the police department.

Many student teachers wonder whether they will be prepared to deal with all the issues and questions that they will encounter in their subject fields. Also, they ask, "Will I be able to manage the class? Will I be able to plan and conduct high quality lessons?" You may have occasional frightening thoughts that the class might get completely out of hand. You may sometimes become preoccupied with special problem cases, including the obviously disturbed child. Having these questions and thoughts is perfectly normal. You are moving forward into what, for you, is uncharted territory.

Then there are the worries related to the unique role of the apprentice: You work in the proverbial goldfish bowl, under the observant eyes of the cooperating teacher and the college supervisor. You know you will learn much from their observations. Will you get used to their presence?

Optimism

Hopefully, your answer to all these questions is a resounding "yes." Hopefully, you have an optimistic outlook on life, and you expect that, come what may in the form of problems, you will confront them as best you can. And if you cannot resolve them at first, you will not blame yourself, lose self-esteem, or become depressed.

In his book *Learned Optimism*, psychologist Martin Seligman (1991) tells us that optimists are not fazed by problems or setbacks. Unlike pessimists who think their misfortune will last a long time and is their own fault, optimists perceive setbacks as temporary and as challenges to try harder to succeed. The difference between the two habits of thought has substantial effects: Many studies show that optimists perform better in school and college, on the job, and at play. They tend to surpass predictions based on aptitude tests, and even their health is better.

Being optimistic in outlook, or acquiring that outlook through methods spelled out by Seligman, can be an advantage for you during your student teaching days and, in fact, for the rest of your life. As an optimist, you will probably regard the diversity of knowledge and skills required in teaching as a great attraction. And you will find that the daily challenges and the bits of the unpredictable that arise from time to time add spice to your working life.

HOW THIS BOOK CAN HELP YOU

We could go on telling about the enjoyment and growth you will experience in your profession. Instead, we have highlighted the demands and pressures of the job because those may be uppermost in your mind. We believe that right now you want help in solving problems you are likely to face and in acquiring skills you do not yet possess. We have written this book with that in mind.

The problems student teachers encounter result from myriad causes. Some problems student teachers unintentionally create for themselves. These may be a result of misjudgment due to inexperience, or of the anxiety that the novel experience of student teaching arouses in them. Some are the problems inherent in the day-to-day life of teaching. Others are peculiar to the special circumstances of being a student teacher, such as feeling inadequate as a result of comparing one's own work to that of the experienced cooperating teacher.

In this book we confront each of these types of problems. We show how they relate to the life of the student teacher, and we provide you with tools: the knowledge and problem-solving strategies that we think will help you contend with these difficulties.

In writing this book we had one objective: to develop material useful to you in making your student-teaching experience optimally rewarding. We have been guided by an orientation of realism. You will be doing your student teaching in the here and now. Your thoughts will be on effectively meeting the day-to-day demands of that job and also on finding a teaching position for next year. We have concentrated on those concerns. We have been straightforward about what you can do to prevent and avoid problems and how you can deal with those that cannot be circumvented. To accomplish this we drew on theory and research and on our practical experience as teachers and supervisors.

You will see that this book serves you in a very personal way. Our goal was to write it so that the pages would have the ring of real life about them. As you read the pages ahead, we think it will be most useful if you regard each one as if it were written especially for you. More specifically, consider the ways in which each idea or thought that is presented bears on your life in the classroom now. Although we expect that what we have written will be useful to you next year and perhaps beyond, our aim is to help you make your life as a student teacher easier and more successful today and tomorrow.

A final point: One of the most important objectives of education—yours and each of your students'—is to reach the point of being an independent thinker. Those free to think and solve problems for themselves have enormous control over their own lives and professional work. You can make much progress toward such independence during your apprenticeship. We believe this book can help you.

JOURNALS: FORMER STUDENT TEACHERS
SHARE THEIR EXPERIENCES

To help you to more fully understand and learn to cope with the real problems of student teaching, we have incorporated excerpts of many student teachers' journal entries. Some were written in the white heat of emotion, perhaps at the beginning of the student teachers' assignments when they were feeling frustrated, inept, or powerless; others, while they were burning with anger over a sense of having been treated unfairly, or close to panic about their difficulties in controlling the class; and still others, at moments of warm satisfaction over seeing progress in their students' work and of pride and confidence as they saw their skills developing.

The journal entries were written by student teachers to serve as aids to themselves. Although the entries were shared with supervisors, they were not graded. Instead, the supervisors wanted the journals to provide their students with opportunity to:

1. Recall, review, and reflect on their daily experiences.
2. Experience release from the emotions of the day.
3. Work at solving problems that they face.
4. Cope with relationship issues, with students or others.
5. Share thoughts and feelings with their supervisor.
6. Recognize and record their growth as professionals.
7. Look to their future as fully accredited teachers.

Dozens of journals were collected during several different academic years. Three states in the eastern and midwestern parts of the country are represented. The journals were written by men and women of diverse racial and ethnic groups who came from families of middle, upper middle, and working-class backgrounds. Although the journal authors ranged in age from 20 to 35, most were in their early 20s. Their assignments were at the preschool, elementary, junior (middle school), and senior high school levels, and their schools were located in urban (including inner-city), suburban, and rural neighborhoods.

The instructions given to students writing the journals quoted in this book were essentially those proposed for your use in chapter 2. They were asked to reflect on their classroom experiences each day and to write about them freely. They were to review events that went well and those that did not and to try to explain why the events turned out as they did. They were encouraged to express their feelings about the day and the people involved. They did—sometimes tearfully, sometimes joyfully, and sometimes with passionate anger. Their openness has made their documents valuable to themselves and to others.

The anonymity of the journal authors has been carefully safeguarded. Names of student teachers, cooperating teachers, college supervisors, and students are pseudonyms. The school names have also been changed, and no localities are identified.

In addition to the journals, we have drawn material from personal interviews with student teachers in several regions of the country. Again, pseudonyms are used and the interview excerpts are preceded by a date.

THE CONTENTS OF THIS BOOK

Part I of this book is devoted to *beginnings,* by which we mean the beginnings of your student-teaching experience. We place great stress on this early stage (and even the weeks before it) in order to help you prepare for early successes.

Two themes that are repeated often are developed at great length in chapter 2: The most effective way to deal with anxieties about new experiences is by preparing for them, and the best way to avoid teaching problems is by thoughtful preparation for the work to be performed. One of the features of chapter 2 is the elaboration of a problem-solving method that you will find useful in your student-teaching period and later as a teacher.

Part II is devoted to the *crucial relationships* of the student teacher. Your success depends on your relationships with the students, the cooperating teacher, and the college supervisor. In the chapters devoted to each of them (chapters 3, 4, and 5), we indicate how to go about building constructive relationships and how to cope with the kinds of problems that student teachers have repeatedly reported. Chapter 6 is about building relationships with parents, the school principal, and others who are important in school life.

Part III focuses on *diversity, curriculum, and classroom management*. Linkage of the three topics is deliberate, because the content of your lessons and their presentation play a big part in forging your students' classroom behavior. In other words, what and how you teach can foster student involvement and discourage disruptive behavior just as easily as it can fail to hold your learners' attention and, in this and other ways, lead to classroom disruption. The problems of classroom control and management are discussed in great detail because we expect, from countless experiences of student teachers, that these issues loom large in your mind.

Part IV addresses some of the *student teacher's special concerns*. These include concerns of "today," by which we mean those prevalent during student-teaching days. Then there are concerns of "tomorrow," such as the stress associated with the approaching end of your college career and the beginning of your preparations to assume a regular teaching position.

CRITICAL ISSUES

- What rewards am I expecting from student teaching?
- What personal resources—resources in me—can I call on to make my student-teaching experience a rich and rewarding one?
- How do I feel about the difficulties student teachers are likely to confront?
- How do I feel about being an apprentice?

2

Preparing For Student Teaching

TOPICS

- Expectations about your class
- Self-expectations
- Preparing for your assignment
- Becoming part of the school community
- Common concerns of student teachers
- The CONTROL-C method of problem solving
- Four stages to student-teaching success
     Stage 1: The early days
     Stage 2: Becoming a member of the teaching team
     Stage 3: Soloing as a teacher
     Stage 4: Feeling like a teacher
- Critical issues

"When I think about teaching my own classes, I'm excited, anxious, and a little scared. Especially I wonder if I can be a real teacher to them, someone they will accept as the equal of their own teacher. I also wonder if the teachers at the school will respect me." Those were James' feelings a few days before beginning his student teaching.

His feelings were normal. It is normal to feel some anxiety in anticipation of a new experience, especially when you are going to be observed and evaluated and when your career hinges on success. Do you remember other first experiences—the first date, the first time you drove a car, or, earlier yet, the first time you gave an oral report in class? Chances are you showed the normal human reaction of anxiety of one kind or another: "butterflies" in the stomach, a bit of sleeplessness, a lowered appetite or its opposite, overeating and some digestive problems, or a combination of these. And chances are, moments after the new experience got under way, your anxiety level dropped considerably.

That is what you can expect about the "firsts" that are coming up: when you first report as a student teacher, when you first lunch in the teachers' room, when you first take over the class for a lesson, when you first teach a whole day.

Anticipating a new experience is usually worse than the reality itself. Worry about failing can grow out of proportion, especially considering that most cooperating teachers will go to great lengths to help you develop as an independent teacher ready to take over the class on your own. The same is true for the college supervisor, who wants to see you through a successful teaching assignment. And the school principal wants that, too, if for no other reason than because your success means a smoother running school.

The students? They are children or adolescents, with all the feelings and problems and stresses that go with their stage in life. They expect and want you to behave like the adult you are. They do not want you to be one of them. Friendly, yes, but not their friend; understanding, yes, but not with the intimacy of a parent or peer; in other words, they want you to be the teacher, the adult who sees to it that they keep to the limits of behavior expected of them. They are not your opponents; on the contrary, most will be friendly to and supportive of the student teacher.

EXPECTATIONS ABOUT YOUR CLASS

"I'm happy when I think about taking over the class. But I guess I'm also apprehensive because I don't know what to expect. It's like the unknown," a student teacher shared with her seminar group.

"What are you apprehensive about?" she was asked.

"That's just the point," she replied. "I know that my fears are groundless. My cooperating teacher is friendly and decent, and she likes being helpful. But sometimes the kind of help she wants to give is not what I want. But that doesn't take away from her wish to be helpful! I don't know. I just don't know what I'm worried about."

When a stressful future experience has a lot of unknowns connected with it, we tend to fill in the unknowns with uncomfortable scenarios that, frequently and thankfully, are far from what actually develops. Here are examples taken from the reports of student teachers.

"I expected the school to be modern, the climate to be cold and impersonal, and the staff to be distant. How different it all turned out! There is a very warm, close atmosphere among the teachers. They made me feel very comfortable. As to my cooperating teacher, she is warm, helpful, cooperative and very understanding. I really enjoy working with her."

This student teacher, a bright young adult, had a bleak outlook about the important experience ahead of her. Fortunately, circumstances corrected her false expectations. Here is another student teacher.

"I thought most of the children would be from middle-class families and that the teacher would be an older woman and probably very set in her ways. As it turned out, the children are great; each is so special. Many of them stay full days because their mothers work. They are all friendly, and most are not the prima donnas I expected. There are 23 children in the class, all from very different backgrounds. The teacher turned out to be young, innovative, sensitive, very open to new ideas, and she's going to be fantastic to work with and learn from."

Not everyone is as pleased with the cooperating teacher and the children as these student teachers were, but hardly any of the worst expectations ever materialize.

The inaccurate expectations of the student teachers just quoted were corrected only after their student teaching got under way. One said, "I sure wasted a lot of energy and time with my worries. And I lost some sleep—not to mention peace of mind—needlessly. Oh well, now it's just water over the dam."

Of course, it does not have to be this way. A student teacher can test out some fantasies and fears. It is reassuring to visit the school to which you are assigned in advance of your starting date. It is better yet to see the classroom and, best of all, to meet your cooperating teacher and the students. "I visited my school back in October," wrote one student teacher, whose assignment started in February, "so I knew more or less what I could expect. The school I found was lovely and the room itself appeared to provide warmth and color and is conducive to learning. That's the way I found it when I started here a few weeks ago."

Often, an early visit serves as fine medicine to reduce anxiety, especially when the picture you get is both positive and inviting. It is true, of course, that early visits do not always reveal the kind of school or conditions that one would prefer. The school might turn out to be old and forbidding in appearance. Worse yet, the teacher might appear to be remote. Worst of all, the children might seem to be so different from yourself that you could be concerned about your capacity to understand and to cope with them.

Your early observations may be disappointing. Still, it is better to know the characteristics of your teaching assignment than to live with untested fantasies. All one can do with the unknown is toss and turn in bed over it. You can deal with the "known." You can prepare for it. Here is an account of a student teacher's expectations and the real life of the classroom that unfolded:

> 1/15: I expected the school to be an old one in a poor neighborhood, and so it was. I had been told it would be like that, so I expected everything that I thought goes with that: poor equipment and very little at that. I also thought it would be poorly organized and, hence, that minimal amounts of teaching would occur. Then, I expected the children would be wild whether in the classroom or on the playground. They would display minimal self-control, that is, a lot of battling, hitting, and teasing. The teacher, I figured, would always be screaming at the top of her lungs and reprimanding the children. You can imagine that I wasn't very happy about that and it surely didn't add to my confidence.

> As it turned out, this old building in a depressed area was very well organized and had many advantages (e.g., a breakfast and hot lunch program, a reading program, a library, and a good gymnasium). The children displayed a lot more self-control than I had expected. They are very verbal and use minimal physical aggression in the classroom. They are also learning self-discipline about finishing their work. The teacher is very firm and consistent with the children. She fosters independence in the children. Nonetheless, teaching here will be a difficult task, as the class is large and there are a lot of cultural gaps as well.

Your foundation courses probably stressed the need to understand the diversity among the students in a school. Chances are you learned the value of demographic information to aid in that understanding. Now is the time to use that knowledge—to find out in advance the composition of your class and to be familiar with the community around it.

Let us sum up. Anxiety in anticipation of a new experience is normal. Some of it is even desirable, to give us a bit of an "edge." More than a little of it, however, is a burden, and we should work to reduce it so that it does not interfere with our sleep, our appetite, or our personal life.

Reality testing, by getting useful information about your school and cooperating teacher, is the best antidote to worry about the unknown. One of the important realities of our pluralistic society is the diversity of our culture, including diversity in the use of language, in ways of relating, and in the values we hold. When you get acquainted with things that are unfamiliar, they can become as familiar as curry, chimichangas, or caviar. To borrow from the classic song, "Getting to know you" is what you need to do, and the best time to start doing that with your cooperating teacher and students is as soon as possible.

SELF-EXPECTATIONS

Have you ever asked yourself, "What do I expect to gain from my student teaching assignment?" What you expect depends partly, of course, on the standards you set for yourself and on your own concept of yourself as a person. Your expectations will also be shaped by other factors, such as the similarity of philosophy of teaching between you and your cooperating teacher, the class composition, and the atmosphere in the school and especially in the classroom.

Let us look at "teaching approach." Assume that your upbringing and your own experience in school have given you a preference for a highly structured mode of teaching. Now you are assigned a cooperating teacher who is generally permissive and loosely structured in class organization. Under these circumstances, you have a right to expect more stress than if your approaches were similar.

You may have difficulty in adapting to the unaccustomed behavior. Yet the experience could turn out to be an enriching one. You may find that incorporating some permissiveness makes your teaching more effective. The same expectation is appropriate in the opposite situation; that is, if you are permissive and the cooperating teacher is highly structured.

Let us look at the second of the three factors that should have a bearing on the expectations you set, the class composition. It is unrealistic to expect all classes to perform in the same way. If you are assigned to a large class in an urban school and the students are behind grade level, it does not mean that you will not accomplish much; it does not mean that you will not be contributing much. Generally it means that your expectations should be in terms of progress and not in terms of level of performance achieved (e.g., grade levels).

One should, of course, set high standards in all professional work but not expect the impossible. In 10–15 weeks as a student teacher, one cannot expect to remedy years of poor school performance and lack of readiness for the grade or subject you are teaching. Moreover, it is not the student teacher's job to do so.

The last of the three factors, school and class atmosphere, cannot be ignored when you set your expectations. If there is tension in the school, a sense of distrust and perhaps quiet hostility among teachers or between teachers and administrators, the children will be affected. If tension is clearly present in the classroom, it will affect the behavior of the children. They will still learn, but probably at a diminished level. Under those circumstances, you adjust and do your best. But bear in mind that you, yourself, cannot control all the forces that determine what happens when you student teach.

PREPARING FOR YOUR ASSIGNMENT

We said earlier that visiting your assigned school and its surrounding area would probably reduce some of your concerns. The other reason for such a visit is that teachers have an advantage when they know the context in which they work and in which the children and their families live, work, and play. To obtain such information, investigate the neighborhood as systematically as possible before you begin your assignment. Your college supervisor can give you a start in obtaining useful information. Your cooperating teacher can help fill in the gaps.

One of us had the good fortune of taking a course in which a useful plan for studying the community was used. (This sociology of education course was taught by Patrick J. Kelley, then at New York University.) The following modified outline indicates the kinds of useful information that you can obtain to assist you in understanding your school's neighborhood and its people.

Exploration and Investigation of a Community

Get a map covering a radius of 10 blocks around the school in which you will be doing your student teaching, and obtain a neighborhood and/or local newspaper, if available.

Using the map and newspaper, plan a visit to the school's neighborhood. If you are assigned to a school in a high-crime area, inquire whether it is safe for you alone, or you and a friend, to walk in. If it is not safe to walk, try to arrange a visit by car. In either case, your aim is to make careful observations. If possible, speak to storekeepers, staff members in neighborhood agencies, community leaders, and people in restaurants, laundromats, and other public places.

Visit community agencies, such as public libraries, hospitals and clinics, human services agencies, police and fire stations, community organizations, and so forth. Speak with community leaders, official and unofficial.

Become acquainted with curriculum resources, such as factories and commercial enterprises; transportation facilities; museums and parks; churches, synagogues, mosques and other houses of worship.

Determine the representation of ethnic and socioeconomic groups in the neighborhood, based on available statistics (from agencies or census or from local college or university library), and on personal observation of street signs, restaurants, and languages spoken.

Note the characteristics of the neighborhood including evidences of problems (e.g., many boarded-up shop windows) and strengths (e.g., friendly interactions among people on the streets).

The information you obtain about ethnic and socioeconomic group representation and about the characteristics of the neighborhood is especially important to your teaching. It can help you understand the conditions under which your students live their daily lives.

The very meaning of education itself varies from social class to social class and from ethnic group to ethnic group. In many instances, a college education, which was obviously important to you, may not mean the same to your students. It may have less value because in the past it was generally unrealizable, or because a child from a family dependent for three generations on welfare support has had no opportunity to know its meaning.

To use another example, children of extremely high-income families are likely to hold a different perception of the importance of education from yours and ours. They do not worry about having a job and income after graduation. Their outlook on life and their experience of life are bound to be different from that of children of lesser means. No one socioeconomic or ethnic group is better than another, but members of each group may experience school, and even the lessons and homework you assign, differently.

BECOMING PART OF THE SCHOOL COMMUNITY

Over the decades the teaching profession has undergone considerable change in the direction of freedom to live one's private life as one prefers. When your grandparents were children, the practices were very different. In most school systems if a woman teacher married she lost her job. But that was not all. Teachers seen serving beer in their homes on a Saturday night found their contracts not renewed.

Those days are past. However, that does not mean that all of the public's social restrictions on teachers have been lifted. The proprieties in a school regarding such practices as speech or mode of dress are generally more conservative than on a college campus. Take dress as an example. Although there has been much change in teachers' attire since the early 1970s when, for instance, slacks were taboo for women in most districts, certain styles of dress are still considered inappropriate in a school building.

We would like to be helpful to you by being able to spell out what the "well dressed" student teacher wears today, but that is not possible. Although the loosening of dress requirements for teachers has its advantages, it poses the following question for you, much more than it did to your counterparts in years past: "What should I wear?"

Our recommendation is to note the dress of the faculty in the school to which you are assigned and, within the boundaries of your own taste, to dress as formally or informally as they as a group do. For your first visit, assuming that you know nothing about the dress codes of the school, you would be well advised to be conservative in your choice of attire.

COMMON CONCERNS OF STUDENT TEACHERS

One of the best prescriptions for mental health is to remind ourselves that we are not alone in our concerns. For that reason we dwell here on common concerns reported by student teachers.

Over a several-year period, candidates for student teaching in one department at the University of Georgia were surveyed about their concerns (Murwin & Matt, 1990). At the beginning of their course in methods and curriculum, and one quarter before their student teaching, they were asked to identify their 10 major concerns about student teaching (S. R. Matt, personal communication, February 21, 1991). The responses of 36 students showed that some or all of the following were very much on their minds:

- Discipline. Uncertain about what to expect . . . and how to handle it . . . and whether their ways of handling problems would meet with approval.
- Student Relations. Anxious that they might not get along with their students . . . might not be liked and respected . . . and that this outcome would develop for reasons over which they themselves might not have any control.
- Faculty Relations. Apprehensive about relations with teachers and winning their respect . . . troubled about what their relationship with the cooperating teacher would be like.
- Lesson Plans. Insecure about preparing adequate and acceptable lesson plans . . . not confident that their plans would be found to be satisfactory.
- Methods and Motivation. Troubled about their ability to motivate and hold their students' interest.
- Self-image. Unsure about their ability to match the expectations of the people who would make judgments about them.
- Materials and Supplies. Teachers in fields like technology, art, and music wondered if the necessary materials and supplies would be available and adequate in quantity and quality.

The students in this study seemed to be saying, "I don't know what to expect and how I'll handle it. Also, I'm not sure whether students and teachers will like what I do, and will like me. I hope I can live up to expectations."

An earlier study (Cohen, Mirels, & Schwebel, 1972), with 139 student teachers, took a different tack but showed some similar findings. The participating student teachers were given a 122-item questionnaire built to assess the common concerns of student teachers during their school assignment. The items covered the broadest possible range—from concerns about getting cooperation from the school's janitor to those about getting too personally involved with the students' problems. The student-teacher subjects were asked to rate each item indicating whether it caused: (a) *no concern*; (b) *slight concern*; (c) *moderate concern*; (d) *great concern*; (e) *such very great concern that it has led me to consider leaving the teaching profession.*

It is comforting to know that only 3 of the 122 items on the common concerns list aroused great concern or very great concern in 50% or more of the student teachers. These three were:

- Obtaining a good job placement after graduation (81%).
- Working with students who don't seem to care whether they learn or not (52%).
- Finding enough time to give adequate attention to each student (50%).

Not surprisingly, the first of the three was about getting a good job after graduation. Student teachers know that their performance and the ratings they get from the cooperating teacher and the college supervisor will have considerable bearing on their success in obtaining a job.

Next came concern about the "unmotivated" students. Implicit in this concern are fears about control of the class if the unmotivated become disruptive. The third greatest concern was worry about the time available for effective teaching. The student teachers wondered if, given the press of time, they would be able to provide attention to individuals, which they were taught was the mark of the good teacher.

It is fortunate in one sense that studies show not all of student teachers' concerns develop and must be faced at once. Fuller (1969) found that student teachers typically experience concerns about themselves first. Until they deal with those, it is difficult for them to focus on the pupil-related concerns.

This seems reasonable. Student teachers need to feel comfortable and secure themselves before they can mobilize their energy and concentrate their attention on the children's problems. However, student teachers, in the midst of the near chaos of the first weeks of adapting, become upset that they are worrying about themselves rather than about the children. This, they believe, is not the behavior of a responsible student teacher. Such a view is a mistaken one; the continuity from self-concerns to concerns about students seems to be a normal process, as Fuller's work suggests. Incidentally, the same pattern emerges in nursing students during their clinical assignments (Packard, Schwebel, & Ganey, 1979). Specifically, they are first concerned about themselves and whether they are performing up to their supervisor's expectations and then, recognizing this, feel bad that they are worrying about themselves rather than about their patients.

Given the results of these studies, remember when you are feeling overwhelmed early in your teaching that there is a tendency to blame yourself, and also to assume that somebody else would be working wonders. Self-criticism is useful because it can help you do better, but self-condemnation is crippling. It drains your confidence while offering you nothing positive. When you are knee-deep in concern, remember that everybody faces challenges of one kind or another during student teaching, most problems are remediable, and conditions tend to improve over time.

Knowing that you are not the only student teacher with worries can be reassuring. Helen put it this way in her journal:

> 3/5: My lesson on plants was timed perfectly today. But I'm still having problems getting the children to listen or respond to me. The student-teaching seminar helped me here. It's comforting to know the rest of my classmates are having similar experiences and problems.

For generations, concerns like Helen's and others discussed here have troubled student teachers. Most student teachers successfully managed or conquered their fears, coped with their stress, and went on to become effective educators.

THE CONTROL-C METHOD OF PROBLEM SOLVING

In embarking on new ventures like student teaching, individuals who feel confident are at a great advantage. They know the realities of student teaching and have some of the concerns discussed earlier, but they are not thrown by them. They are able to keep their fears under control because they are confident that they will manage to cope successfully with whatever comes their way. As we said in chapter 1, student teachers who train themselves to think optimistically will not blame themselves for setbacks. They will not retreat into helplessness and depression. Instead, they will be challenged to find ways to confront problems more successfully (Seligman, 1991).

One way to reinforce your optimism is by having the wherewithal to deal with problems. You don't have to be Superman or Superwoman to feel that way, you just have to develop skill as a problem solver. For that purpose we have developed a system that you might want to master. We call it the CONTROL-C method.

CONTROL-C is an eight-step process that may look complex but actually is simple and straightforward. As you will see, it is just a logical way of coping with problems that teachers encounter.

Assumptions

Following are the three key assumptions about CONTROL-C:

1. Usually there are several ways to cope with a problem in teaching.
2. To cope effectively with a problem, you must appreciate the perspective of everybody involved.
3. Not every problem a student teacher faces is solvable.

After these assumptions are discussed, the CONTROL-C method is presented.

Assumption 1: Usually There Are Several Ways to Cope With Problems. Ours is the scientific age. When we have a problem, we go to the expert to solve it. Our thoughts are so dominated by a belief in the invincibility of research that we have become accustomed to thinking there is a right answer to everything. Such simplicity rarely exists in the problems that student teachers face. Usually there are many reasonable approaches to problems, with no one alternative more obviously right than the others. Each possible approach has its own likelihood of success, its own payoffs, and its own costs. CONTROL-C was designed to help you select your best alternative for a given problem.

For example, consider Johnny, a bright youngster who finishes seat work quickly and then interrupts the work of slower-paced neighbors by conversing with them. There are many ways to deal with him, such as moving his seat, assigning him more work, scolding him when he talks out of turn, using him as a messenger, developing his talent as a peer teacher, or challenging him with an independent study project. There is no one obviously correct solution, however.

Ideally, student teachers select their approach after considering several factors including their values as educators, their understanding of the child's needs and interests, and their assessment of the relative merits of each choice. If one plan fails, the student teacher can choose another.

Assumption 2: To Cope Effectively With a Problem You Must Appreciate the Perspective of Everybody Involved.   For example, finding an effective solution to Johnny's disruptiveness could involve a number of people, including Johnny, his mother and father, the student teacher, the cooperating teacher, the principal, the school counselor, and the student teacher's college/university supervisor. Each party has his or her own needs, goals, and so forth, and these affect how each sees the situation and what each wants to do about it. Some of their needs may not be immediately obvious, but if one surmises that they are there, one might be much more effective in problem solving.

Everybody wants Johnny to be a more effective learner and less disruptive to the class, yet everybody is also influenced by covert (that is, not immediately obvious) needs and goals. The following list shows what some people's needs might be in Johnny's case. Psychologists sometimes call these covert needs hidden agendas. All people have them in situations that relate to their work and personal lives, which means in virtually all their relationships. There is nothing wrong with hidden agendas. Having them does not mean these people do not want to help Johnny. Quite the contrary, they all want to help him function better in school. However, if each person were aware of the hidden agendas of the others, the group might be better able to do what they all want—to help Johnny. The possible covert goals of those involved with Johnny's problem are as follows:

1. Johnny: To get attention from teacher and classmates.
2. Johnny's parents: To be judged by school people as concerned and good parents.
3. The student teacher: To appear patient and competent when dealing with Johnny, to the cooperating teacher and college/university supervisor.
4. The cooperating teacher: To appear to the principal as a skilled teacher who is having difficulty because of Johnny's personality (and not because of his or her handling of Johnny).

5. The principal: To portray himself or herself as a concerned administrator who cares about each student.
6. The school counselor: To show progress in diagnosing and helping Johnny.
7. The college/university supervisor: To demonstrate the usefulness of academic knowledge in problem-solving.

Assumption 3: Not Every Problem a Student Teacher Faces Is Solvable.
Regrettably there is not a Hollywood happy ending to every classroom problem. However, most situations can be improved to the point where those involved are comfortable. For instance, Johnny may never be the most obedient pupil, but if he and the class are handled appropriately, his behavior can be modified so that he is much less disruptive.

An example of an unsolvable problem may apply to a cooperating teacher who is hypercritical and whose behavior is not truly cooperative. Forming a perfect team with such a person may be too much to hope for, but a growth-promoting working relationship can be established that is at least tolerable, if not comfortable.

Using CONTROL-C

Your mind is the most important tool you have at your disposal as a problem-solving student teacher. When inevitably you face a problem, apply CONTROL-C. The raw material for CONTROL-C is the information you collect. You process this information in steps that allow you to gain a deeper understanding of the problem and then to solve it in a thoughtful way.

The eight steps of CONTROL-C are:

C   Collect a bank of information.
O   Ongoing identification of problems.
N   New information collected.
T   Take others' perspectives.
R   Review coping procedures (solutions).
O   Overview of problem and of alternative coping procedures (solutions) shared with others.
L   Link all information.

C   Closure on one procedure.

Now we explain each step.

C: Collect a Bank of Information

We suggest you collect your bank of information by keeping a daily journal of your student-teaching experiences. Enter key events of the school day and your thoughts, feelings, and reactions to these. Record what you consider positive and what negative, what you could have done differently to make things better, and what you could do to avoid problems in the future. Also enter important events in your student-teaching seminar and your reactions to those events. Effective journal keeping involves both a logical thinking process and a more free-flowing reflection on the range of emotions emanating from your classroom experiences.

Across the many miles and the time that separate us from you, we can sense your groaning reaction to the thought of having one more chore a day. We can sympathize with such a reaction. To keep a journal or not is your decision. We can only point out the advantages. The journal (a) helps make CONTROL-C work more effectively, (b) encourages you to regularly devote a few moments to think through the events of the school day, (c) provides you with a regular opportunity to relieve stress by venting your feelings, and (d) develops a document that reveals your growth as a teacher.

Carmen provides a strong argument for keeping journals in the document she was required to keep during her student teaching:

> I just reread some of my earlier thoughts from the beginning of the month. Sometimes it's easier for me to explore things on paper. When I look back on my thoughts after a time interval, I see that not all of my ideas are logical. That makes this sort of thing valuable to me. I've been doing this journal-type thing since spring quarter. I wish I had kept a journal of my thought-notes during my three weeks in the classroom winter quarter. It would be interesting to see my changes on paper. Easier, too. I've gone through a lot of changes since then. I'll bet this is much more interesting to me than to you! [Her college/university supervisor.]

Example of C.   See the excerpts of journals found throughout the book.

O: Ongoing Identification of Problems

Problems inevitably develop during your student teaching assignment. As difficulties arise and as you encounter situations that need remediation, use your journal to make an accurate statement of what concerns you. Describe the difficulty or concern briefly, preferably in a sentence or two. Be sure that you are describing the problem rather than presenting a presumed cause or a proposed solution.

Example of 0.   My cooperating teacher will not let me teach enough to satisfy me. [Not: My cooperating teacher doesn't like me and that's why I'm not teaching enough to satisfy me.]

N: New Information Collected

New and banked information that pertains to the difficulty or concern is organized. Using your journal or memory, list factors that could be playing a role in the situation. Put all possibilities on paper so you can review and reflect on them, now and later.

Example of N.   Journal entries on different dates that provide information that might be relevant to the concern or difficulty include: "I didn't control the children today during my first lesson." "We had a long class discussion today, got off into six different directions, and covered only half of what we were scheduled to do." "Mrs. P. didn't want to go to lunch with me today. I don't think she likes me." "She complained about the kids she gets from State University, that they're never prepared."

T: Take Others' Perspectives

Remember the issue of "hidden agendas" discussed earlier. Try to get into the shoes of everyone else involved, and try to understand and appreciate their perspectives on a given problem. Use whatever information you can to posit what is in their minds.

Example of T.   Mrs. P. doesn't think I'm ready. She is afraid I'll ruin her class. She may assume if I observe her for a few more days I'll be better able to control the class. Mrs. P. is so much older: Maybe she treats all her student teachers this way, protecting them like the children in her class. The university requires that I take over the full class for only 4 weeks. Maybe Mrs. P. thinks that's all the time I want in front of the class.

R: Review Coping Procedures

Generate a list of alternate ways of dealing with the difficulty or concern. In doing this, consider what you learned in the previous steps and the resources at your disposal.

Example of R.   I could talk to Mrs. P. about my early performance, or ask her to let me teach. I could ask her why she hasn't let me teach. I could ask my supervisor to talk to her and explain that it's OK if I take over the full class earlier than the last 4 weeks of the term. Or after the next lesson I teach, I could ask her directly for criticism.

O: Overview of Problem and of Alternative Coping Procedures

Share the problem and your alternative coping procedures with resource persons, such as your college/university supervisor, cooperating teacher (if the problem is not directly related to them) or friends. Have the resource person help you review your thoughts about the problem. Once they have the relevant information, they may be able to provide a fresh view.

Example of O.   You plan to speak with your best friend, a student teacher in another school, and your supervisor, in that sequence, to seek ideas about how you might obtain more time teaching the whole class.

L: Link all Information

After reviewing the complete set of information developed through CONTROL-C, consider each alternative approach and the likelihood that it would improve the problem. After identifying the advantages and disadvantages of each, take into consideration all the people involved and the effect each approach would have on them and on you.

Example of L.　Drawing on your thoughts and the information you gathered from various sources, make a chart like the one in Table 2.1.

C: Closure on One Procedure

Choose an approach, plan its use, and determine how you will evaluate the success of the approach selected.

Example of C.　Based on the information on your chart, you finally decide to ask Mrs. P. directly why she has not allowed you to teach more frequently. You reasoned that this direct approach might solve your problem, build your confidence, and enable you to win respect from both Mrs. P. and your supervisor. The specifics of the plan you developed involved your staying after school the next day to raise the issue with Mrs. P. You would measure success by comparing the number of lessons you teach to the whole class next week with what you taught this past week. If no increase occurred, you would revert to the chart and select another approach.

We give the CONTROL-C procedure prominence here because we know you will inevitably encounter concerns, issues, and problems in student teaching. We also know that you will benefit by having CONTROL-C at your disposal. Once you try using CONTROL-C, you will find it is not much more difficult to use than the sound reasoning you apply in various situations in other areas of your life.

FOUR STAGES TO STUDENT-TEACHING SUCCESS

We conclude this chapter with a description of four stages of development typical of the life of the student teacher and the kinds of concerns, issues, and problems you are likely to encounter. This is not to say that your experience will follow each stage exactly, or that each will be equally prominent. However, you can expect to find at least elements of each stage, perhaps more of some than others, during your teaching assignment. In each stage you will find that CONTROL-C can help you deal with the inevitable problems

Stage 1: The Early Days

The first days are no honeymoon. They can be overwhelming, especially because student teachers try to absorb so much information very quickly. They drive themselves: must become acquainted with each child, must learn the class routine and procedures, must master the materials the teacher uses, must learn the teacher's techniques. Besides trying to master all that, they want to please the cooperating teacher. Feeling overwhelmed and seeing the cooperating teacher handling everything in stride, they feel awed. "Can I do it?" they ask themselves.

TABLE 2.1

Problem Analysis Chart

Alternatives	Likelihood of improving situation	Advantages	Disadvantages	Effect On			
				Me	Mrs. P.	The students	My supervisor
1. Talk to Mrs. P. about my early performance							
2. Ask her to let me teach							
3. Ask her why she hasn't let me teach							
4. After next lesson ask directly for feedback							
5. Ask my supervisor to talk to Mrs. P.							

Stage 2: Becoming a Member of the Teaching Team

Through observation and immersion in class activities, student teachers begin to get a more accurate picture of their class and its teacher. They begin to see the students as individuals and, at the same time, to gain a sense of the wholeness of the class, a group that operates as a unit. The cooperating teacher is not a name on an assignment sheet anymore but, rather, a real live person. Effective as that teacher may be, he or she is not imbued with superhuman powers, but is simply an able person who, being human and working with humans, has to cope with problems. Student teachers start to generate ideas about what they would do differently if this were their class. They now begin to feel like part of the class. The class recognizes them as members of the teaching team. And student teachers, perceiving their cooperating teacher as a person, have feelings that stem from their interaction, including feelings of warmth, respect, and anger.

Stage 3: Soloing as a Teacher

The preliminary period is over, and student teachers try their wings. They solo! All of the topics and problems discussed so often in the college classes, and fantasized and dreamed about (including an occasional nightmare?) are now real life, here and now, today. Preparation, presentation, timing, movement of students from one activity to another, assisting one group while monitoring the class, discipline, and discipline again—all these confront student teachers at one time.

By Stage 2, student teachers' morale had risen rapidly. In Stage 3, unless they are careful, their morale can nosedive. If the student teachers want to feel bad about something, there is always something to feel bad about. For instance, if they compare their performance with their cooperating teacher's, they will surely find themselves inferior, yet they may fail to attribute this inferiority to the differences in their experience. But they need not make this comparison. They can, instead, find positive things to take note of, such as the progress they have made and their success each day in coping with something they were unable to cope with before.

There are no yardsticks for student teachers at this point, only feedback from the college/university supervisor, cooperating teacher, and the children, which they can reflect on and learn from. There are three patterns to choose from in this stage: Some feel defeated by the situation, label themselves failures, and give up; others feel defeated, but place the blame elsewhere, usually on the cooperating teacher and sometimes on the college for having prepared them poorly; but most student teachers feel okay about Stage 3, viewing it as just a passing phase, difficult indeed, but one that they will weather successfully, in part by using a problem-solving system like CONTROL-C.

Stage 4: Feeling Like a Teacher

After passing through the storms of Stage 3, student teachers settle down to the job of working with their students and, in the process, transform themselves into teachers. Their time with the cooperating teacher will be drawing to an end. From here on, whole days are theirs to plan and execute.

From the weeks of classroom experience, they have begun to develop their own style and, further, they have come to feel at home in front of the class. They know there is much more to learn, but they accept the reality that one does not become a master teacher in 10 weeks or even 10 months. Above all, now they have much more confidence. When the new school year rolls around and they take over their own classes as full-time teachers, they know they will be able to handle the job.

CRITICAL ISSUES

- What am I expecting of myself as a student teacher?
- What do I know about the community of my assigned school?
- What can I do to become part of the school community?
- What are my chief concerns about student teaching?

PART II

Relationships

3

Building a Good Relationship With Your Cooperating Teacher

Success in student teaching begins with a good relationship with your cooperating teacher. With that, you will put yourself in a strong position to learn and to become an effective teacher. It will also lay the groundwork for a supportive letter of reference that will aid you in securing your first position.

We start with a step-by-step discussion on building an effective bond, followed by discussion of how to avoid potential relationship problems and how to deal with such problems when they arise. The last section in the chapter deals briefly with substitute teachers, whom you may encounter during your student-teaching assignment.

THE FIRST MEETING

That first meeting with your cooperating teacher is important. You can do much in advance to make it a successful one. Here are some suggestions:

Don't Make Prejudgments

Before and after student-teaching assignments are announced, you may hear your classmates voice very subjective evaluations of different cooperating teachers: "Hartman is good, but Hellman is a loser." "I hope I don't get stuck with O'Shea down at Lincoln School," somebody will say.

If you hear your prospective cooperating teacher so evaluated, we advise you to ignore the comment. Without prejudgments, you will be better positioned to enter your first meeting with an open mind and with the expectation that, in due time, you will get along and develop an effective teaching team.

Psychological Readiness

The situation is most ideal if you come with confidence in yourself and in your ability to succeed. If you cannot muster that degree of confidence now, you can work to prepare yourself psychologically and, as a result, to show yourself as willing and able to assume classroom responsibilities.

A central factor in psychological readiness is coping with your anxiety about your teaching assignment. Let us assume that every time you think about the meeting you get nervous. If you deal with the situation by deciding not to think about it, the worry will indeed go away for the moment. However, such a strategy also prevents you from planning for the meeting. Not thinking about a stressful upcoming event is a widely used defensive approach; regrettably, it is also self-defeating.

The alternative, admittedly easier said than done, is to take the feeling of nervousness as an indicator that something important is about to happen and gear yourself accordingly. Such an approach reduces your tension. It also serves to increase the chances that you will plan for the important event and be more successful.

How can psychological readiness help you harness the stress associated with your first contact with your cooperating teacher? First, set aside time to think about what you want to learn. Jot down specific skills you want to develop, content areas in which you want to prepare units, discipline techniques you want to use, and so forth. Next, think about the first meeting with your cooperating teacher. Plan your part in it. What do you want to know from her or him? What do you want to tell her or him? Finally, rehearse the questions you want to ask and rehearse each of these aloud, as if you were saying them at your first meeting with your cooperating teacher.

The Cooperating Teacher's Perspective

Because you will probably know little about your cooperating teacher, it will be difficult to anticipate the dialogue between you. One way you can deal with this ambiguity is by imagining somebody who is both your boss and your instructor. Those are the cooperating teachers' roles. Now, imagine that you were in that position. What characteristics would you want in your student teacher? Would you be pleased to have a student teacher who conveys excitement and enthusiasm about teaching?

While you are still in the cooperating teacher role, consider what else you would want. The instructor part of you would probably prefer a person who exhibits an appetite for learning as well as an eagerness to use you as a resource person. The boss part of you, in contrast, wants a person who is willing to roll up his or her shirtsleeves and work hard and smart in the classroom. If you have these qualities, be sure to communicate them one way or another during the meeting.

Scheduling the First Meeting

Although there is much you can infer about your cooperating teacher, you will not begin to get the information necessary to substitute facts for assumptions until you meet. When you are given your cooperating teacher's name, it is wise to telephone and request an opportunity to meet. It is good to do this as early as possible.

The ideal first meeting would be a leisurely one, held after school at a time and place convenient to you both. Such circumstances would allow you to set a pattern of useful communication and thoughtful sharing of ideas. If ample time has been set aside, you could also exchange ideas about education as well as discuss practical issues related to your role as student teacher.

Unfortunately, the ideal is frequently not possible. Some student teachers will not know their assignment until the day before they are to begin. Others will have sufficient notice but a cooperating teacher who prefers not to meet until the term begins. If the cooperating teacher seems to be putting you off in scheduling a meeting, remember it may not be for the reasons you assume. For instance, he or she could be slow in establishing relations or, at the time, very busy. Whenever it takes place, make that first meeting the first step in building a solid relationship.

At the meeting you will form your first impressions of your cooperating teacher. You will see whether the teacher is open and comfortable or restrained in interacting with you. You will probably learn something about the teacher's orientation toward education and style of running the class: for example, highly structured, following a well-defined schedule, or loosely structured and flexible.

Before and after meeting your cooperating teacher, remind yourself that a single conference can give only a first impression. If the meeting went well, you may feel fortunate in being assigned an effective and personable teacher. If you thought it did not go well, remind yourself that even if your assessments were accurate, feelings often change as students and cooperating teachers become better acquainted and more comfortable with each other.

THE FIRST DAY

Although you may be too busy to realize it, your first day as a student teacher is a special milestone in your life, as well as an important transition point in your professional career. It deserves special attention. Whether things go well or you end up needing two aspirins before noon, take a moment to celebrate the occasion.

Alice, who was not able to meet her cooperating teacher prior to her first day, described her initial impressions in her journal. Note that she made observations that she expected would be useful when she began teaching:

> 1/6: It was a pleasant day. I met Mrs. L., my cooperating teacher, who appeared to be friendly and highly concerned with her pre-kindergartners. I was also introduced to the children, who seemed to be happy and most of them eager to learn.
>
> I observed all day long and noticed how some of the children had very short attention spans. That should be useful to me when I begin teaching lessons. Since I was observing, I didn't have much interaction with the children. They tended to be a little shy with me yet.
>
> Overall, I think I'm going to enjoy student teaching at Glen Avenue School.

Alice was obviously pleased. Some student teachers leave school after the first day in a state of ecstasy, whereas others are disappointed because the school, the cooperating teacher, and/or the children were not what they had anticipated. To some extent, Joyce felt this way, but she had hopes too:

> 1/6: This wasn't what I expected at all! I guess I'm really disappointed with the situation I think I'll be in at this school. Well, it's only for 10 weeks. With a big mental psyche maybe I'll make it. I like the other student teachers. And, if I'm not crazy, I feel an air of disappointment from them too. The staff seems friendly towards us all, but I receive negative vibrations towards me as a Black.
>
> The class and I will get along fine. The school day in this classroom is so regimented! That's one thing I'd like to change. The kids are always in their seats. The fact that I'm Black may not upset them much, since I'll be the teacher. But, with the staff things might be different. It's going to be hard working with Mr. P. . . . He's so set in his ways and he seems to be against change. Hope I'm wrong!

To state the obvious, first impressions are not necessarily accurate, and it is a mistake—a very serious one, in fact—to set your expectations on the basis of your initial experience. Why? Expectations prepare us to act as if the "expected events" were inevitably going to occur. Then, without our necessarily being aware of it, by our actions we may help make them occur.

For example, if, on the basis of very limited experience, I expect my cooperating teacher to discourage me from voicing my views by putting me down every time I utter a word, I will end up censoring myself and speaking only when necessary. Put another way, I will make my expectation come true and, at the same time, I will limit my chances to learn from my student-teaching experience. Instead of making premature judgments, I should go into the situation with a positive outlook.

STAGES IN YOUR RELATIONSHIP
WITH YOUR COOPERATING TEACHER

If your student-teaching experience is like that of those who kept journals, most likely your relationship with your cooperating teacher will pass through many stages of development. At each stage you will face certain challenges and have unique learning opportunities. To help you prepare to take best advantage of those opportunities, we trace the development of the cooperating teacher relationship, using the stages outlined in chapter 2.

Stage 1: The Early Days

In getting started, much time is spent trying very quickly to absorb a great deal of information. So much is new and so much must be learned. You must channel energy into (a) becoming acquainted with the students and learning their names, (b) becoming familiar with the learning styles and personal characteristics of each class member, and (c) adapting to the pace of and atmosphere in the room. The "I'm overwhelmed" feeling may develop, and, if so, expect to feel drained by day's end.

You also will want to invest energy into building the student teacher–cooperating teacher relationship. As the journals we collected suggest, this relationship does not develop automatically. Although some cooperating teachers take the initiative, others do not. In such cases, it is in the student teacher's best interest to do so.

As days go by and you feel more comfortable with both class and teacher, you will want to assume more responsibility. By then, your cooperating teacher will know you better and may be ready to have you teach. When you reach this point, a student–cooperating teacher planning–goal-setting meeting is useful. At such a meeting, you can review your classroom involvement to date and identify areas in which you would like to work. Perhaps through give-and-take discussion, the two of you can develop your learning goals.

Sandra asked Darla, her cooperating teacher, if she would be interested in having a planning–goal-setting meeting. Darla thought it was a great idea, and it was she who suggested a luncheon. Much was accomplished, as Sandra described in her journal:

> 1/26: Darla and I went to lunch. The first part of the meeting turned out to be more of a social situation than anything else. Later, we did discuss my position in the class and Darla was concerned how I was or wasn't enjoying the observation days. She informed me I could begin teaching lessons on Monday and we planned the procedure for the day. We also set up a series of long-range goals. These were for me to:
>
> a: rearrange the reading corner and that side of the classroom;
>
> b: plan a nutrition unit;
>
> c: fully acquaint myself with all materials in the room;
>
> d: design a unit on the senses;
>
> e: review the science manual and classroom laboratory kit and start science with kids;
>
> f: individualize with Stephen and Kevin;
>
> g: work on being a creative teacher;

h: create a backlog of 5-, 10-, and 15-minute classroom activities;

i: by the middle of March, see how much of the above has been accomplished.

For Sandra, building an effective working relationship with her cooperating teacher, Darla, was easy. Most student teachers who call upon their social skills and the knowledge acquired in their courses will also find this task easy. In fact, they will find it much like forming a friendship with a willing person who shares common interests.

Not every student teacher will be this fortunate, however. You may be wondering: "What if I cannot seem to build an effective working relationship with my cooperating teacher?" "Will he or she ever warm up to me?" You may be asking yourself, "What can I do to improve the relationship?"

First, reassure yourself that others have been in a similar position and succeeded in bringing about change. Next, use the CONTROL-C method to think about the problem systematically. In analyzing the situation, consider not just the first possibilities that come to mind, but a range of them, including those that involve your cooperating teacher's style and behavior as well as your own. For instance, ask:

1. Is your cooperating teacher by nature a reserved person who takes time to warm up to people?
2. Is your cooperating teacher an unwilling participant in the student-teacher program?
3. Are you your cooperating teacher's first student teacher and, if so, is he or she learning how to make the cooperative effort work?
4. Did you do or say anything your cooperating teacher might have thought was out of place? If so, could that account for the difficulty you are experiencing?
5. Do you represent a threat to your cooperating teacher because of your personality, appearance, or some other trait or quality?

The CONTROL-C procedure may lead you to discuss the problem with a classmate, a friend or your college/university supervisor. They may help you consider alternative coping methods or, if necessary, your supervisor may intervene on your behalf. As you know, the supervisor's job is to help as well as evaluate you. Supervisors know that a poor relationship with a cooperating teacher deprives you of an optimal learning experience.

Stage 2: Becoming a Member of the Teaching Team

A little more secure in the classroom, the student teacher now recognizes the cooperating teacher's substantial professional ability while also discovering that the halo of perfection has disappeared. Cooperating teachers are not perfect. They make mistakes, and they do some things differently from the way the student teacher was taught. For example, they do not handle June's disruptive behavior head-on and they seem to ignore Harry who, with all his potential, will soon turn 16 and drop out unless somebody persuades him to complete high school.

A frequently voiced concern during this stage relates to the cooperating teacher's classroom style and philosophy of education. For example, Ernest wrote in his journal, "The teacher is so traditional. . . . She shouts at the kids all day. . . . Even an adult couldn't sit still for as long as those kids have to."

Student teachers airing such criticisms note the differences between their philosophy of education and teaching style and those of their cooperating teacher, and they often hasten to add comments like, "I'm not going to teach my class that way." But making such observations and declaring that one is going to teach in a different way does not eliminate their worry. They wonder whether they can learn from a mentor whose approach seems so different.

Fortunately, student teachers do benefit from an experience with a teacher whose approach is very different from theirs. Richard is a good example. Although he first feared he would be unable to tolerate a semester-long relationship with his cooperating teacher, after several weeks he found that his classroom experiences were helping him crystalize his own thoughts about teaching:

2/5: School went well today. I have vowed to myself I will not teach in the same manner employed by Allyson. . . . My obedience to this vow remains to be seen. Also the question comes to mind, how will I teach?

. . . How? I am really not sure, but I will try to avoid shouting . . . and asking them silly or irrelevant questions when they act up.

I will try to let them look at more books, have their work areas less cluttered, and come up with more imaginative ways of introducing a lesson's learning objective.

The reason we confidently state that you can learn in any cooperating classroom is that you are the key ingredient in what is learned. Regardless of your assignment, you can derive great benefits from your interactions with your students. It is true that with certain assignments you will have more extensive experience and more opportunity to experiment, but wherever you are, if you commit yourself, you can develop professionally.

At some point during Stage 2 you will probably compare yourself with your cooperating teacher. This may occur when you are reflecting at your desk, or in class when your cooperating teacher calls on a student you might not have selected to answer the question posed to the group. When you do compare yourself with your cooperating teacher, you will invariably find differences, some of the most obvious of which are discussed here.

First, you two obviously differ in years of experience and perhaps in the kind of training you received. You have come on the scene with fresh ideas from your college or university that may contradict the ideas and practices that your cooperating teacher has developed through the "school of hard knocks."

Second, you have different roles and responsibilities in the classroom. Your main job is to learn. In contrast, although the cooperating teacher has some responsibility for instructing you, his or her first responsibility is to the class, to see that certain instructional goals are achieved.

Third, the two of you may have different personalities, work styles, and so forth. You may be energetic and bubbly, whereas he or she may be quieter and steadier, or vice versa.

These differences, and others, may create divergences in the ways you approach students and in the preferences you have on how lessons should be taught, class order maintained, and routines conducted. As a person without the year-long responsibility of maintaining discipline, you may be critical of aspects of your cooperating teacher's approach. For example, you might think he or she shouts too much, is too tied to routines, and is too whole-class rather than group-oriented. After you have drawn these mental conclusions, you may well be tempted to suggest changes to your cooperating teacher or to indicate how you would handle things differently. Should you? Resist that temptation and instead:

1. Avoid being judgmental and assuming the cooperating teacher's way is wrong and yours is right. Both approaches may have advantages and disadvantages. When he or she handles a situation or teaches a lesson in ways that are different from how you would have handled it, enter that in your journal and list the pluses and minuses of both approaches.

2. With an open mind, approach your cooperating teacher to discuss his or her approach. Ask "Why?" questions and share your perspective. You may find that your cooperating teacher is insightful and has well-thought-through reasons for selecting the approaches used.

3. Follow your cooperating teacher's way, unless you have permission to experiment. Do so for several reasons, including the fact that you are a guest in the classroom. If you give the cooperating teacher's approach an all-out effort, you can see how it works for you. With that experience, the two of you can assess whether that approach works for you or whether another approach would be worth trying. For example, one of the authors was assigned a male cooperating teacher in an inner-city school. The rough-tough masculine approach to disciplining children did not work well for her. As a result of several discussions, the two of them worked out a plan she could use for disciplining, which was comfortable for her but also consistent with his approach.

The journal entries that follow show that differences in teaching approaches, which seem terribly important in the early days and weeks, generally get resolved satisfactorily as time passes. Discussions of methods, discipline techniques, and differences in style become more fruitful and comfortable as the student and cooperating teacher get to know each other as people. As far as trying new approaches is concerned, often what happens is this: After the student teacher wins the confidence of the cooperating teacher, he or she is allowed to experiment. Marsha reported this:

2/19: When I first observed Mrs. H.'s split first and second grade class, I saw she was much more strict and traditional than I wanted to be. Her room was very orderly. She asked the children to raise their hands before they talk and tried to stress manners. I don't object to an orderly class, but it seemed to me that the children were too regimented. They all sat in their seats and were not allowed any paper or objects in their hands.

I think that they need quite a bit of direction to begin with. Also, they do need help in working quietly. But then gradually, they could work in groups, and be given a little more "room." Those are thoughts which occurred to me at the start. . . . Within a month Mrs. H. and I had a good relationship. She let me open things up more and try some of my ideas. She was surprised at how well they worked, even though I let the children go some.

When you get permission to try things your way, the results are not always satisfactory to you and/or your cooperating teacher. For example, Phyllis tried to give the students more freedom and, when she did, she was pleased with the results. However, her cooperating teacher was not at all happy about what developed. The two of them spoke about their different views on classroom atmosphere and about what was tolerable in terms of control. Phyllis hoped they could define a middle ground between them, but they were not able to. Wisely, Phyllis accepted the fact that she had to run a "tight ship" for the rest of the term.

Although many students are fortunate because they are assigned to cooperating teachers who give them opportunities to experiment, not everybody will find this. If you are not permitted to try your way of teaching, bear in mind that the cooperating teacher is the boss. The relationship is not an equal one. The cooperating teacher has the authority and you have only that which is delegated to you when you teach a lesson. In any situation, when somebody must yield, and the cooperating teacher is not willing, then you must. When you have on-going conflict with your cooperating teacher, you always lose, one way or another.

In summary, if you are convinced that you are not getting the chance to use yourself effectively, try CONTROL-C and talk with your cooperating teacher and/or supervisor. Then, if it becomes clear that there is no way of obtaining the teaching opportunities you want, think about next year when you will have your own class.

It seems appropriate to conclude our discussion of Stage 2 with a brief report of two studies much related to the issue of student teacher–cooperating teacher differences over teaching. The purpose of the first study was to compare the orientations toward educational practice of student and cooperating teachers (Harty & Mahan, 1977). The investigators used the Educational Preference Scale to assesses the participants values regarding the nature of knowledge, the nature of learning, the nature of the learner, and the purpose of schooling. Individuals' scores on this instrument show the direction of their orientation, whether toward conventional or emergent forms of education, whether against or for progressive education. The Scale was given to 159 student teachers prior to and after their 16-week student-teaching experience. It was also given to the cooperating teachers halfway through the students' 16-week assignment.

The results were clear-cut. The student teachers were more liberal (progressive or emergent) than their cooperating teachers before they began their classroom assignment. By the end of the teaching, their orientation had shifted in the direction of their cooperating teachers. In fact, a substantial number of student teachers ended up with more conservative scores than their cooperating teachers. The investigators concluded: "Student teachers tend to become more like their cooperating teachers with respect to their expressed orientations toward education as a result of a 16-week student-teaching experience" (p. 40).

This change occurs, we believe, not because cooperating teachers force it on student teachers. Rather it occurs because of a bias toward conventional, custodial forms of schooling in our communities and in our society at large (Sarason, 1982). Student teachers discover this during their apprenticeship.

In the second study, 191 student teachers were compared with two other groups: students taking educational methods courses who would soon student teach, and students earlier in college preparation, some of whom were planning to be teachers (Hoy & Woolfolk, 1990). These three groups were compared with respect to the following orientations about controlling and managing a class of students: (a) The custodial orientation that calls for "an inflexible and highly regimented setting concerned primarily with maintaining order," and (b) The humanistic orientation that calls for "an educational community in which students learn through coopera- tive interaction and experience" (Hoy & Woolfolk, 1990, p. 281).

The results were similar to those of the first study: The student teachers became more custodial in orientation and the other students remained unchanged in orien- tation. These two studies indicate that the socialization process that goes on even during the brief period of student teaching seems to shift students' outlook toward tighter control. "The ideal images of college preparation apparently give way to the instrumental necessities of maintaining order and running a smoothly functioning classroom" (Hoy & Woolfolk, 1990, p. 294).

Stage 3: Soloing as a Teacher

This is it! Although student teachers learn much by immersing themselves in the life of the classroom and observing the process of teaching and learning, the heart of student teaching is in teaching itself. You learn most when your teaching is accompanied by constructive criticism. Student teacher–cooperating teacher rela- tionships often get rocky around the time that criticism is given and received. Sensitivity and fortitude, respectively, are essential to giving and receiving criti- cism. If you feel resistance within you when your cooperating teacher begins to offer criticism, tell yourself, here's an opportunity for me to learn how to be a better teacher. He or she is not evaluating my worth as a human being, but rather how I might be more effective in a realm of functioning that is important to me. With practice, the process of receiving criticism in a healthy way will become second nature to me.

Few of us get a great deal of experience in giving and receiving criticism in a professional setting. This lack of experience can cause problems that manifest themselves when cooperating teachers prepare to provide feedback to their student teachers. The kinds of problems that may emerge range from cooperating teachers holding back on providing feedback to providing only negative feedback. These and other commonly encountered problems are:

1. Receiving no feedback from your cooperating teacher;
2. Getting only negative feedback;
3. Being criticized while you are teaching and in the presence of students;
4. Having criticism of you publicized;
5. Getting angry at the cooperating teacher; and
6. Finding yourself in a difficult relationship with your cooperating teacher.

Each of these is discussed, in turn, with an eye to helping you overcome such a problem should you encounter it in your relationship.

Receiving No Feedback.   Perhaps the most frustrating problem is not receiving verbal feedback. Without it, you do not know how well your cooperating teacher feels you are doing, leaving a gap you must fill by wondering and guessing. This hampers your learning, often forcing you to search for signs of approval instead of concentrating on your students.

Joyce had problems getting feedback and commented in her journal on how that made her feel:

4/8: Today, I was supposed to take the class over for the entire day. The only thing I wasn't supposed to teach was history . . . (after lunch). And that is how it went. The day went along great. Everyone got along and I feel my lessons were successful. The children really got involved with the math lesson. My first one! Boy, I was glad. Sometimes I wonder what Mr. P.'s bag is. He glares at me with approval (I think) but he'll never say anything. But then the glare could be envy or dislike. I wish he'd say something because as it is now, I don't feel at ease with him watching me. I just don't know what he's thinking.

What can you do in a situation like Joyce's? Here are general suggestions that may help:

• When you have a good opportunity to talk, meaning that students are not present and your cooperating teacher is not busy, ask specific questions about your work, various class procedures, the functioning of individual youngsters, and so on. Remember to phrase your questions so they do not sound critical or threatening. Stress instead your interest in satisfying your curiosity or in learning about the art of teaching.
• Ask about the possibility of establishing a regularly scheduled time to discuss your progress as a student teacher.
• Receive any criticism you get graciously. If you appear intimidated, angry, argumentative or annoyed by feedback, you will make it harder for your cooperating teacher to criticize you and, in fact, may discourage future sharing.

At the core of these suggestions is the idea that you will need to take the initiative. We recognize that the notion of asking directly for criticism is often anxiety provoking, even in cases where the student teacher and cooperating teacher have a fine relationship. Ed's journal entry illustrates his concern about receiving specific feedback from his cooperating teacher:

> 4/4: Mrs. R. is fantastic. She spends so much time talking with me, suggesting, and giving me books to read. I also feel comfortable with her because I feel that we have ideas and beliefs that "mesh" and work together well, with the main objective being the benefit of the kids.
>
> I still wonder if I am doing enough. . . . Does Mrs. R. expect me to do more? Does she think I'm lazy or afraid to take on more? I feel as if I am not asserting myself enough with her, that I should ask her more. I guess I am a bit afraid to suggest taking over more . . . than I do, and I can see that I am slowly doing more and gradually taking my place.

Ed needed evaluative information from Mrs. R. but was afraid to ask for it. As a result, he had needless worry and spent time feeling he was not meeting her expectations. When he finally asked, he felt reassured because Mrs. R. was very pleased with his work.

There are at least three ineffective ways to get feedback on what you want to know. Although they are widely used, we do not recommend them. The first is "dropping hints." You know how that operates. In a matter-of-fact way, you say, "Something just came to mind." Then you mention it and hope the cooperating teacher will catch on and tell you what you want to know. Sometimes hint-dropping succeeds, but you cannot depend on it.

The second method is to start a conversation and "hope." This involves talking first about an issue related to what you want to know and hoping the teacher will catch on and move to your topic. This is not a reliable approach, as an entry from Vicky's journal shows:

> 3/8: I made plans for today and informed Mrs. B. of them. But things didn't turn out as planned. I was very upset at one point when I told the children to go to their small groups and Mrs. B. decided they should have some exercise. Since I had already told some children (Group I) to get their books, there was a lot of confusion. ("Are we supposed to get our books now or get in a circle?" etc.) Besides the fact that she interrupted my plans and completely undermined my authority in the classroom, she chose to play an exercise song that half the children refused to participate in because the other half of the children get so rowdy. . . .
>
> Later, when I asked her if she had any comments about what I had done today (I was hoping she would bring up this part of the day so we could discuss my intentions), she only said she liked what I had presented, especially the Bear Hunt.

Vicky started a conversation and "hoped," but the conversation did not turn to what she wanted to discuss. As a result, the air was not cleared and she went home frustrated. Whatever caused Mrs. B. to interrupt Vicky's plans was left unclarified, so a repeat of the incident at a later date was possible.

The third ineffective method is "mind reading." Mind reading is not a prerequisite for being a cooperating teacher! This method is unreliable because it assumes the cooperating teacher knows what you want feedback about—or that you want feedback at all.

Getting Only Negative Feedback.   A hazard of student-teaching is encountering a cooperating teacher who gives you only negative feedback. What problems can this cause? First, people want to hear good news about what was right as well as the bad news about what was wrong. When you hear one without the other, your opportunity for learning is accordingly reduced. Second, hearing only negative criticism can erode your confidence, even if you have the strongest of egos.

If you find yourself receiving only negative feedback, and getting very angry or frustrated about that, you should take action. A good initial step is to mobilize yourself so that you are able to determine exactly what your options are. Use CONTROL-C. Think the situation out systematically. Ask whether you need the positive words from the teacher to learn better, to build confidence, or as an ego boost in general. The information you generate this way will help you plan your course of action.

In one journal entry Leslie reported facing negative criticism and, after analyzing her situation, she concluded that she needed positive feedback to improve her teaching. She said to Mrs. R., "I need to know what I'm doing right so I know what not to change." Mrs. R. smiled and replied, "You are doing everything fine," but that was all the positive feedback Leslie got that week or the next.

More thought about the situation led Leslie to decide that Mrs. R. was not the "positive feedback type," and that she would have to learn without hearing from her the positives that she craved. Instead, because her need for "positives" stemmed from a desire for feedback to improve her teaching, Leslie decided she could obtain her own feedback by watching her students.

After each lesson she presented, she would ask herself, "What did I do well? Did they learn what I intended to teach them? Did they seem challenged and effectively stimulated by the material?" She also would look at their papers to document the reliability of her observations. Did a good many of the youngsters master the material taught, as evidenced by their seat work and homework?

Leslie also made good use of conversations with her supervisor and informal talks with her friends as a way of further determining whether her progress in student teaching was on track.

Although Leslie did not change Mrs. R.'s behavior, she did develop a plan that made things tolerable. She also wondered why Mrs. R. would not give her positive feedback. She thought, "Perhaps Mrs. R. had been taught to avoid complimentary comments; perhaps, unknowingly, she might be experiencing me as a threat because of my high energy level; or, perhaps Mrs. R. is going through difficult times in her personal life."

Without further speculation, Leslie made peace with the situation. She accepted Mrs. R. for what she was and learned to use the children as an indirect source of information to evaluate her work.

Like Leslie, Lorraine was concerned with negative feedback she was receiving and the doubt it had caused in her about her competence. Lorraine's journal entry shows how she worked at understanding possible hidden agendas in her cooperating teacher's negative feedback. Note how liberating it was for Lorraine when she sensed that it was a personal quality in Mrs. C., rather than one in herself, that had resulted in the flow of negatives:

> 3/4: Today went all right, and for the most part I taught for the entire (day). . . . I really like when Mrs. C. gives me corrective criticism or suggestions, but some times I feel as though she is stressing or pointing up to me that she has had much more experience. In a subtle way, at times she makes me feel inferior or not as intelligent, and I'm beginning to realize that this is just her personality.

As you might expect, when Lorraine came to this realization, she was much more able to profit from Mrs. C.'s expertness and also from her criticisms. Lorraine managed to deal with the negative-feedback situation without asking for help from her supervisor. This is not always the case. For example, there are times when the amount and intensity of negative feedback from the cooperating teacher is such that it is defeating to the student teacher. Kate's journal entries, written over a period of a few days, describe what it is like in such an extreme case:

> 2/25: As I was leaving today, Mrs. N. said, "I can see by your face that you're not happy about today." I said, "I don't like the way things went." She answered, "Neither did I." I was glad she had answered me honestly. But at the same time, I think I was hoping more for reassurance.
>
> Essentially my dissatisfaction came from the fact that whenever I tried to do something with the class today I never seemed to have their full attention. They wouldn't listen to me when I asked them to be quiet, etc. Mrs. N. said that I lacked control. (I don't know if I would choose that word. To me it connotes a dictator.)
>
> On the way home I began developing a "fear of failure" feeling and I started dreading tomorrow morning. But after I sorted out my thoughts I realized my teaching strategy was not totally at fault.
>
> 2/27: As I walked out of the building today, the tears started pouring down my cheeks. I had held it all in for almost 3 hours, enduring the worst day of my life, and I was now ready for a good cry. When I got home I was crying so hard I couldn't even explain what had happened.
>
> It took me all afternoon to sort out what had occurred, and I'm not sure now what brought about my noontime discussion with Mrs. N. She told me (the obvious) that I am responsible for the children or I will be when I take over full time.
>
> [Mrs. N's criticisms included:] . . . I tend to get engrossed in one activity and have trouble keeping track of everything else that is going on in the room (a character flaw, perhaps?). I am not disciplining the children. And she went on and on, the criticisms pouring out all over me. I tried to explain that I need time to get everything coordinated and that by the time I took over I was sure things would have improved.

I also tried to point out that because she always overpowered me I did not jump right into discipline situations. I would be standing there trying to talk with a child who had done something. Seeing it, she would be right behind me, with a "Stop it now!" directed at the child. Yes, the kid would stop, my discussion was over or I felt I might as well not bother. Anyway, our talk ended with her telling me that she didn't think I would make it and my numbly saying, "Don't worry."

I was so upset when the children walked in for afternoon classes. I don't remember how I taught my lessons. How could she do that to me? Hours later I'm still upset. I'm hoping that by morning Mrs. N. will be calmed down, the whole thing will be forgotten. Maybe she was having a bad day, because I think many of her comments did not take into account the fact that I am still learning and need time to absorb everything.

For the next few days, Kate went through a great deal of suffering with Mrs. N. During this difficult period, she sought and received support from her supervisor, who eventually spoke to her cooperating teacher. Kate's persistence and the aid of Kate's supervisor paid off, as the following entry shows. Note that it concludes with thanks to her supervisor:

3/2: No more tears. Today was so much better. Mrs. N. liked my plans a lot. She was pleased with the way the day went and I was pleased too. The encouragement she gave me built up my confidence and I could teach again.

She told me that she could have cheered me up . . . but that then I wouldn't have done the soul searching I needed to do. Strange reasoning, in my opinion. There must be an easier way than coming close to a nervous breakdown.

Now I realize that perhaps we just weren't communicating, and I really didn't understand what she expected of me. I just hope there isn't a repeat. Although I would know what to expect, I don't think I could go through it another time. Thanks for the hours you spent.

Being Criticized While You Are Teaching.   Two things we know for sure: (a) you want criticism of your work but not while you are teaching a lesson, and (b) you want assistance in learning to control the class, but not in the form of having the cooperating teacher step in during your lesson. Nobody benefits from being contradicted in front of others. When this does happen, not only do you feel put down and worry that your authority has been undermined, but you also have to rebound from those feelings quickly so that you can overcome the interruption and maintain the flow of the lesson.

To some extent, you can take steps in advance to try to prevent your cooperating teacher from stepping in while you are teaching or handling discipline problems. The most important preventative measure is forming a healthy relationship with your cooperating teacher. If you accomplish this, chances are good he or she will feel better about electing to withhold criticism until the two of you can have a private discussion. Realistically, however, even when a solid rapport exists there are times when the cooperating teacher may unknowingly countermand your directions.

Let us first look at an instance where the cooperating teacher, perhaps unknowingly, gives a set of directions that contradict the ones issued by the student teacher only moments before. Sheryl's diary entry describes an incident during her fourth day of student teaching:

> 1/8: The day didn't start out well. We were going to the museum and the bus was due at 9:00. I told the class to keep their coats on—why have them in and out of the coat room? Mrs. R. came and screamed, "What's going on? Take your coats off and hang them up now." She really laid it on and made me feel stupid and sorry for the kids.

The incident struck Sheryl hard because it seemed at the moment to halt the progress she was making toward achieving something important to her: establishing her authority and winning respect from the class. The episode resulted from lack of communication. Sheryl had not had a chance to tell Mrs. R. that she had told the children to keep their coats on. Of course, Mrs. R. could have assumed that or even inquired of Sheryl, but she did not. Fortunately, the events of the next few days proved Sheryl wrong in thinking she had lost face with the children.

At the time of an incident like Sheryl's, it is natural to feel that single episodes like this one are very important. Generally, they are not. However, when episodes of this kind recur, there is reason for concern. Here are specific steps you can take to help prevent being repeatedly interrupted, contradicted, or countermanded:

1. Learn the class rules.

2. From the beginning, try to establish a before-the-school-day-begins routine of speaking to your cooperating teacher about the day's plans. Besides what has already been scheduled for you to do that day, find out if there are any other specific tasks your cooperating teacher might want you to handle and the thoughts he or she has about these.

3. When you are observing, attempt to train yourself to know at what point your cooperating teacher reacts to events. For example, note at what point he or she speaks to a student who has been restless or disturbing, and how long after a group of youngsters becomes noisy does he or she put a stop to it.

Rose, who had been having trouble with in-class criticisms, reports how, by learning and applying class rules, she saved the children from criticism and herself from embarrassment:

> 3/3: Spring may be here at last. We went outside today for the first time. I really had the urge to slide down the sliding board with the kids, but I had the feeling Mr. N. would not approve. So I stood around with the other teachers on the playground and occupied my time by observing the large-muscle coordination of the children. I saw a lot more about their physical coordination out there where they were free to run around than I could ever have observed within the confines of the classroom. I also tried to absorb all their playground rules. Mr. N. has a lot of rules that I am unaware of until I let one of the children break a rule and he hurries over to correct the situation.

(I, of course, always feel like a jerk.) So before we went out today I decided to learn as many as possible, so that I wouldn't end up embarrassed and the children wouldn't be needlessly confused. Mr. N. seemed pleased to list them for me.

Student teachers differ in their predominant emotional reaction when they feel their cooperating teacher repeatedly and inappropriately interferes with their lessons. Although some will be embarrassed or hurt, others will be angry or even infuriated. The least effective reaction is to slough it off, trying to convince themselves with, "I don't care—it doesn't bother me one bit."

Such a situation should be confronted, but not impulsively. An impulsive confrontation may lead to irrelevant talk about personalities or to a diffuse, angry barrage, instead of a directed discussion of the situation. By using CONTROL-C, student teachers can get in touch with their reactions and use them as motivators to speak directly and firmly for their position. Having thought the issues through, they are more likely to focus on the incidents when they were interrupted, how they felt, and the relationship between the incidents and their learning.

In the next example, we focus on a situation where the student teacher was repeatedly criticized in front of the children. Although this example merits attention in its own right, here it illustrates how a student teacher can use feelings to motivate a search for solutions. Note how Alice handled her problem over a 2-week period:

2/10: As I walked out of the doors of Glen Ave. this afternoon, I felt as if I had been a complete failure. Though I spoke with Mrs. L. about the day and accepted my criticisms well, I still felt something was missing.

Because I was 10 minutes late I was scolded by Mrs. L. for being irresponsible as an adult. The children were restless throughout the entire day. I got very upset because Mrs. L. got angry because the day did not go smoothly. She criticized me in front of the children and before I had done my Valentine story.

I told her that I would appreciate criticism after school. She said, "No, I'm going to tell you what you do wrong whenever I see you doing something wrong." I further explained that I could not function to the best of my ability if she did not save her criticism for later. "Well, that's the way I am," she said, "and besides, if I said something to you after school, I would just blow up."

I told Mrs. L. that I am student teaching for the purpose of learning, and it seemed as if she wasn't allowing room for any mistakes. She neither agreed or disagreed but continued to talk about how I had done this wrong and that wrong.

This was a start for Alice and Mrs. L. Two weeks later they made further progress:

2/24: Each morning Mrs. L. writes assignments on the board. Today she put my lessons at the end, because yesterday I lost control of the group and she couldn't do anything with the children and had to punish them because of me. I asked her if she felt this was fair. "No," she said. When I asked why she punished them then, she said, "Because they must learn, and learn to listen."

I explained my feeling about having my lessons put at the end. I felt as if I was being punished for making a mistake. I asked her how I was going to develop control if she didn't give me a chance. Agree? She agreed. Then she put my lesson back on the board at the top, but she warned me, "The children must learn, and if you can't keep control I'll have to take them."

Mrs. L. didn't interrupt during the lesson, perhaps because Alice had handled the situation so well. Alice's success, in this instance, illustrates that forcefully but diplomatically stating your side of things can be effective.

Having Criticism of You Publicized.   Any real professional understands that criticism should be private, shared only with the student and the college supervisor. Yet that is not always the case. Remember a game called "telephone"? It was a favorite of Scout leaders and camp counselors. The way you play it is the first person whispers a secret to the second, who in turn passes it on to the next. By the time the story gets around, the last person announces the message as he or she has heard it. Typically, it ends up vastly different from the original.

Dorothy faced a situation in which she was not getting constructive feedback from her cooperating teacher. Instead, as with the telephone game, the cooperating teacher was telling another teacher who was, in turn, passing the information on to her student teacher. This student teacher was a friend of Dorothy's and kept Dorothy posted on how Dorothy's cooperating teacher was feeling.

Dorothy was never sure how accurate the information she heard was and, moreover, she wanted direct feedback. Dorothy's supervisor intervened, asking the cooperating teacher if she would give Dorothy more feedback.

Getting Angry at the Cooperating Teacher.   The student teacher's partnership with the cooperating teacher has the potential for being intense. You will know soon enough whether the mix of your personality and your cooperating teacher's has the potential to lead you to uncontrollable anger. Because favorable outcomes rarely follow outbursts, if you spot such potential, plan a method of keeping your temper under control.

The following may be useful to you in preventing a volatile situation:

- Wait at least one day before you react to an upsetting situation.
- Ventilate your feelings daily in your journal and then, using CONTROL-C, develop suitable means of handling them.
- Talk the situation over with your supervisor and with friends and get their reactions to your proposed ways of handling it.
- Remind yourself that next year the class you will teach will be your own.

Becky was ready to explode with anger at her cooperating teacher, but instead she kept her temper. Following several of the steps previously suggested, here is how she handled the situation:

3/9: Class-wise today was OK, but I had some problems with my cooperating teacher. She voiced her opinions on what I planned to teach when I take over the class. She told me exactly what materials I should use, rather than let me use my own plans, and exactly how I should go about it. I became annoyed, frustrated, aggravated, and just plain angry. But I kept my temper and said nothing and went along with what she said. I will be planning activities for all reading groups, as well as teaching them (these activities) to the individual groups.

After my first week, she informed me, the aide will no longer help me. I will be completely on my own. I understood her logic of wanting me to have experience teaching without an aide, because, true, I might not have one. But for three weeks? I think that's a little ridiculous. I have to work my butt off while they are lollygagging in the teachers' room. Blah! I have decided I will try it for one week or 1½ weeks, but no more. After that, if the aide doesn't help I'm going to Mr. Y. and tell him he is paying his teacher and aide to smoke cigarettes and gossip in the teachers' room. I know I will cause "fireworks," but tough stuff. I have my limit too! Today was a terrible day. I was MAD!

Becky did not vent her anger on her cooperating teacher, which was fortunate because, as Becky's later two journal entries show, her initial concerns and fears did not materialize:

3/10: Today was all right. My teacher came out of her witch act today. She was nice. She even offered to help me with my lesson plans for next week. And she gave me my very own plan book. Hurray! I'm going to let bygones be bygones because after all I still have to work with her and teach her class. And she has to give me my grade. I explained to her that I will be unable to stay for the afternoon tomorrow, because of a prior commitment. She understood. So I hope we are on the road to a better relationship.

3/14: Today was the first day I took over the class completely. My lesson plans are now done for a full week and my cooperating teacher is pleased. The day went pretty well. I came in extra-early to be organized, and it helped a lot. I planned the activities for reading groups, but we continued to teach as is. I taught my group, Mrs. C. taught hers, and Mrs. A. taught hers. . . . I was pleased. I left tired! But pleased.

Finding Yourself in a Difficult Relationship With Your Cooperating Teacher.   Ann was successful in building a relationship with her cooperating teacher despite an unhappy beginning. Ann experienced herself as a low-keyed person and presented herself in class that way. Unfortunately, at least as she perceived it, she was placed with Mrs. K., a vivacious "snappy" teacher, who wanted Ann to be a carbon copy of herself, even though she declared that every teacher should develop her own style.

Ann's success did not come easily. She worked very hard to attain the good relationship she wanted. And she spent many long hours discussing her situation with her supervisor.

She found herself uncomfortable with Mrs. K. and unable, she thought, to talk with her. To complicate things further, Mrs. K. had already established a close relationship with the classroom teacher's aide. This left Ann feeling like an outsider.

The first time she was able to get the teacher's ear at all was the day the aide was absent. Ann took advantage of this situation, for she felt she had to grab at every straw.

The first day Ann asked for feedback on her science lesson, the cooperating teacher responded with, "How do you feel about it? How would you mark yourself?" Ann's silent reaction to those questions was that she wanted Mrs. K.'s opinion, not questions. At this point Ann was not ready to evaluate her own lessons.

Ann and her college supervisor discussed the initiative she could take to improve communication. First and foremost, they decided, she had to be open and honest if she expected to establish a good relationship. She had to communicate her needs to Mrs. K., one way or another.

Ann knew she would have to ask her cooperating teacher for time to discuss her feelings, time to discuss future lessons, time for feedback, and suggestions for improvement. To get this she had to be flexible and willing to come in early or stay late. The situation, she came to realize in discussion with her college supervisor, was unlike social ones she was accustomed to, and she had to make a distinction between her personal and professional life.

When Ann's cooperating teacher turned down a request for a meeting, Ann had to ask again, although in her social life she would not have done so unless the turndown had been accompanied by an explanation and a request for a rain check. Instead, Ann persisted. She ended up treating Mrs. K. to lunch.

With support from her supervisor, Ann continued to arrange meetings and make progress with Mrs. K. About a month into her assignment she made this comment in her journal, "I am starting to build up a very nice rapport."

Ann learned that she had to compromise on certain things while she was in Mrs. K's classroom; this included working with the children in a style that was acceptable to Mrs. K. She came to realize that sometimes you do things because your cooperating teacher expects it, but that you do not have to incorporate these things in your mode of teaching in the future. In fact she wrote, "One good thing I'm learning is exactly what I don't want to do as a teacher!"

The process for Ann was turbulent. At times her spirits were so low that she doubted whether she would ever succeed as a teacher—or even if she still wanted to be one. But Ann pressed on, saying, "I don't want to adopt her style. It isn't me; I'm not the snappy type. However, I probably do need to improve my voice inflection, and I am going to work on it." And so, out of persistence and effort, Ann built her relationship, won her cooperating teacher's respect, and received a top grade!

After Ann's last day at school, Mrs. K. asked to see the university supervisor. The supervisor thought that Mrs. K. was coming to discuss Ann's grade, but instead, Mrs. K. opened a floodgate of feelings. This is the story as it unfolded:

Mrs. K. began apologetically, explaining that this was the first time she had a student teacher. During the early days she found it hard to relinquish her class to someone else, even the student teacher she had requested. "I was very unsure of myself from the start," she explained.

When Ann tried her first lesson, Mrs. K. was shocked at her quiet but diligent style. "But she is so different from me," Mrs. K. thought. That observation led her to remember what had been said by the supervisors at the introductory tea: Each teacher has to be himself or herself. So for the next few days, Mrs. K. tried not to impose herself as a model. Instead she tried to allow, indeed to encourage, Ann to do things her own way. However, that did not work. Mrs. K. saw the children changing under Ann's leadership. Discipline was loosening. The class was falling apart. She saw all her months of efforts "going down the drain." Eventually, Mrs. K. reached her limit and found it hard to refrain from imposing her standards on Ann and directly on the class.

Ann responded to Mrs. K.'s silent (and not so silent) impositions as harsh criticism of her teaching ability. It was then, with the help of her supervisor, that she undertook her campaign to improve communication and persisted until she set up the luncheon appointment. At that time, however, Mrs. K. explained during the conference, "I hadn't realized Ann thought I thought she couldn't teach. . . . I tried to interfere as little as possible. It was difficult to hold myself back. I thought my class, my children, were at stake, but I did hold myself back and much to my surprise it was not as disastrous as I had anticipated. Then when the end of the term came, and Ann began tapering off in her teaching and I began getting back into the act, I had another surprise. I didn't find teaching or disciplining to be a problem. . . . The children were exposed to both styles of teaching, and I think they grew and developed as a result."

In reflecting on the term that had just ended, Mrs. K. also mentioned with satisfaction that although Ann's style was different from hers, Ann had nonetheless acquired some of her ways. Mrs. K. mentioned that even the children noticed this and had said to Ann, "That's the way Mrs. K. would do it."

The conversation ended with Mrs. K. and the supervisor agreeing about how important it is for the student and cooperating teacher to establish rapport. Mrs. K. said that unfortunately she and Ann did not have instant success, but at least they made it. Smiling, the supervisor said that in some cases it never happens.

We have seen both perspectives in the two-sided experience of forming the student teacher/cooperating teacher relationship. Basically, the essence of Ann's and Mrs. K.'s problem is a universal one, and it reduces itself to this: Student teachers must function in established classes and under the direction of others who, over the years, have developed their own way of teaching. On the other hand, cooperating teachers must share their classes with someone new, someone different, probably younger and more idealistic, and surely less experienced—characteristics that are likely to lead students and cooperating teachers to have different perspectives.

Stage 4: Feeling Like a Teacher

By this point, the major problems you will face during student teaching are probably behind you. With the end in sight, what was negative in your experience will seem more tolerable and under control; concomitantly, what was positive will begin to get the weight it merits. Gerald describes what he experienced:

5/17: Just a couple of weeks left. So much stuff to do and learn. Oh, well, there is always next year in my own class. My own class. I have to write that to believe it will happen.

This is my second week of planning and doing the whole day. Before I couldn't imagine how I could [manage] the whole day. Now it seems so natural. Mrs. R. was gone part of the afternoon, and I felt like it was next year. I've learned so much from her—even the hassles we had now seem unimportant to me. I'll miss her, but I feel I'll be ready to do it on my own next September.

Some "Feeling Bads."   As the term progresses and you take over more teaching duties, many thoughts will come to mind, including some that you may find surprising. We review a variety of these here, primarily so you will know that they are normal and typical.

1. Feeling bad because you want the cooperating teacher to leave you alone in the room. This feeling is particularly annoying if you have had a good relationship because, in this case, you may feel guilty wishing him or her away. Vicky made this entry in her journal, "I can't believe it. Even after 3 months she (the cooperating teacher) still never leaves the room, and I wish she would every once in a while."

2. Feeling bad about having to teach a lesson you think lacks excitement or having to teach a concept using an approach you believe is ineffective. Laura provides an illustration: "The day basically went well. The one activity that I was requested to do was pretty bad. It was a filmstrip on maps and globes. The kids were bored with it and so was I, but I had to do it. There are a lot more interesting ways to present maps and globes."

3. Feeling bad because you see time being used ineffectively. Vicky complains about an excessive use of films: "I'm also getting a little upset with the practice of always going into another teacher's classroom when she has a film to show. I think it's great to get films but not necessary to see every one in the school. Just because the class next door may be discussing climate and is seeing a related film is no reason to take my class to see it when we could be doing other things that we never seem to have time for. . . ."

4. Feeling bad about being successful and worrying about whether your cooperating teacher will resent your success. Brenda shares, "I am beginning to feel more confident and I love the children. I really hope that Mrs. C. does not resent or mind my taking over sometimes, because I don't want to offend her. I decided that I wanted this to be a good learning experience, and I hope we can really make it one."

These feelings hardly deserve to be called problems. They sometimes develop during student teaching, and will not be problems if you reflect on them and put them in perspective.

HOW YOU AND YOUR COOPERATING TEACHER MAY DIFFER IN ASSESSING YOUR PERFORMANCE

Rarely do any two people agree 100% in assessing performance, especially if one is the novice performer and the other is the expert mentor and evaluator. Jane Williams (1995) designed a survey study to test this issue in regard to student teaching. Using an instrument containing 54 specific student-teacher performance items, she administered it twice to 200 Tennessee State University student teachers and their 200 cooperating teachers. All in all, she found statistically significant differences on 23 items. In most of those differences the cooperating teachers gave more favorable ratings to the student teachers than the student teachers gave to themselves. At the second administration, the 9th week of student teaching, the cooperating teachers gave more favorable ratings than the student teachers did to the following: Their lessons were not boring; they got students actively involved; they seemed to have had time to plan adequately; and they managed all the paper work.

Not until the 9th week did differences in the assessments occur that Williams considered to hold a high potential for causing conflict between the cooperating and the student teachers. According to the cooperating teachers, the student teachers were having trouble managing small groups and revising lessons while teaching if lessons were not going well. As Williams pointed out, these are instructional skills that are acquired with experience. They are not likely to be in the repertoire of beginners. They probably showed up at 9 weeks rather than at 3 weeks because the cooperating teachers gave their student teachers longer teaching opportunities at the latter point.

Two points should be noted: first, that cooperating teachers in this study generally saw the work of the student teachers in a more positive light than did the student teachers themselves; second, that cooperating teachers may not be mindful of something that most of them probably know, namely, that some essential skills can only be acquired through experience over time. Remind yourself of these two findings during your student teaching assignment to help you keep your morale high and your self-assessment on target.

RELATING TO SUBSTITUTE TEACHERS

The chances are good that your cooperating teacher will miss at least a few days of school. Most likely on those occasions you will be teaming with a substitute teacher.

A day or two with a substitute usually provides a good learning experience, for the simple reason that a new set of circumstances is introduced. Treat the substitute's replacement of your cooperating teacher as a quasi-experiment. The substitute is the one variable that has been changed while everything else has been held constant: the students, the physical setting, your presence, and so on.

Of course, the substitute's personality and skills as a teacher partly determine the kind of opportunities you will have, as do several other factors (e.g., whether the absences happen early or late in your experience, and whether you have lessons ready the day your cooperating teacher is out).

Also remember that in a sense you will be in a position similar to a substitute's in the near future. You will be as new to those in your first class as a substitute is to the children in your cooperating class. Be attentive to how the substitute introduces himself or herself and to the methods he or she employs. Assess the substitute's approach, and note whether it is one you would be comfortable with.

Before looking at problems you might encounter with substitutes, let us look at the bright spots in the picture. Whether you end up teaching (with a substitute observing) or watching a substitute teach is not as important to your learning as it may seem at the moment. By observing, you can often gain some otherwise unavailable insights. Laura reports:

> 3/19: The substitute today was fantastic. She was so bright and cheerful. The minute she walked into the room, you knew things were going to be good.
>
> In fact, Mrs. J. was one of the most enthusiastic teachers I have ever seen. After seeing how effective she was, I wanted to work on my own enthusiasm even more.

Laura saw a style she wanted to emulate, and she was exposed to certain techniques that she might not have otherwise seen. By contrast, Stan had a useful day because he saw what he did not want to be as a teacher and what effect cynicism can have on a professional's performance. He entered the following in his journal:

> 1/4: I worked with a substitute teacher who informed me that teaching was boring. It was evident he was not at ease or content, for his introduction of concepts was hastily completed, which led to impatience when Anne and Blanche and several others . . . asked several questions. He failed to follow the lesson plans Mrs. H. had left for him. I can imagine how much damage a permanent teacher could do to a class if she or he didn't want to be there.

If you are scheduled to teach lessons on the day a substitute covers, you also could find yourself with an opportunity for constructive criticism from still another professional. If your initial contact suggests that the substitute is willing to observe, you could explain how eager you are for feedback and how valued his or her opinion would be. You may also get a chance to teach for an entire day, with the substitute acting as a backup on an as-needed basis. Such an outcome can be exhilarating, as Irene reports:

> 2/26: Today was absolutely fantastic! Mrs. L. was out sick today, and I felt I was the teacher and not just an assistant. She called me last night and told me about the things she had planned. She said that it was completely up to me whether I wanted to do them or give it to the substitute. I decided that I wanted to try to handle the entire . . . [day] and fit her plans into the ones that I had. The day went very well. The substitute was there but always in the background. I accomplished everything that I

wanted to and . . . the day was over before I knew it. The more time that I spend in the classroom the more I dream about having a job in September doing what I want to do.

Finally in the substitute's presence, you might feel more comfortable experimenting and trying ideas you believe your cooperating teacher would not be comfortable with. Sheryl reports such a situation, and what it meant to her:

1/21: Today Mrs. R. was absent and so we had a substitute, Mrs. T. The class behaved better for her than for Mrs. R., and I think it was because she didn't yell constantly over what I feel are unimportant things. She also put extra work on the board for them to do. All the children were afraid they wouldn't get done, which was a new twist.

. . . At the end of the afternoon we had extra time, so we sang "Puff the Magic Dragon" and played two popular songs one of the boys brought. The kids really liked it. It took about 10 minutes and it was a nice way to end things. However, I don't think I would have done it if Mrs R. was here.

Of course, any number of problems can arise between substitutes and student teachers. Sometimes the situation is such that you choose to overlook them, other times you may decide to take action. An example of each is provided in the journals of Carl and then Dorothy. Carl wrote:

2/19: Today we had a substitute. Was today ever horrendous! I had to raise my voice more today than I've had to in the past four weeks. It seemed as though their "routine" was broken by Mrs. B.'s absence. They behaved in ways they never had (i.e., acted dumb to the previously established rules and routines).

The substitute was a sweet person, but she constantly interrupted me and challenged my authority on several occasions. I only hope it really is for one day. I got the impression she wasn't working with me but against me at some points. An example of this feeling of opposition . . . [was] her reinforcing behavior that was contrary to the established rules in the class, like talking, etc. . . . I'm really thankful it's only temporary.

Carl wrote off the experience, knowing his cooperating teacher was returning in the next day or two. He could have been more assertive, but at the time felt it was not worth the risk of causing friction. However, a few days later in a seminar he reported that if it were to happen again, he would have privately approached the substitute during lunch and said, "You know, while I was setting up the first lesson you interrupted me to discipline Brad. I felt the kids saw that as your challenging my authority. What do you think?"

Dorothy did take action, as she reported in this journal entry:

2/8: Miss K. is gone for the entire week due to some illness. The substitute is an elderly lady. She is very sweet, but as she said, "The children are too much for me to control." The main problem was that she continuously sent students to the principal's office. This is not appreciated by Mr. R. (which I will hear about when Miss K. returns), and I don't think it helps the class. Therefore, I discussed the problem with the substitute.

She said this was the last means of control and that she felt it necessary. After we talked, though, no more children were sent.

Dorothy took action in the interest of the class and also of herself and Miss K., because of the principal's anticipated reaction. The substitute did not welcome Dorothy's comments but seemed to respect her for speaking her opinion. Further, Dorothy's comments changed the substitute's behavior.

Another important factor is *when*, during the course of your student teaching, your cooperating teacher is absent. Working with a substitute later in your apprenticeship, when you know the class and feel ready and willing to teach, often provides you with a different experience than working with a substitute earlier. Here's Carla's comments:

2/7: More adventures! Mrs. P. was gone today and they couldn't get a substitute. That's fine; I would rather have the class alone at this point.

We have been discussing issues frequently encountered during short periods of time working with substitutes. Occasionally student teachers find themselves spending substantial numbers of days with one or a series of substitutes. If that happens, the important concept to keep in mind is that these days represent a significant proportion of those you will have as a student teacher. Use these days as best you can for your own learning.

Elaine had experience with a lengthy absence of her cooperating teacher and wrote the following:

5/16: Mrs. R. told me today she has to go to the hospital. I know I can handle the [full] responsibility . . . because I did it the week she was out and part of last week. But I feel bad. I learn a little more every day from her and feel I'll be missing out. Besides, I'll miss her—I've gotten close to her. Well, the substitute they will be getting in her place will have much to offer on things too.

The presence of student teachers, especially after they are familiar with the children (and vice versa) is reassuring to cooperating teachers who face the need for a prolonged absence. Often, knowledge that the student teacher will be there to provide continuity is enough to sway conscientious but ill teachers, who might have otherwise come to school against their best interest. That they have that much faith in you will make you feel good.

YOUR STUDENT-TEACHING ASSIGNMENT AND THE REALITIES OF SCHOOL LIFE

By their very title, cooperating teachers are those professionals who cooperate with your college or university and with you, for the purpose of providing you real-life experience in an apprentice-master teacher relationship. Cooperating teachers are selected for the role because they are considered skilled.

Although cooperating teachers want you to have a rich experience, they are subject to the policies of the school and under the direction of the principal. In a school that values teachers who maintain quiet and order and a highly structured teaching plan, cooperating teachers are unlikely to encourage you to use a teaching approach that carries the risk of disorder. That does not mean that cooperating teachers object to the approach on professional grounds—or would prevent you from trying it under any circumstances. It means only that they accept (even if begrudgingly) the realities of professional life in their school.

Realities like that will be very much part of your life, both as a student teacher now, and as a teacher with your own class in the near future. Perhaps the most helpful advice we can offer is that you make peace with the real limits you face in today's schools. Give yourself permission to function at your best within the boundaries of freedom of action available to you. Whatever limits are imposed on you by your cooperating teacher, your supervisor, or your cooperating school, remind yourself that there is still much you can learn.

Delight in the fact that you are a student teacher, and that you are teaching in a real community and a real school. That community may have social and moral values similar to or different from yours. That school may have educational values similar to or different from yours. Your cooperating teacher may have an instructional orientation similar to or different from yours. Whatever the case, accept it and tell yourself, "This is my one and only student-teaching experience, and I'm going to make the most of it."

Be good to yourself. Devote yourself to gaining confidence in teaching in ways that circumstances permit. Except for those your cooperating teacher permits you to try, save your innovative ideas for your own future class. Record in a notebook those good ideas that come to mind that you know your cooperating teacher would not want you to use in class. That way you will have them available when you can use them, next September or in the years ahead.

In summary, from the first meeting, recognize your cooperating teacher as a potentially helpful person. Understand at the same time that that person will be affected by your responses. If you show that you are eager to benefit from advice, you are more likely to have good rapport. If, instead, you always react annoyed when criticisms are given, you will make life difficult for your cooperating teacher and for yourself. And you will probably discourage him or her from offering you helpful suggestions.

Even with the best of intentions and the greatest of efforts in the relationship with the cooperating teacher, there are always occasions that call for problem solving. When you encounter problems, remember that your supervisor and a method of problem solving like CONTROL-C are invaluable resources.

CRITICAL ISSUES

- How do I feel working under the watchful eye of another person?
- What can I do to raise my comfort level when I'm teaching?
- How do I normally react to constructive criticism?
- What can I do to get the most benefit from constructive criticism?
- If I believe I am being unfairly assessed, how can I cope with that constructively?

4

Building a Good Relationship With Your College/University Supervisor

College supervisors are a special group of people. Typically, they are knowledgeable about the schools in the community where you will teach and are familiar with the problems of daily classroom life. They have a good working relationship with principals and teachers, which is helpful not only during your student teaching but also in your job hunt. Because of their practical knowledge of teaching, they are a rich resource to the student teacher.

Who are the people who serve as supervisors? All of them have had experience as teachers, some for many years. Having themselves been student teachers, they also understand the experience of being in that position.

Supervisors differ in experience, personality, educational background, and approachability. Regardless of the mix of those qualities, your supervisor will be interested in your professional development. You will want to develop a trusting professional relationship with that person, whoever he or she is.

HOW YOUR SUPERVISOR CAN HELP YOU

College supervisors have a broad set of responsibilities and often carry a heavy load. Their tasks may include:

- scheduling and holding observation sessions for each student teacher, including meetings with cooperating teachers and principals involved;
- writing reports on the observations they make;
- conducting a seminar for student teachers;
- planning and hosting professional–social activities for student and cooperating teachers;
- maintaining cordial relationships with principals, department heads, and other school personnel (this for its own purposes but also as the college's "ambassador");
- serving as a confidante, problem-solving aide, resource person, and supporter to student teachers;
- keeping records, including supplying information to the registrar for official school documents;
- keeping informed of position openings for teachers;
- evaluating student teachers and providing official letter grades, often in conjunction with the cooperating teacher;
- composing letters of reference for student teachers.

The supervisor is very much a middle person, an agent of the college working to satisfy the needs of many people. Here are some student-teaching issues that arise as supervisors perform their duties.

As Classroom Observer and Constructive Critic

Your college supervisor will observe your teaching at least several times. On those days, "put your best foot forward" by functioning in the classroom much as you would on any other day. Most supervisors want to observe you and your students under typical conditions in the natural setting of the classroom. That is reason enough to operate in your accustomed way.

But do this for another reason too. To differ greatly from the normal routine adds new dynamics that may lead you and your students to feel uncomfortable. This, in turn, may invite the unpredictable to emerge. The accustomed routine puts both you and your students at ease and increases the likelihood that you will teach at the same level as on other days.

Although an observation day should be treated like others, the days preceding it should be treated differently. Your supervisor in the classroom sitting among the students represents a new condition for which you want to prepare. In doing so, bear in mind that your supervisor's several visits allow you to demonstrate the diversity of your skills.

As at other times, prepare your plans and materials thoroughly and well in advance. Prepare yourself psychologically, by mentally picturing the day unfolding. In effect you will be previewing the expected sequence of events.

Imagine yourself entering the room in the morning with carefully planned lessons well suited to your abilities and the students' needs. When your supervisor arrives, picture yourself handing her or him a copy of your lesson plan for the day, including your aims and behavioral objectives for each lesson. Then, because your classroom has an accepted procedure for introducing classroom guests, imagine making the introduction. Your cooperating teacher smiles; so does your supervisor.

If at any point a negative thought comes to mind, banish it. For instance, if you start thinking that you have chosen the wrong lessons, reassure yourself immediately. Remind yourself that the class has previously responded well to lessons like the ones you have planned. Remind yourself that you are well prepared.

Picture yourself remaining effective throughout the observation period. Imagine the supervisor asking, "Do you have time for critical feedback now?" The words "critical feedback" ring in your ears: You remind yourself that this is the evaluation your supervisor promised to give you after the observation. You are alarmed again, but only momentarily. You remember that your supervisor has your development as a teacher at heart, and wants to help you become the best teacher you possibly can.

Playing out the imagined scenario of a forthcoming observation is an effective preparatory mechanism. It helps you deal with the worry and stress evoked by your thoughts about the supervisor's scheduled observation. Some uneasiness is natural under the circumstances. Your supervisor is there to evaluate you; you alone are in the spotlight, and you want to excel.

Returning to the preparation of your materials and plans, try to do this well enough in advance to discuss them with your peers. Then, after benefiting from their input, you can discuss them with your cooperating teacher. The consultation will help you gain confidence. However, keep in mind that you may do this and still be nervous. That is the time to remind yourself that you are well prepared. Phyllis wrote:

> 3/8: I was tense about the observation at the beginning . . . in the back of my mind I was hoping that the children would be easily managed and my lesson would go all right. As it turned out, an early part of my lesson failed but everything else seemed to go well. Afterwards my supervisor gave me some good advice which I have really thought about, and now even the failures of the day seem unimportant.

Because Phyllis prepared extensively, much of her nervousness passed once she began her lesson. Further, she was well enough in control of herself so that she was not devastated when—early in the period—her lessons did not go as planned. Under the pressure of being observed, that minor misfortune would have upset some student teachers. But Phyllis had prepared for contingencies and thus was able to handle the situation.

Phyllis' nervousness was short-lived. Stephanie was never able to free herself of anxiety, even though her supervisor had worked especially hard to make her feel comfortable while being observed. Stephanie wrote to her supervisor in her journal after two successive observations:

2/25: Today I must admit, I was a little edgy and nervous. It's funny, but I feel very comfortable and relaxed speaking with all of you in college, but I felt nervous just knowing that I was being observed by you, Mrs. S. Also, the lesson I had planned did not go according to my plan, though it went pretty well. . . . I was very glad that you spoke with me immediately afterward and gave me many interesting suggestions.

The next month, she still experienced substantial anxiety about being observed, although she was becoming a more confident and able teacher:

3/30: Today I must admit again I was a little nervous. As I explained to you, Mrs. S., you're one of the nicest people I have ever known and I feel very comfortable talking outside the classroom, but I guess that just knowing I am being observed can throw me a little. Well, anyhow, my day was planned and everything went pretty smoothly. Afterward, I felt very comfortable speaking with you, because I felt by criticizing and making creative statements about how I could improve certain things you were helping me. One other thing that I felt very pleased about was when you told me that you thought I had good control and was doing a good job teaching. As you once said in a seminar—a little praise never hurts anyone!

Although intelligent and insightful, Stephanie could not manage to free herself of anxiety about being observed. But that was not disabling because she managed to keep it at levels that did not materially affect the quality of her work. Although Bev taught in a situation similar to Stephanie's and Phyllis', because her level of anxiety was higher and she was unable to control it, her student-teaching experience was less satisfactory. Bev wrote:

6/2: . . . I'm a high strung person . . . the presence of my supervisor and at times my cooperating teacher made me uneasy, and unsure of myself. I had the most faith in myself when no one was there. and I feel that's when I did my best work.

Bev assumed that because she was high strung, the presence of adults observing her in the classroom would inevitably affect the quality of her teaching. Once Bev accepted this assumption as fact, she handcuffed herself. Instead, she should have used a logical problem-solving procedure, like CONTROL-C, to tackle her anxiety.

Although Bev performed adequately as a student teacher over the course of the term, she did not develop in a most important personal way, that is, in terms of her confidence in working under the observation of others. Our profession is a public one. Our classrooms, in sharp contrast to the offices of our fellow profession- als—lawyers, physicians, and dentists—are always open to the scrutiny of others. Next year Bev will have to work at making herself more comfortable with her principal and with parents who come to observe her class.

If you find your stress level uncomfortably high during an observation, and this continues in second and third observations, take action. First, apply CONTROL-C. Identify factors related to your anxiety. Second, as part of the CONTROL-C process, talk with a friend or, better yet, with your supervisor. That is what Nancy did, initiating contact with her supervisor through the following journal entry:

1/20: I feel very loving and warm today. I like myself. I was thinking about our talk last week: You must think I'm immature. It's really weird that I can't talk with you. I'm usually pretty open. I guess I'm intimidated by roles. Nope, that's not it, because I basically feel that you deserve no more human respect than anyone else. I respect the fact that you have gone to school a lot longer than I and are valuable and helpful as a resource person. But I'm not in awe of professors. I wonder why I am uncomfortable, uptight with you. I'm sorry.

When Nancy discovered that she had considerable difficulty in dealing with the student teacher–supervisor relationship, she treated her problem in an effective way. Although some might have been tempted to delay taking action, Nancy immediately raised it with her supervisor, and the two of them together were able to help Nancy resolve this difficulty successfully. As a result, Nancy was able to capitalize on the guidance and insights of her supervisor during her student-teaching assignment.

Carole, in contrast, never gave her supervisor a chance to be of any help. The problem arose early in the term when Carole had a direct conflict with her supervisor. Unlike Nancy, Carole did not foresee the value of tapping her supervisor's resources and took no steps to resolve their differences. Instead, she simply let things drift, trying without enthusiasm to please her supervisor by her behavior in class. Let us follow events that took place in Carole's relationship with her supervisor, starting with comments in her journal about their first meeting:

2/8: Wednesday was the first session with my supervisor. . . . I brought up the question of the role of the student teacher in the classroom, giving my opinion that it is a dual role: (1) the cooperating teacher aided the student teacher by contributing to his development and guiding him, and (2) the student teacher contributed to the cooperating teacher by bringing new approaches and developments that were being introduced in university classes. My supervisor stated, "But most teachers and principals would not agree with you." I answered, "But ideally this is what we want." Her response was, "But ideals don't exist in city public schools." This is a 7-credit course and I have already antagonized the supervisor. That's all I need today!

One month into the term Carole had already been having a difficult time with her class. Frustrated by classroom conditions she had no power to change, Carole seemed to release her frustrations in her first session with her supervisor by defining the student teacher–cooperating teacher relationship in a "radical" way. She did this without forethought about how her comments might be perceived by her supervisor, a person charged with the responsibility of maintaining good relationships with the cooperating teacher and school.

Carole would have been better off if she had recognized what was really going on inside herself. She was frustrated by her mixed success in the classroom and could have benefitted greatly had she asked her supervisor to observe and discuss with her how best to approach the situation. Fortunately, Carole's supervisor returned to her school the next week. This time Carole handled the situation differently:

2/17: Mrs. W. stopped in briefly for a conference with the other three student teachers and me. We had an interesting conversation. She'll never really see things my way, but at least I used my head more today in the discussion. That helped us to be more open with each other.

The relationship between Carole and her supervisor had taken a step forward. She knew that her supervisor would be making four visits to her classroom, and that her grade for student teaching would be based on the outcome of these. Carole wrote about the next visit:

2/29: My opinions about my supervisor have changed somewhat. At least I must admit she's a well-meaning person. I also must realize that she had a rather strange first encounter with me. The things I was saying weren't things one would normally say to a supervisor just like that.

As far as Mrs. W.'s actual observation went today, there is nothing particularly exciting to say. My lesson went well. . . . I spoke to her briefly right after the lesson. She commented that I should be more dramatic. Things should be gre-e-e-e-at and w-o-o-onderful when kids get them right. Mrs. W. was surprised (and she said so) at how well things seemed to be going in the class. She mentioned that after our first talk she was a little disturbed and had prepared herself for the worst.

Carole's classroom assignment was not an easy one. As the weeks went by she realized that her cooperating teacher, although considerate, was not overly committed, what with holding a second job, going to graduate school, and being a parent. Carole's learning experience would have been richer had she learned more fully to tap what her cooperating teacher did have to offer.

Carole's second observation went poorly. Her supervisor arrived early, the class had been having a bad day, and in teaching her lesson nothing seemed to go right. Although the third observation was better, the final one, she felt, was a great success:

5/9: Today was my last observation. I must admit that it was a relief to have it over with. I learned my lesson well. I put on a show for her, and she obviously liked it. The kids really enjoyed the African folk dancing lesson. You can tell. It just shines all over their faces.

Each time Carole had been observed she went through severe anxiety and tension, made worse, most likely, by her doubts about her relationship with Mrs. W. Had she employed CONTROL-C at the outset, she would have spared herself unnecessary pain and gained more from her student teaching assignment.

Carole's experiences offer many lessons. One is this: The student teaching experience is brief (although at times it may feel endless). When you identify a problem in your relationship with your supervisor, try to correct it immediately. Carole knew a problem was brewing after the first meeting, and she expressed her concerns in her journal. If at that point she had obtained information about the purposes of student teaching, she would have learned that they did not include providing continuing professional education to the cooperating teacher, even if that sometimes is a by-product.

If Carole had used CONTROL-C and sought this information, she would have confronted questions such as the following (all related to her February 8 journal): Where did I acquire the concept of the dual role? What did I mean when I responded to the supervisor, "This is what we want"? Whom did I mean by "we"? What motives were involved in confronting her? Why do I think I antagonized her? What will I do now? Presumably, faced with those questions, Carole would have evaluated her motive in challenging her supervisor and would have acted to correct any damage done. Why did Carole allow herself to remain alienated from a professional whose help and support could have been greater than it was—which was considerable under the circumstances? Think about that question. By supplying your own reason you can alert yourself to motives that might hamper you in making full use of your supervisor.

Three further points are worth noting. First, Carole had moderate success in overcoming the initially poor relationship. Although this improvement was partly due to her supervisor's professional behavior, Carole's efforts were helpful too, even if they were primarily driven by concern about her course grade and not by the desire to make the most of this unique experience.

Second, an important aspect of professional development is strengthening one's skills of communication with peers and supervisors. During a successful experience, the student teacher learns from interactions with the supervisor and cooperating teacher as well as with students. Because the student-teaching assignment is of such short duration, you would be wise to set to work immediately to make the best of it, even if you are not happy with your supervisor or have a difference of opinion about educational issues. An important principle in working with others is to recognize and utilize their strengths and learn from their weaknesses.

Third, Carole's supervisor, like yours, wants her student teachers to be successful and to have the kind of experience that will help them become effective teachers. Besides caring about students, supervisors take pride in the quality of their own work and are concerned about their professional reputation, both of which depend partly on the success of their student teachers.

As a Problem-Solving Resource

The journals we collected contain hundreds of examples of supervisors making suggestions that aided student teachers in solving a variety of problems, such as developing materials, teaching lessons, and coping with different kinds of students. Although the assistance they provided was similar to that offered by the cooperating teachers, supervisors had the advantage of different perspectives: first, of seeing many teachers at work in different schools and school systems; second, of bringing to their observations in any given class the fresh outlook of the outsider; and third, of knowing the most advanced outlook on teaching.

An important specialty area of supervisors is in helping student teachers deal with difficulties in their relationships with cooperating teachers. Here we explore three examples that illustrate this supervisory role.

Brent, whose student-teaching experience seemed to be going well, came to see his supervisor because he was unhappy about the grade his cooperating teacher had given him. He thought that he had established good rapport in the classroom and that his work had been well received by both the class and the teacher. True, he might have been a little weak in disciplining, but Mr. H. had never expressed any dissatisfaction; in fact, he had praised Brent often. "So why the mediocre grade?" he asked himself.

The supervisor supported Brent's questioning of the situation. After some discussion it was agreed that the supervisor would take the initiative and set up an appointment with the cooperating teacher. This was done and, after the usual niceties and a general discussion of Brent's classroom work, they turned to the subject of Brent's grades.

It turned out that this was Mr. H's first experience as a cooperating teacher, and he had decided it would be wise to mark Brent low on the first grading period and then on each successive marking period to grade him progressively higher. Mr. H. felt this would be advantageous because it would show Brent's growth during his student-teaching experience. After a constructive discussion during which the supervisor explained to Mr. H. the consequences of his well-intended actions, he decided to change Brent's grade to one that reflected his actual performance.

The supervisor intervened directly in Brent's case. More commonly, supervisors will help you solve problems by sharing their ideas or perspectives. Ann's cooperating teacher wanted Ann to work with the whole class, but Ann felt she was ready to work only with groups. The supervisor could see that Ann's protests and worries were not consistent with observable fact, even reported fact, for Ann herself had written:

> 3/10: I also had quite an experience reading a story to about one hundred children while they waited for the film to be ready. I'm not sure how I did. They were all quiet, so I guess I must have been doing something right.

Ann's cooperating teacher kept urging her to "feel self-assured." Ann insisted that this feeling would come to her only with time. The supervisor scheduled a series of appointments to discuss with Ann just what was involved in being self-assured.

The supervisor argued against the position that you were either self-assured or not. She noted that Ann was hardly devoid of self-assurance, reminding her of the previous journal entry, although it was written as if Ann were reluctant to admit her assurance. The supervisor explained that teaching the whole class would bring Ann success that, in turn, would yield greater self-assurance.

A supervisor can also help you better understand some unexpected reactions on the part of experienced teachers. The example we use is a poignant one, illustrating as it does the harsh fact that it is not only students who are victims of stress when the college supervisor comes to observe. Unfortunately, some cooperating teachers feel that they themselves are being observed and assessed.

Following are reports written by Leslie about two of her observations and her cooperating teacher's reaction to them. We have also included in brackets the comments the supervisor wrote in Leslie's journal:

> 3/9: I was quite anxious to see how Mrs. J. was going to react with my supervisor in the room. After the assembly program, the kids were very excited. Mrs. J. was getting nervous because they weren't being quiet. She kept giving me these frantic looks. I don't know what she wanted me to do, because I certainly didn't expect them to sit like angels after having attended such an exciting program. [Supervisor: I thought the kids were great.]

> 3/31: Mrs. J. was so hyper when I reminded her my supervisor was coming tomorrow. It really bothered me. She told me to make sure I had control. I don't know whether she expected them to sit around like silent bodies or what, but I didn't like the idea that she wanted them to be little angels just because there was going to be a visitor in the room. At lunch Mrs. J. suggested I tell the children to be extra quiet to help me out during my observation. I told her I didn't want to do that and she assured me that she used to do it and it worked out well.

> [Supervisor: her reaction—it is a pity, but I see it time and again, though usually not carried to this degree. I think it's basically a lack of security which I can understand in a student teacher but not in an experienced one. You handled the situation well. I hope you will not allow these experiences to interfere with your learning from her. She does have much to offer.]

Only pressure of great intensity would lead professionals to be so concerned that, instead of being a source of strength and security, they add to the student teacher's anxiety. Because some cooperating teachers see the success of their student teacher as a reflection of their own ability, they unknowingly create unrealistic expectations about what their student teachers should achieve.

Granted that some cooperating teachers have to contend with their own problems, we urge you to concentrate on the strengths of those assigned to help you, even as you recognize their frailties. Leslie had been incensed by her cooperating teacher's suggestions about asking the children to be "extra quiet" and made an appointment with her supervisor to discuss her annoyance. When they met, the negatives poured out. As Leslie came to understand her own attitudes, through talk and her supervisor's input, she became less self-righteous and more understanding of Mrs. J. Then, she was able to recall the various ways Mrs. J. had been helpful and could appreciate her, despite the inappropriate advice in this instance.

As a Source of Emergency Help

"May I phone you at home?" supervisors are often asked by their student teachers. If your supervisor makes no mention of that possibility early in the term, ask about it, and if the supervisor approves, obtain the home number and the preferred calling hours. If a telephone number is given, unless you are instructed otherwise, use it sparingly—only for genuine emergencies, by which we mean that you are very troubled and cannot resolve a dilemma or reach a decision necessary for the next day.

In an interview, Tracey, who worked in an urban high school, reported the following:

2/16: I came home late one afternoon and spent several hours over-organizing my kitchen and wrestling with the question of whether to call my supervisor. Finally, at 10:00 p.m. I made the call to Mr. A. The teachers are meeting tomorrow to discuss unionizing and my cooperating teacher invited me to come. In fact, it seemed more like a request than a polite invitation. She said, "You might as well learn now about what teachers have to put up with in terms of bureaucracy." I have mixed feelings, however. I would like to get a job in this district next year. My husband works downtown [in city government] and I don't want to alienate the principal who I want to write a letter of recommendation.

Mr. A. and I had a long talk. When he finished he said, "I'm glad you called me about this decision. It's the kind of thing teachers must think long and hard about. I do have one question," he added. "If you knew about the meeting for a week, why did you wait so long to call me?" I didn't have an answer for him then. But after a little bit of thought, however, I figured it out. I was hoping the issue would just disappear, so I wouldn't face the decision at all.

As a Seminar Leader

In many colleges the supervisors conduct a seminar for student teachers. This seminar, designed to supplement the practicum, differs from other college-level classes in several important ways. First, there are typically no exams and sometimes no letter grades. Second, all the students are having the same kind of preprofessional experience, although their learnings may be very different. Third, student teaching, and that alone, is the major focus of the class. Fourth, the major objective of the seminar is to give the support (professional, academic, and psychological) that will help student teachers be most effective and profit from their experiences.

How can you best use this resource? First, use it as an incentive to organize the thoughts and feelings you have about your classroom. Prepare for your seminar beforehand by reviewing the classroom events of the previous days. The process of making such preparation may help you gain fresh insights into what you have been experiencing and may also ready you to participate more actively. With the help of the seminar group, you will be able to see that the stimuli you experience every day in class with your students are not just a mass of unrelated events. They fit together and relate to theories that you have studied.

Second, use the seminar to discuss problems you are confronting. Be open with your thoughts and feelings. Some student teachers are hesitant to be frank, feeling that such disclosure will reflect badly on them. However, the fact is that if they are experiencing a particular difficulty, the probability is high that other student teachers are too. They will be pleased and perhaps relieved that you mention it, as will the seminar leaders who want active participation by the group in order to have useful sessions.

Third, the seminar provides an ideal forum for exchanges. Participants in this sharing derive benefits not only for the present but also for the school years ahead. You can share and trade ideas, lessons, methods and materials, and teaching strategies (e.g., finding a way to involve students in a science experiment, or to help manually awkward pupils in industrial arts, or to encourage mainstreamed students to participate in physical education activities.)

Mark spoke of the benefits of sharing in his seminar: "The second period English class is awful. Four senior girls sit in the back corner and giggle. I know one or two of them have a crush on me. I brought the matter up during seminar and found that several other students, both male and female, faced the same difficultly. Together we figured out several ways to tackle the problem."

As a Support Figure

The college supervisor also functions as a support figure, sometimes by being a good and sympathetic listener. Student teachers may need such support. They have been working toward this gateway to teaching for years and may have exaggerated notions of what they can accomplish. Anthony, for example, first had hopes of changing his cooperating teacher's class in ways he felt were pedagogically superior. He comments:

> 3/3: I have become aware of something, that is, that any changes that are going to be made in the class are only going to be incremental.

Anthony expected Ms. V. to change in his direction, and he expected to be able to teach exclusively in his own way, not Ms. V.'s. His next comment suggests that he felt there was something inherently wrong or undesirable about trying out the cooperating teacher's "routine:"

> 3/10: I'm a little worried. I seem to be getting the idea that I will be following Ms. V.'s routine when I finally take over. I realize the children need some type of a steady schedule, but frankly there are times when I'm bored with her routine.

With help from his supervisor Anthony came to understand the following:

- The class routines had been established before he arrived.
- Ms. V. and the class would have to work together after Anthony finished student teaching.
- He should try to accommodate himself to fit her teaching style.

With support from his supervisor, Anthony had an "aha" insight. To be an effective teacher, he had to develop his skills in recognizing and taking the perspective of others. His supervisor explained that from Ms. V.'s perspective, he was a guest. From the perspective of the students, the issue was not whether Anthony was bored by Ms. V.'s lesson, but how they, the students, were reacting.

WHAT SUPERVISORS LOOK FOR

Your supervisor probably will inform you of his or her expectations at the outset of your experience as a student teacher. If he or she does not, it would be appropriate for you to ask.

Even without asking, you can be sure of some important dimensions that will be taken into account in evaluating you. Your college supervisor will want to see you develop the basic qualities of the professional—qualities that all educators value. Promptness, for example, is essential. Reliability in other matters is also of vital importance.

If you are ill and cannot work, or if your car breaks down and you will be late, phone the office to inform the principal and your cooperating teacher at the earliest possible time. If you are scheduled to prepare some material for school or to give a report at the college student-teaching seminar, have it ready by the due date. If you are annoyed with the cooperating teacher or the supervisor or both, do not allow your anger to build silently; on the other hand, do not resort to angry outbursts. Bring the matter up directly and professionally.

Absences should be reduced to essentials. A person who phones in ill repeatedly is not one who is going to be wanted or recommended for a position. Someone who schedules medical and business appointments during school hours is going to leave an indelible impression on the supervisor and cooperating teacher, and not the kind that leads to good ratings when grades are due or when reference letters are written.

Natural and normal appreciation of what others do for you should be expressed. Supervisors, being human, get satisfaction from knowing that advice they gave you about some home economics equipment or about a more effective way to use a recently released software program meant something to you. They also like to be appreciated when they help you understand that your cooperating teacher, although perhaps lacking a diplomat's tact, is nonetheless pointing out a way for you to improve the questions you raise in class or to make better use of science equipment. And if their interactions with you are not rewarding and their critiques not penetrating, they want to know that, too, and early.

Before turning to the final section of this chapter on evaluation of student teachers, we want to elaborate on some conditions in your classroom that are beyond your control. Your supervisor knows that you will be constrained by the existing conditions.

THE CLASSROOM CONDITIONS THAT SET LIMITS

As we have said before, there is no one right way to teach. Each of us formulates a personal approach. It is based on our beliefs, experiences with teachers in schools and college, interactions with students in our classes, and the influence of the school system in which we teach. How we teach may also depend on some factors beyond our control. For example, the physical structure of our classroom or the school's rules may limit us. Further, important limits are imposed by the classroom climate already established by the cooperating teacher and others in the school.

Here we review three studies that speak to limits that exist in cooperating classrooms. These studies are valuable because they point to subtle factors often overlooked by student teachers.

As a rule, student teachers have been exposed to many different kinds of teacher behavior. As elementary and secondary students themselves, they have experienced diversity, and as college students they have learned about varied instructional techniques. They have a right to wonder, in advance of their beginning to take over the class, whether there is some way of knowing if certain kinds of teacher behavior are likely to be more effective than others.

Probing questioning, so important to the teacher's behavior, was studied by Copeland (1978). The kind of probing teacher questions Copeland examined were those that followed a student's verbal statement and were based on the substance of that statement. Such questions were intended to encourage the student to go further into the thought previously expressed. Copeland wanted to find if there was support for either or both of the following:

1. Cooperating teachers, by asking probing questions, encourage student teachers to use the skill.
2. Cooperating teachers, having accustomed the students to the skill by using it prior to the arrival of student teachers, foster and support the use of that skill by student teachers.

Copeland used 32 student teachers who had been trained to ask probing questions, and 64 experienced teachers (Grades 2–5), 32 of whom were high users of probing questions and 32 low users. Of the student teachers, 16 were assigned to high users as their cooperating teachers and 16 were assigned to low users. That means that half the student teachers had cooperating teachers who served as models of teachers using probing questions, and the other half did not. In the meantime, the other 32 experienced teachers (16 high users of probing questions and 16 low users) were teaching their own classes without having any student teachers.

After 3 weeks, the student teachers were asked to spend 30 minutes each day for a week teaching reading groups in another classroom, classrooms taught by those other 32 teachers. The question now was: Which student teachers will ask probing questions during those 30-minute sessions with the reading groups? Will it be those student teachers whose cooperating teachers had served as question-asking models?

The findings were as follows:

1. Student teachers who taught reading groups in classes accustomed to hearing probing questions used them themselves, whether or not their cooperating teachers in their regular student-teaching class used them.
2. Student teachers who taught reading groups unaccustomed to probing questions did not utilize them extensively, whether or not their regular cooperating teachers provided models of the use of that skill.

The conclusion of the study is that the ecological system in the class (what the students are accustomed to) has a large influence on what skills a student teacher uses. Students become accustomed to behaving in a certain manner in a certain class and are likely to respond to their student teacher much as they do to their teacher.

This important study demonstrates that your ability to experiment in your cooperating class is limited by the style and approach to which the students are accustomed. This finding makes sense at an intuitive level. Keep it in mind early in the term when you are trying to establish yourself as a disciplinarian. To hold their attention and to maintain the necessary order for learning, find out what practices they are accustomed to.

Classroom climate, a subject of much interest to teachers and student teachers, was studied by Hearne and Moos (1978). The researchers went to 19 high schools (11 general and 8 vocational-technical) to study the relationship between subject matter and classroom climate. To do this they gave the 4,000 or so students and their teachers in the 207 participating classes a 90-item questionnaire. This was designed to measure the extent to which the following nine characteristics were present in their classroom:

1. Involvement: Assesses the extent to which students have attentive interest in class activities and participate in discussion.
2. Affiliation: Assesses the level of friendship students feel for each other.
3. Teacher Support: Assesses the amount of help, concern, and friendship the teacher directs toward the students.
4. Task Orientation: Assesses the extent to which it is important to complete the activities that have been planned.
5. Competition: Assesses the emphasis placed on students competing with each other for grades and recognition.
6. Order and Organization: Assesses the emphasis on students behaving in an orderly and polite manner, and on the overall organization of assignments and classroom activities.
7. Rule Clarity: Assesses the emphasis on establishing and following a clear set of rules, and on students knowing the consequences if they do not follow them.
8. Teacher Control: Assesses how strict the teacher is in enforcing the rules, and the severity of the punishment for rule infractions.
9. Innovation: Assesses how much students contribute to planning classroom activities, and the extent to which the teacher attempts to use new techniques and encourages creative thinking in the students.

As you examine Table 4.1, note that the researchers grouped the participating classrooms listed in column 2 into the categories (based on the nature of the subject matter taught) listed in column 1. The characteristics of the climate they expected to find in each category is listed in column 3 and what the students reported about climate in columns 4 and 5. As you examine the table, you will see that in some cases, but not in all, they found the climate as they expected.

These results illustrate several important points:

- Each class has its own climate.
- Students tend to describe it similarly.
- Classes offering the same subject matter tend to have similar classroom climate.
- The class you enter for your student teaching will already have a climate of its own.
- Studying the dimensions of classroom climate described in the table will suggest the kind of climate you might find in your student-teaching class.
- Bearing in mind the results of the previously mentioned Copeland study, you will undoubtedly work most effectively if you operate within the limits of the classroom climate already established by your cooperating teacher.

Student brinkmanship is another behavior to consider in connection with classroom climate. The term has been defined as behavior that students engage in to resist school authority, in other words, to resist you, the teacher.

The term "brinkmanship," and the concept of being on the brink or on the edge, well describes the student behavior involved—for example, the clowning, giggling, chalk squeaking, book dropping, and enthusiastic hand-waving instead of hand-raising—all of which are done by the students at a level that is not really punishable. Students know they can get away with this brinkmanship level of behavior and, in doing it, they express and release some of their hostility to authority.

Newman and Licata (1986–1987) studied the relationship between such behavior on one hand and teacher and classroom climate on the other. Their subjects were students and teachers in 122 classes in a large, urban-suburban school district in the midwest. Both teacher and student samples were representative of the diversity seen in today's schools.

The findings of this carefully designed study suggest the following useful hypotheses:

- Students are less likely to use brinkmanship if they feel positive about the teacher as a considerate person and about the classroom climate. In other words, they tend to be less hostile and not engage in brinkmanship if they find the teacher is friendly, respecting, and warm, and if they find the classroom climate favorable (cohesive—students interact and feel friendly with each other; satisfying—students like their class and work).
- The frequency of student brinkmanship is inversely related to classroom routinization. Teachers can reduce the incidence of brinkmanship by increasing the amount of time given to following well-established, orderly routines.

Implicit in Newman and Licata's study and their discussion of their findings is this advice to student teachers: While you are developing a positive teacher–student relationship (based on "consideration"), rely heavily on routinization. Initially, to establish routines, the teacher sees to it that students know what work is to be done

TABLE 4.1

Classroom Categories and Expected and Observed Characteristics

(1) Classroom Category	(2) Classroom Subjects Assigned to Each Category	(3) Expected Characteristics of Classroom Climate in Each Classroom Category	(4) Characteristics Rated High by Students in Each Classroom Category	(5) Characteristics Rated Low by Students in Each Classroom Category
Realistic	Auto repair, carpentry, electronics, general shop, machine shop, power mechanics	Asocial, conforming, frank, genuine, materialistic, persistent, practical, stable, thrifty, uninsightful	Involvement, affiliation, competition, rule clarity, teacher control, innovation	Task orientation
Investigative	Algebra, biology, chemistry, geometry, mathematics, physics, physical science, science	Analytical, curious, independent, intellectual, introspective, introverted, passive, unassuming, unpopular	Task orientation, teacher control	Involvement, affiliation, innovation
Artistic	Art, band, composition, drama, English, French, German, Italian, literature, music, Spanish, theater	Complicated, disorderly, emotional, imaginative, impractical, impulsive, independent, intuitive, nonconforming, original	Innovation	Competition, rule clarity, teacher control
Social	Civics, economics, government, history, political systems, social studies, sociology	Friendly, helpful, idealistic, insightful, persuasive, responsible, sociable, tactful, understanding	None stood out in the analyses	Task orientation, rule clarity, teacher control, involvement, affiliation
Conventional	Bookkeeping, clerical office practice, retailing, shorthand, stenography, typing	Conforming, defensive, efficient, inflexible, inhibited, obedient, orderly, persistent, practical, prudish	Task orientation, competition, rule clarity, involvement, affiliation	Innovation

Note. Portions of this table are from Hearn and Moos (1978, p. 113).

and when it is to be done. Once the relationship is established to your satisfaction, you can then reduce your reliance on routinization and use it in ways consistent with your teaching philosophy and approach.

HOW YOU WILL BE EVALUATED

Evaluation will be important throughout your professional career. Understandably, at this point in your life you are mostly interested in the evaluation that will be made of your student teaching. Therefore, our comments about evaluation focus on that. Nevertheless, the general principles of evaluation apply equally to those assessments made by your cooperating teacher and those you will make of your students' work in your classes this year and in the future.

Evaluation involves the process of making judgments. Your cooperating teacher and university supervisor (with different degrees of influence depending on institutional policy and individual differences) will make judgments about your student teaching.

Those judgments will be of two types. The first, known as *formative*, will be made for the purpose of advising you. They will advise you, not grade you. Your mentors, as a result of their observations, will indicate to you, perhaps through questions or direct comments or a combination of both, some of the ways in which you could be more effective. They may, for example, suggest how to arouse more student interest in classroom activities, or how to manage the class with fewer discipline problems. Their aim will be to help promote your development as a teacher—or, as we might say, to help you "form" yourself professionally.

The second type, known as *summative* evaluation, will be made to indicate by means of a grade whether you have successfully completed student teaching. This will be a judgment of your all-round effectiveness, taking into consideration your strengths and weaknesses. This type of evaluation can be thought of as a form of "summing up" your current level of performance.

One of the greatest gifts you can give yourself is to recognize that the evaluation you get at this time in your career is worth a fortune. Two experts are going to share their time, observations, and advice "for free," something you are unlikely to get to this extent at any other time in your career.

If you find in yourself a feeling that you want to avoid their observations and hide your usual practices from them as much as possible, then think of the following example: A young singing artist, hopeful for a career in opera, goes for a lesson with an expert teacher who will listen, advise, and listen again. Can you imagine that young singer thinking, "I pay that teacher $100 a lesson, but I want to hide my usual style, and when I get advice I won't take it because I think the teacher is wrong"? Student teachers should not allow themselves to get that uptight about being observed and evaluated or that close-minded about another person's point of view, even if they believe the observer holds a different philosophy of education.

As we said, you may never again get this quality of evaluation (repeated observations by and feedback from two experienced teachers). A leading expert

(Raths, 1982) explained that although claims are made that teacher evaluation is an ongoing process in the schools, in practice this is more rhetoric than fact. Unless there are major changes in the future, you are likely to be observed and evaluated only by administrators and only infrequently during the course of your career.

As far as *student teaching* is concerned, several researchers set out to investigate how student teachers are being evaluated on the national scene (Fant, Hill, Lee, & Landes, 1985). By drawing on prior studies, they identified eight factors. We describe each of the eight factors because you may well be evaluated in those terms and because you may find them useful.

1. Clarity: Objectives clear and understandable to students, content well organized, important points stressed, reviews and summarizes.

2. On-Task Behavior of Students: The percentage of time students are involved in learning, in contrast with time spent in trying to keep order or discussing unrelated topics. (This is not an argument against discussing the circus coming to town or the World Series, but for managing a high proportion of on-task time.)

3. Use of Feedback: How often and how well students are given high-quality feedback about their work.

4. Task-Oriented: The class climate is task-oriented, meant for learning, not entertainment. Learning objectives and tasks are clear, class starts and ends promptly. (A business-like atmosphere does not exclude humor and lightness.)

5. Warm, Supportive Environment: Teachers are kindly in their relationships with students, showing respect and acceptance of all of them. Students feel that the teachers are available to help them.

6. The Flexible, Adaptable Teacher: Can change as situation demands it, and can adapt plans as student responses dictate.

7. The Enthusiastic Teacher: Excited about learning and students know it. (This teacher quality is believed to be important to motivation and students' tendency to concentrate on learning tasks.)

8. High Expectations of Students: High expectations are thought to foster higher student achievement.

SUPERVISORS AS EVALUATORS

Your supervisor will of course consult with your cooperating teacher prior to assigning you a grade. As we noted in the chapter on cooperating teachers, the study by Williams (1995) showed that on a survey questionnaire of 54 student-teacher performance items, where there were differences, generally the cooperating teacher gave higher ratings than the student teachers gave themselves, especially at the 3-week mark of student teaching. At the 9-week mark, two unfavorable ratings by cooperating teachers stood out: handling of small groups and ability to revise lessons while teaching if the lessons were not going well. If your cooperating teacher should be unaware that these more difficult skills of teaching come with experience, your supervisor is likely to point that out. In any event, these are skills that you will want to work on, perhaps by seeking the advice of your cooperating teacher and supervisor and also by evaluating yourself.

As a student teacher, one of the great benefits of evaluation is the opportunity to learn how to evaluate yourself. You might find it helpful in this respect to use a format like the one described by Hanhan (1988). With this format, in advance of a mid-semester conference with one's supervisor, the student teacher is asked to reflect on 13 questions, for example, the times of the day and/or week that are the easiest and the hardest; areas in which one feels pressured and those that are smooth-running; a description of some of the students; and a view of one's role as teacher. The student teacher is asked to prepare a question about an area of personal concern about teaching, which is to be discussed at the conference. The self-knowledge from the conference is believed to breed self-confidence. It also helps to establish a mode of dealing with problems.

From such a process you stand to gain an enormous amount. From reflecting on specific questions about your student-teaching experience and discussing it with your supervisor, you stand to gain three of the major objectives of supervision: self-confidence, self-knowledge, and problem-solving skills.

CRITICAL ISSUES

- How do I feel about being observed by someone who will grade me?
- What can I do to manage to "be myself" when I'm being observed?
- What can I do to get the most benefit from my student teaching seminar?
- What benefits can I get—and give—from sharing experiences with other student teachers?

5

Building a Good Relationship
With Students

The first day. Ms. V. introduced me to the class. I looked them over . . . like a sea of faces. I smiled and they did too. I just hoped I'd be able to be a good teacher and that I would have some beneficial impact on their lives.

These were the thoughts of one of us authors during the first day of student teaching. In fact, by the end of the term this student teacher did have "some beneficial impact on their lives." As a student teacher you, too, can have a positive impact on your students and make significant contributions to their development.

Students are the central characters in the classroom. Your objective is to give them the best possible opportunities for learning. As we have said, because you are a guest in your cooperating teacher's classroom, you must work within limits set by her or him. Nevertheless, you are still free to do meaningful things. Most importantly, you are free to develop a relationship of trust with the students. You can do this with the class as a whole by acquiring a reputation for fairness, and with individual youngsters by helping them learn.

You are free to strengthen these relationships by establishing the practice of making comments to individual students that give them recognition and a feeling of self-worth—and not just to the most able learners, but to all students. You are free to demonstrate your interest in them by making their classroom experiences exciting, in part by relating learning to their lives. You have many opportunities to help enrich your students' learning experiences and, in doing that, you will gain confidence in your ability as a teacher.

LEARNING ABOUT THE STUDENTS IN YOUR CLASS

Start looking at individual students from the outset, preferably on your first day at school. Guard against having your attention predominantly focused on the obvious ones, such as the attractive, or the very vocal, or the undisciplined ones. The quiet and restrained students deserve just as much attention. All students—fast, average, or slow—have something that interests them. It is worth discovering that something, whatever it may be, in order to make use of it in your teaching.

How well you know students partly determines how much they will achieve in your class. When you know students' current level of development, then you know what assistance they need to make additional progress. Just as in the work of the physician, diagnosis is needed before you write the prescription (i.e., plan of action) that will enable you to help students take the next steps in intellectual and social development.

Here is Ruby, in her first week as a student teacher, working at getting to know the students so that later she can more effectively assist them in learning. Her journal entries are instructive for another reason, too:

1/6: Kids—I'm getting to know them better, to know their names and personalities. A lot of them have problems or unusual home situations that they want to tell you about; questions aren't necessary, they just want to be listened to. Felicia likes to tell about her family, and even though it doesn't seem ideal, she seems happy about it. Stan is supposed to be in a primary special class, but because there is no room he is in a regular third-grade class. Mrs. W. says that he cannot do a lot of the work, so a lot of it isn't assigned to him. He seems bored.

My first impression was that Stan needed personal attention. I didn't question the idea that Stan has learning difficulties, but he does a lot of the work that the other children do and with just a few minutes of personal attention he has done work for me that wasn't expected.

Daniel is another child that I am concerned about. Mrs. W. says that he consistently receives Fs on his work and has expressed her dislike for him because of his attitude. She says his family is on welfare and his mother is a real "slut." My first impression of Daniel was that he was a nice boy who needed a good one-to-one relationship and a lot of motivation. Today on the multiplication test Daniel missed 8 out of 12. After the test he asked me his score. I showed it to him and he said, "I had both of my fingers crossed hoping I'd get a hundred. I haven't got hardly any hundreds all year."

1/7: Mrs. W. seems concerned about my interest in Stan and Daniel, and I'm afraid she feels that by showing concern for them I'm questioning her success in teaching them. Today in the lounge the principal mentioned a chance at getting help for some of the kids. Mrs. W. told him Daniel had already been tested and still no outside help has been made available to him.

After going back to the classroom Mrs. W. and I talked about Daniel a little more. Mrs. W. explained that there wasn't time for her to give Daniel 15 minutes of personal attention each day. I agree. But Stan and Daniel need that attention and help, and the school system has a responsibility to provide it for them.

Yes, Ruby made the kinds of observations an effective teacher makes, but she was not being helpful to herself by her self-righteous attitude. Sensing that her cooperating teacher felt threatened, by approaching her in a sensitive manner, she could have made this a more successful learning experience for herself and more helpful to the children. Because it was early in the term she might, for example, have asked Mrs. W. for suggestions on how she could help Daniel and Stan or, alternatively, developed a plan and asked for Mrs. W.'s reaction.

People sometimes get a false sense of self-worth because they recognized something another person missed. They feel superior because of another person's errors. Ruby should feel good because she got to know her children and learned about their needs, but not because of what may be seen as her cooperating teacher's inadequacies. As all teachers come to learn, when there are 20 to 30 children in a classroom, even the best of us cannot single-handedly be aware of everything that is important, not to mention attend to all that needs to be done.

Returning to the subject of understanding the students and their classroom needs, skill in making accurate diagnoses does not come automatically. The classroom is an active and busy place. So much is going on that one's mind tries to adapt by unwittingly stereotyping the students and treating them according to certain expectations—one child is responsible, another a doll, this one the quiet one, that one the bully, the troublemaker, or the dull one.

Juan's comment addressed this point:

3/7: My day brings me into contact with over 120 different kids in my classes and 1,000 more in and around the building. During my first few days I formed impressions about many of the kids, and the impressions tended to stick. I was really surprised yesterday when Jacki—who I thought was a tough-too-cool lady—came up to me after class and asked for extra help. Was I surprised! I had to revise my thoughts about her and now I'm wondering about all those early impressions.

Let us look at how other student teachers experienced stereotyping and what they did to correct it. Making a last entry in her journal, immediately after her student teaching ended, Patty reflected on her experiences:

6/6: In the beginning, I watched the children closely, finding that certain ones appealed to me more than others. I guess this must be quite a natural, automatic feeling, but I knew these feelings shouldn't influence my attempts to reach all the children. To deal with this, I tried to talk more with the children I thought would be harder to handle.

I would ask them questions on an interpersonal level, and in handling discipline, I talked to the child individually, hoping to build some rapport. In doing this, I hoped to let each child know that he was equally important to me, and that his feelings and behaviors were given my attention. I found incidents where, because of my attempts, children began to respect my feelings too, and a rapport grew. However, I also saw some of the children could have been given more of my support.

I found getting to know the needs of each child to be quite difficult. In order to find a child's level of maturity or ability, I once again related to each child on an individual level. Observation is another technique I used to see the development of the children socially. I'm quite sure that sometimes I interpreted, underestimated, or expected too much or too little from some children. I feel that if I would have had more time with them, I would have understood more.

Anyway, I was very conscious of showing the children that I did care for each as a person. In group activities, I tried to build confidence in certain children by allowing them to perform successfully. When I showed them my pleasure, they became pleased with themselves.

Rita recognized a tendency in herself to attend to certain types of children and to neglect others. Her journal entry is unusual in that she found herself paying special note to shy children:

1/28: I have a tendency to attract and pay more attention to the shy and introverted children. . . . Since both of those girls [referred to earlier in her journal] are extremely outgoing, I think I might have been passing over them. I'll have to correct that.

Today seemed destined to "prove" to me the difficulties of finding a balance in your relationships with children in the classroom. How can you accept, without rejecting, those children who want to almost cling to you so that they can learn to be independent and yet also friendly and at ease? How can you relate to the child who seems to be afraid of you, without intruding? Perhaps the answer is just to be friendly and at ease to all and let time and their individual personalities decide the outcome.

Elaine, a talented young student teacher, took the problems she faced in stride. No wonder she did, the way she saw the children as individuals. In reviewing her student-teaching experiences she reports:

5/25: My feelings about my children and my profession are fantastic! Each of my children was beautiful in a unique way. Each was capable of a certain amount, and I made each know that I believed in that capability. I always tried to include all of them, especially those who were less secure about themselves. They all knew that I liked them and have no doubt that they all liked me. Being with them was a great ego trip.

My greatest faith in myself as a teacher concerns my ability to love and understand each child equally, and deal with them accordingly. I enjoy very much, and am proud of, the profession that I have chosen. There is something very special about working with children.

It is because of all this that I want to teach. I value myself, and what I am doing, and I have faith in my abilities. Student teaching succeeded in backing up my confidence.

You can guard against stereotyping students by being alert to instances when this might occur, and you can actively work to circumvent it. For example, at the end of the first few days of your student-teaching assignment, note which students you observed and the time spent watching each. After a few more days note whose names you know and whose you do not. Every half-day or class period single out one student for your attention, go to him or her, say something supportive, have a conversation, and/or ask a question. Every week or so develop a list of strengths and weaknesses of several students and a program to correct a weakness of those in most immediate need of remedial help. For example, youngsters who daydream during class assignments could be helped with occasional positive reinforcement when they are concentrating on work: "You are really coming along, Chris" or "Good work."

RECOGNIZING THE DIVERSITY IN YOUR CLASS

Cultural Differences

Looking at the faces of the children in many American classrooms, one is left with the impression of the "United Nations." So many of the world's people are represented here. This raises a challenge to the teacher to understand the cultural differences and how they are played out in the classroom. Next we present useful information about three large segments of the American student population: Asian Americans, Hispanic Americans, and African Americans.

The fastest growing population is the Asian American. During the 1980s it grew by 80%, or twice as high as Hispanics and six times greater than the growth of African Americans (Carrasquillo & London, 1993).

We use the term "Asian American" as if they were a homogeneous group. In fact, there are distinct differences among the Asians who come from more than two dozen countries of Asia and the Pacific Islands, among them Cambodia, China, Japan, Korea, Laos, Samoa/Tonga/Guam, Thailand, and Vietnam. We can not spell out those differences here. For more detail describing the Asian groups, as well as other groups in our schools, see *Parents and Schools: A Source Book* (Carrasquillo & London, 1993).

Those authors point out several facts useful to teachers. For example, most Asian children are raised in highly disciplined and sheltered home environments; to live harmoniously, they do not aggressively promote themselves, and they guard the expression of their emotions; teachers are respected, and their directions are carefully followed; Asians value education highly and their children are urged to excel; Asian students may show the impact of practices in Asian schools where passivity is promoted and where students listen, do not ask questions, and memorize lectures and lessons, consequently doing well academically. Remember, these facts are but guides to help teachers gain perspective on how Asian children may look differently at the classroom than their non-Asian teachers. Of course, one must look at each student as an individual.

As with Asian Americans, the term "Hispanic" applies to a heterogenous group, coming, as they have, from Cuba, Dominican Republic, Mexico, Puerto Rico, and Central and South America. In terms of numbers, the largest groups are the Mexicans, Puerto Ricans and Cubans, in that order, with Dominicans fourth. With the exception of the Cubans, most of them did not bring with them educational and commercial skills that would aid in their adjustment. On the average, Hispanic families are larger than non-Hispanics, and a higher percentage are headed by a female parent with no husband present. They have lower median incomes, and more of them in 1989 were living in poverty (26.2%) compared with non-Hispanics (11.6%; Carrasquillo & London, 1993). For the children, 40% live in poverty, compared with 15% for Whites (U.S. Bureau of Census, 1992.)

Hispanics have a higher incidence of below-grade-level enrollment than other populations. As a result, they tend to be older and bigger, are more likely to be bored, have lower self-esteem, and are at greater risk of early drop-out (Fracasso & Busch-Rossnagel, 1992).

Teachers who are unacquainted with cultural differences, including child-rearing practices, are likely to misunderstand the behavior of many Hispanic children. For example, the "polite, retiring and deferential behavior toward school personnel . . . is frequently misunderstood as docility, obsequiousness, and passivity by the unknowing observer" (Fracasso & Busch-Rossnagel, 1992, p. 91).

Improved classroom interaction appears to be vital to improved learning. In a review of studies on Mexican American students and classroom interaction, Losey (1995) said the research suggested that teachers could ensure greater involvement of students. To do that, teachers needed to (a) use collaborative learning techniques, for example, with students working together as teams; (b) introduce material that is both challenging and related to the interests of the students; and (c) accept and appreciate the students' language usage. This is good advice in working with students in general.

In the next chapter we dwell further on Hispanic values that are relevant to the parent and student-teacher relationships. Here we add that the children generally come to school without preschool experience and enter a world that is different linguistically, cognitively, behaviorally and emotionally. These differences can easily undermine their self-esteem. Bear that in mind. To counteract it, you can demonstrate your value of the Hispanic heritage. Within limits of your knowledge (which you can continue to expand), you can use "the Spanish language, foods, music, dances, and celebrations as examples in class" (Fracasso & Busch-Rossnagel, 1992, p. 93).

Again, we stress that these observations are reported by us to alert you to group tendencies that may or may not apply to individual students in your class.

As with the other groups, African Americans constitute a heterogeneous group. Although all of them or their ancestors came from Africa, some by way of Caribbean islands or Latin America, there are marked cultural differences among them that distinguish various ethnic groups (Carrasquillo & London, 1993). An obvious difference between the Jamaican-born and the native African American is in dialect.

Considering African Americans collectively, their median income is 43% lower than European Americans, and the proportion of them who are poor is three times greater than Whites. Furthermore, 44% of African American children live in poverty (U.S. Bureau of Census, 1992).

Many African American families, even among those of low-income, have high aspirations for their children. They want to see them achieve well. The children benefit from a collaborative relationship of school and parents, and they need support and positive expectations and a positive classroom climate. These are needs that you as a teacher can strive to satisfy.

Further useful information on diversity may be found in Procidano and Fisher's handbook for school professionals, *Contemporary Families* (1992). Here are the names of the four parts of the book, out of a total of five, and the chapters in each part that are relevant to this section:

I. Family Configurations: dual-wage families, single-parent families, step-families.
II. Families of Diverse Ethnic and Cultural Backgrounds: Hispanic, African American and Korean.
III. Families in Stressful Situations: in poverty, facing death and serious illness, effects of divorce on children's adjustment.
IV. Families with Vulnerable Individuals: learning-disabled children, families of children with chronic illness, children and parents with psychological disorders.

Diversity in Temperament

When you observe a class of students of any age seated at their desks, you find marked individual differences in behavior. Some students sit quietly, others periodically shift their positions in their seats, while still others seem to be in almost perpetual motion, moving restlessly from one position to another. To a considerable degree you are witnessing evidences of difference in temperament.

Psychiatrists Chess and Thomas (1987), who pioneered work in this field, defined temperament as the behavioral style of an individual. It is the "style" of behavior, not the "why" (what motivates them) or the "what" (the content and abilities that go into behaving). They found that normal children from early infancy differ in nine categories of temperament, such as:

1. "Activity level," which refers to motor functioning. Even from infancy some children tend to be active in their behavior, whereas others show this trait to a low degree. You will see some children wiggle continually as they work, whereas others sit still.

2. "Approach or withdrawal," which refers to the individual's initial reaction to any new stimulus, be it food, people, places, toys, or procedures. You will see some

students stand back, not ready to respond to a new stimulus until they have grown accustomed to it, whereas others go out eagerly to meet a new situation.

3. "Rhythmicity," which refers to the regularity of the individual's behavior. Some children, from early infancy, eat, sleep, eliminate waste, and socialize almost by the clock; others, the arrhythmics, at the opposite extreme of normality, do these irregularly. Some students will settle in for the class period, grow restless toward the end of the lesson, and show other signs of being influenced by their "internal clock," whereas others will behave in a studious fashion, regardless of what the schedule is or whether lunch time is at hand.

Attention span and persistence are two more categories of temperament with educational significance. Knowing some of the ways in which people differ is important. It explains, for example, how perfectly normal children, who are arrhythmic but assigned to rhythmic teachers, can become behavior problems without anyone's realizing that at the root of the situation is a difference of temperament—probably present from birth. Further, knowing about temperament enables you to recognize that you will have all of these types in the classroom, and you are also one of these types. You will find it useful to be aware that different behavior—very active or very inactive, eager or leery about meeting new experience, very rhythmic or the opposite—is still normal and may be more or less unchangeable in some students, even into adulthood.

You may want to do what Barb described in her interview: "After learning about temperament in class I went to the library and read more. Then I mentally classified myself and several of my students. I saw where I meshed with some of them and where I didn't. Then I developed plans to deal with what I call the 'temperament gap.'"

DEALING WITH TROUBLING AND TROUBLED STUDENTS

For your needs as a student teacher, it is helpful for you to become aware of the difference between troubling and troubled students. The troubling students are those whose behavior creates difficulty for the class and the teacher; their actions distract or disrupt the ongoing teaching–learning process. Troubled students are those who are unhappy with themselves and their lives and who often have great difficulties in interpersonal relations.

Troubling students will "identify" themselves to you quickly. Troubled students, however, can go unnoticed for a long time. Carla told about an experience 2 months after she started that made her first realize the nature, and something of the depth, of the problem of one troubled boy, Christopher:

3/3: One thing happened today that did upset me. When the kids were lined up waiting for the buses some punching occurred. I asked the children to stop, saying that I thought we were all friends in our class and that I was upset they were doing something that might hurt a classmate. At this point one little boy, Christopher, said that nobody liked him. I said that I didn't know why he said that—that I really liked him (he's really a very sensitive and likeable child). I was hoping that some of the kids would also contradict him, since they could all hear him, but nobody spoke up.

Christopher always sounds as if he has a cold and does not enunciate any sounds well. I feel this is a big factor in his lesser communication with classmates and maybe a reason why he feels "unliked" by his peers. I feel bad for the kid. I really do like him and would like to make him feel more comfortable with his peers. I'm not sure how to go about it, however.

Although Carla applied her common sense knowledge of human behavior, she did not understand that (a) she was indeed on the correct road of helping Christopher in the classroom by her interest and sensitive understanding; and (b) this kind of problem is not quickly remedied. Her supervisor, after rightfully complimenting Carla for her handling of the situation, explained that Christopher did not need pity or sympathy. He needed understanding and the kind of creative teaching that would give him experience with success.

Troubling children and adolescents vary in how troubling they are. Some discussed here might be considered tame compared with those who act out their anger and frustrations in overt acts of aggression against classmates and even the teacher. These "tame" examples are useful, however, partly because they are much more frequent than the very serious cases, but also because their greater simplicity facilitates learning the principles involved in acquiring effective coping techniques.

For example, consider the principles implicit in Mrs. S.'s management of a situation described in Jean's journal:

1/19: Through observing Mrs. S. handle an emotional incident today, I learned how to handle it. The incident consisted of Margaret telling Mrs. S. that another girl had called her a bad name. Mrs. S. asked Lauren, the accused, to apologize to Margaret. Lauren walked over to Margaret but couldn't say that she was sorry; and then Mrs. S. said to her (very effectively), "Lauren, it's so easy to say nasty things, but very hard for us to say we're sorry." I thought that the lesson was well conveyed and made a positive impression on the child. Had the situation been mine to handle, I'm not sure I would have been able to do such a good job. Now, however, I feel that this can be incorporated into my way of thinking.

Before you read further, consider how you would have dealt with the problem. Did you wonder why Mrs. S. did not first ask Lauren if she was guilty as charged? In all probability Mrs. S. saw enough of this student's behavior to assume the report was correct. Furthermore, Lauren did not deny it. Mrs. S. was effective because she was not riled up by the use of a "bad name" and was not vindictive. Being clear headed, and in command of herself, the adult was able to express matter-of-factly the kind of human wisdom that hits home, no matter what age group it is applied to.

Besides having the desired impact on the children, Mrs. S.'s behavior, when followed consistently, has long-term consequences. With regard to this episode,

Margaret had the satisfaction of knowing that her teacher would protect her against abuse in the classroom. She would not have to accept abuse and internalize it (i.e., "swallow it," which is never good for mental health) or carry on some kind of a fight in the class and suffer bad consequences.

Lauren learned that antisocial behavior was unacceptable and also that her teacher was a human authority figure who did not condemn or humiliate her, but could actually understand and reflect her difficulty about apologizing. Also the rest of the students, or those within earshot of the incident, learned all of these lessons, although at lower levels of intensity than the leading characters. The troubling student can be the bane of the student teacher's existence. Because your effectiveness in the classroom depends on your success in coping with troubling youngsters, we deal further and concretely with it in other chapters.

Whatever the age group or class level, coping with the troubling student requires an attitude of respect combined with clear and unrelenting firmness. That is why a basic principle of this book is that success for you really means fostering your own development, so you can feel and react like the adult authority figure and class leader you are perceived to be by your students. If you are like most student teachers, it will take you time to make a transition—to move from the relatively passive and subordinate role of student that you have had for years to the active and superordinate role of teacher. That change is probably the most crucial professional adjustment you will face during student teaching.

PREVENTING PROBLEMS

We refer again to Jean's journal about Mrs. S.'s handling of the situation involving name-calling. Besides reaffirming her position as a fair, humane, but forceful teacher, Mrs. S. avoided unnecessary confrontation and subsequent damaged relationships and negative attitudes. She did not threaten, "Now, Lauren, either you apologize to Margaret this minute or I'm sending you to the principal." Never—yes, we use the absolute here—compound problems by creating unnecessary confrontations. They do nobody any good.

Student teachers must also guard against whatever vestige remains in them of a childlike grudge (e.g., she did it to me, now I'll get back at her). Once the offending student is punished, the episode is terminated, even if the offender shoved you or used an obscene word. For the sake of your professional effectiveness, the experience of such unpleasant interactions should be the occasion to think more about preventing them.

There are many ways to prevent avoidable problems with students no matter what their age. A few are mentioned here, first by Roger:

5/18: Mrs. M. feels it is more beneficial to reward good behavior than to reprimand bad behavior, and I agree with this. While this is something I try to keep in mind, and remember to do at times, it comes more naturally to me to ask a student to stop an inappropriate behavior than to praise another for an opposite, acceptable behavior. However, I will continue to work on this.

Bored students find ways to stimulate themselves. Sometimes they do it by provoking classroom trouble. Laura found a creative way to deal with one boy's boredom:

> 2/15: Leonard is extremely bright. For the most part, the group activities are below his level. Today when we were going to have a story I decided to let Leonard read it for the class. He did great. It solved the problem of his being bored, and the kids enjoyed it too.

At the end of her student teaching, in a discussion with her college supervisor, Dorothy said that a most valuable lesson for her was learning to listen to the children. She discovered this principle after the following incident:

> 3/25: I felt so bad today. Actually I felt like an ogre. Tracy asked me to go to the bathroom twice while she was doing seat work, but she had just gone to get water. I said, "Wait till you finish coloring." Well, a few minutes later she peed in her pants and gave me this look. I told her I was sorry. I just hope Tracy doesn't hold it against me. I took her aside and said that I was really sorry.

From her experience, Dorothy learned the value of listening and trusting as problem-preventing tools. Nancy learned from hers how, in the future, to avoid the kinds of problems that develop when a teacher has unrealistic expectations:

> 2/2: The kids put on their plays for the other ninth-grade English classes today. We explained that these were works-in-progress, not finished productions. The second-period group's play was a fiasco, but fun. They were disappointed and mad at themselves. Definitely a learning experience.

> I'm more relaxed and accepting again now that it is over. I think I was taking these plays too seriously and expecting too much. The "mad" notes the kids wrote me, after I asked them to, said I was asking too much, and I think they're right. We went into these plays with the idea of having fun and learning to work together. I got too hung up on technical things. I guess it's been a learning experience for me, too. I hope so.

Rewarding good behavior, making class interesting, and listening to the students are teacher behaviors that Roger, Laura, and Dorothy learned are important. Those teacher behaviors help make for good teaching; at the same time they are likely to prevent problems. They also contribute to a positive atmosphere and to a sense of community in the classroom.

The feeling of community in schools has been found to be very much related to highly important student characteristics. In a study of 24 elementary schools, when students had a sense of the school as a community, they tended to have positive attitudes toward school, motivation for school work and behavior appropriate to learning. "Sense of community," in this study, meant "caring and supportive interpersonal relationships in the classroom (e.g.,'my class is like a family') . . . caring and supportive relationships throughout the school (e.g., 'students in this school help each other') . . . and student autonomy and influence on classroom norm setting and decision making (e.g., 'students have a say in deciding what goes on')" (Battistich, Solomon, Kim, Watson, & Schaps, 1995, pp. 631, 633). Working to create a sense of community in a classroom, especially in a school that has that feeling of family, is a major preventive activity.

HOW STUDENTS AND STUDENT TEACHERS FEEL ABOUT EACH OTHER

Expect certain thoughts about your students to cross your mind. Some of them will be pleasant, such as the interesting and exciting way they responded to a lesson. Some of them will be troubling, such as using a difficult student as an excuse for a failure. In a very human way we may even have fantasies (or dreams) in which we eliminate the person. If you tend to be excessively self-critical, you may condemn yourself for thoughts such as these. Remind yourself that such transient thoughts are natural and widely experienced.

The other side of the coin is being troubled about how the students feel about us. A student teacher who has an excessive need to be liked by the class members is at a great disadvantage. Stephanie appears here, in the first of two journal entries, to be expressing warm feelings about the children:

2/17: Today was my first day back in over a week. I really missed the children, and it made me feel good knowing they remembered me. Since I had written out their Valentines before I got sick, I brought them in and the children liked the late surprise. I was sorry that I had to miss their Valentine's Day party, but they told me all about it. I even got some Valentine cards from the children. It was nice.

Almost 2 weeks later, however, Stephanie's journal puts her behavior in a different light. Her report suggests that her need to have the attention and affection of the children was excessive and not constructive:

3/9: Yesterday when I met the afternoon class . . . I walked around, spoke with them, and by the middle of the session, a few of them were even fighting with one another to hold my hands.

We all want to be accepted and liked, and if this happens, it makes the student teaching experience that much more pleasant. The problem here is not Stephanie's gratification over the children's apparent feelings about her, but that she could report with obvious satisfaction that she was so liked that they fought over her. This is not a teacher devoted to the needs of the pupils but, rather, a teacher inducing the pupils to satisfy her needs. Needs like this that dominate our classroom functioning interfere with the kind of clear thinking we, as leaders in the classroom, must engage in if we are to see to it that the students have the necessary opportunities for learning.

That very kind of clear thinking enabled Erin, then about 2 months into her student teaching, to use a child's ordinary drawing as a projective technique. By doing that, and by avoiding self-centered temptation, she gave a child an opportunity for emotional release. She herself was able to get important insights about the child that would otherwise have been difficult to obtain:

> 3/19: Today went great. I had the children draw something they like to do and then tell me a story about it. Some of the children were very creative, and I gained a lot of insight into how well they express themselves. This one little girl did two pictures, one with me in it and one about home. I wanted to ask about the one with me, but I decided I'd learn more from the other one. Her story about that painting was amazing and I felt it reflected a lot. In it she had different objects and whenever she went to play with one, her mother would yell at her or beat her. It was amazing how well she could tell me a story about this picture, and it probably reflected her home.

Erin's supervisor praised her for creative use of the pictures and for developing hypotheses about the meaning of the girl's statements. However, she urged her to treat it as no more than a hypothesis and to discuss her observations with her cooperating teacher.

HOW FRIENDLY SHOULD YOU BE?

One question that comes repeatedly from student teachers is, "How friendly should I be with the students?" Our answer is: A teacher is not a friend. Teachers and students have different roles in the classroom and different responsibilities. Being a close friend with students conflicts with being a teacher. Contrast friendliness—an attitude of interest in the students' welfare and support for their efforts—with that of being a friend, which means being a peer, a co-equal involved in the personal lives of others.

Some student teachers deal with their uncertainty in the class by seeking approval from everybody. If they have a great need to "win" the students' favor, and if they work toward this goal, they may find themselves unable to manage their class. Arnold wrote about his cooperating teacher's warnings:

> 4/11: I asked her about my control over the fifth-period class. She told me that I was getting too close and that the guys may soon treat me as a friend more so than a teacher.

Beth talked with her cooperating teacher about being a friend with the children. Here is how she thought about it and what she did:

> 1/9: Ms. W. discussed with me the issue of being too much of a "friend" with children. Ms. W.: "If you become too much of a friend, the children will run over you." I agree, but where is the happy medium? I feel she is too extreme.

Later in this journal entry Beth described how being too friendly with a student disadvantaged her as a teacher:

> 1/9: How do you handle discipline problems? For example: Alice said Donna took her black crayon. Donna denied it. How do you handle this? I responded by saying,

"Donna, Alice said you have her crayon. Will you please give it back?" Donna said she didn't have it. I asked her again, very nicely, but Donna continued denying it. When I told her to clean out her desk she immediately returned the crayon. Looking back, I can see that I was too cautious, still talking to Donna as if she was a friend of mine rather than a child. Maybe Ms. W. isn't too far off. I'll have to try her way.

ANALYZING YOUR CLASSROOM WORK

It is true that teachers are sometimes expected to accomplish the impossible. Take presenting a lesson, for example. Imagine finding material and an approach that will hold the attention of 25 or more youngsters long enough for you to get key points across, to have them understood and digested. Teachers have to do that several times daily with children and adolescents and, as Amy reported, it does not always work:

> 3/2: I began a unit on space today by reading the children a short story about a mouse and what happens when she sees the moon's reflection in a puddle of water. I also hung up a skylab poster. I was pleased with the poster because the children took to it right away. The story however had its ups and downs. At one point the children seemed really interested in the story. Then a few of the children became very disruptive and the whole class began to lose interest.

> I think the whole problem with the lesson, though, was when I stopped to speak to the disruptive ones and when the story was interrupted by an interesting but lengthy point. Some children lost interest then. I also think the interested children began to mimic the behavior of the disruptive ones.

> One good aspect of the lesson was that it gave me feedback in the sense that I now know what direction I need to go to hold all the children's attention. To prevent some children from becoming disruptive.

Amy continued her analysis of the situation in her journal, as she explored the many parts of that experience. She approached the problems in a logical way as a rational adult.

You, too, will want to analyze problems you face in your class in this way, using a logical problem-solving approach like CONTROL-C. You will also want to devote time to understanding your students and to reflecting on the kinds of relationships you have with them, individually and as a group. This is a helpful way to learn about yourself and to grow as a professional.

As you examine your work, do not be hard on yourself, no matter what flaws or mistakes you discover. No teacher, not even a masterful teacher, has a succession of perfect days, a fact your cooperating teacher will certainly validate.

As you are analyzing your classroom work, bear another fact in mind. If school curricula were designed mainly around the interests of young learners, and if those learners were conditioned to a less authoritarian system, student teachers would not have to be so watchful about maintaining their position of authority. But student teachers do have to be watchful. Anthony found that out. After a particularly difficult day with his class, he asked his students why they "listened" to Ms. V., and not to him. He raised this question to the whole class. With the frankness that students can be depended on to give, they told him that Ms. V. gets angry and shouts. Anthony wrote:

> 4/19: I have found it hard to raise my voice and to keep from smiling. But I began to see that I had to try and see what would happen if I did. It worked, I'm glad and sorry to say. It sure made life easier, but it left me with a dilemma. Maybe when I have a class of my own I will be able to condition them to respond to me as the teacher without my having to shout. But it won't work here.

We agree that Anthony's hope is justified. It is possible to teach and control a class in that way. Some teachers do. A teacher can be the complete leader with a smile and without shouting. But a student teacher may not be able to do so in the class to which he or she was assigned—especially if the children have been trained to respond only to scolds, reprimands, threats, and other forms of intimidation.

We work with an imperfect educational system. Doing so is simply an everyday feature of life. Our present educational system is all we have. Although it is being improved, at a snail's pace, we must make the best we can of it. That means we use it as effectively as we can to help children and adolescents obtain the best possible education under the prevailing circumstances.

CRITICAL ISSUES

- Am I seeing students accurately or seeing "stereotypes"?
- To what students am I partial?
- How do I think they see me? What gives me that impression?
- What am I doing to avoid problems from arising? What else can I do?
- In what ways have I used problem solving approaches like CONTROL-C to understand my relationships with the students?

6

Building Relationships With Parents, Principal, and Others

TOPICS
- Getting to know the parents
  - The American family
  - Culturally different parents
  - Parent–teacher meetings/parents' open house night
  - Individual parent–teacher conferences
  - Individual parent conferences for special needs
  - Parent visits during the school day
  - Parental reactions to a student teacher
  - The absence of parent–teacher contact
- The principal
  - As classroom observer
  - As school leader
- The other teachers
- The staff
- The custodian
- A note on next year
- Critical issues

In fantasy and in real life, absent characters sometimes play important roles. Hamlet's father, offstage except for his lone, ephemeral appearance as a ghost, plays a central part in that great drama. In a one-woman play about poet Emily Dickinson, members of the audience sense that they are witnessing a drama involving many characters. Yet, all the other characters, some of them very central to the story, are "offstage."

How much that is true in the classroom! Neither parents nor principals nor department chairpersons are physically present, but each has a voice as to what goes on in class. Together, they determine some of the important limits within which we work: the composition and size of our class, the curriculum we teach, the standardized tests we administer, the values we stress, the topics we may or may not discuss, and often even the mood children are in when they arrive at school. Other important absent characters include fellow teachers, vice-principals, the superintendent, and members of the school board.

GETTING TO KNOW THE PARENTS

Most teachers have personal contact with parents under several different circumstances: Parent–teacher meetings and parents' night, individual parent–teacher conferences on "conference day," parent–teacher conferences for special needs students, and informal parent visits during the school day. Selected groups of teachers such as teacher-coaches, band directors, drama coaches, and so on, may work closely with parents, particularly when parents provide support groups for these activities.

Drawing from several chapter headings in a book quoted earlier (Carrasquillo & London, 1993), we start with some principles that apply to virtually all parent–school and parent–teacher interactions. Given the goals you and your school undoubtedly have, these principles are relevant to your needs.

1. To help students be successful: Ability, effort, and parental involvement are needed. The first two are obvious, for students do need to acquire the ability to do the class work, and they surely need to exert the effort to gain the level of success they are capable of achieving. The emphasis here is on the third, parental involvement. Even if parents are unable to provide direct assistance, either because of their own limited education or because of language deficiencies, their high valuation of education, their encouragement, and their support are significant forms of "parental involvement," and they are instrumental in helping their youngsters to be "successful students."

2. To help schools be successful: Increasingly, educators are recognizing that to have successful schools, a partnership between parents and educators is vital. The partnership means that the school administrators and staff are interested in parents' involvement in their children's education, including their ideas about the curriculum. It also means that parents are actively encouraged to participate in conferences with teachers and at parent–teacher meetings.

3. To help empower all parents: Empowerment in this context means helping parents become better able to influence the school (and the school system) their children attend. It should involve "planning new, positive relations between and among parents, the school, and its community" (p. 103). Parent empowerment can result in higher quality schools and communities.

4. To help parents develop a positive self-concept: This is a particularly potent challenge, because the self-esteem of some parents may be undermined when coming for a school conference or visit for one or more of the following reasons: minority group membership; low socioeconomic class membership; meager com-

mand of English; limited education; unhappy childhood school experiences. The implication is clear: What is needed is school staff behavior that warmly welcomes parents, that sensitively encourages their participation, and that demonstrates genuine interest in their children's welfare.

"Schools, families, and students get stronger when parents and teachers take collaboration into their own hands." That is the title of an article in Research and Development Report, the publication of the Center on Families, Communities, Schools and Children's Learning (1995). The Center is a consortium of seven colleges and universities dedicated to the kind of change implied in the title of the article. The article itself reports on the exciting changes in eight schools across the country that set about the business of reaching out to the least connected parents and involving them in a partnership with teachers. In one school, among other changes, a team of home visitors worked with parents on home learning activities and connected them with resources in the community. Another, also among other changes, improved home/school communication by installing telephones and answering machines in classrooms and establishing a homework hotline system, allowing parents to find out about homework assignments and also about upcoming events in the school. The reactions of many of the parents are reflected in this statement by one of them whose child attended a school in a racially and economically mixed neighborhood: "Becoming active . . . has given me a sense of empowerment, a sense that my voice makes a difference, and also the sense of being an important part of a team" (p. 3). Her statement also was consistent with the positive findings in the case studies of the eight schools (Palanki, Burch, & Davies, 1995).

The American Family

The students in your class will probably come from families of varied make-ups. Statistics indicate that close to 10 million children now live in stepfamilies, and millions more dwell in single-parent homes. Thus, in the average class you should expect students who have experienced the divorce of their parents and the subsequent change in their family unit at least once. You may also have several students whose family is in the midst of this kind of emotional upheaval, or who have lost a parent, or whose biological parents never married.

Some students may come from intact homes where only one parent works outside the household, whereas others will have both parents working. Still others may be living with aunts and uncles, grandparents, foster parents, or adoptive parents; others may shuttle back and forth between households, or live with one parent and regularly (or perhaps never) visit the other parent.

The variety in family life is great. Whatever familial arrangements you experienced growing up, now you need to accustom yourself to looking out on the world with a different perspective. For example, you may face the challenge of looking through the eyes of a child whose parenting comes from a mother who was 15 at the time of the child's birth, or you may have to cope with an only child who is unaccustomed to sharing toys and turns with peers.

In approaching issues like one-parent families—or other potentially sensitive areas such as religious, cultural, and ethnic differences—teachers consider the particular learning needs of the classroom group. Whatever the age of the students, teachers can contribute to their awareness of the diversity of backgrounds and ways of life of all people. This is not to say that one should discuss the advantages of one way of life over another; a teacher's responsibility is simply to build awareness and respect of such differences. This is particularly necessary if their textbooks refer to intact families and a way of life detached from one or many of the students.

When classroom activity calls for writing cards or letters to parents or guardians, bear in mind the circumstances of *all* students. If your art activity is to make Father's Day presents, it would be wise to ask those who do not live with their dads what their preferences are. For one student the solution might be to make two father's presents—one for her natural father and one for her stepfather. A second student might elect to make a father's present and give it to a grandfather. In other words, take action that will give you the feeling that you have made things right for all your students.

Elementary school teachers, who deal with smaller numbers of students, are more likely to know about the stresses and strains in the children's families. By contrast, high school teachers, dealing with many more students in their classes, are unlikely to have that knowledge. They need to be sensitive to the possibility that a marked change in the performance or behavior of students may be due to difficulties in their families.

With your cooperating teacher you may conduct conferences with parents. The *process* of conducting conferences with married parents, divorced parents, parent substitutes, young parents, single parents, and stepparents is not different from that with traditional (dad works, mom stays at home) parents. That is, the teacher listens carefully to get a broader picture of the life of the student and is empathic, showing a genuine interest in the parents' and parent substitutes' concerns.

The *content* of conferences about students from nontraditional types of families may well be different from the content of conferences about students from traditional families; that is to be expected because some of problems are related to familial status. For example, the son or daughter of a single-parent family is more likely than others to get less after-school supervision, and to have available fewer parental hours of help with school work or of advice about friends and behavior in general. There are exceptions, of course, and in some single-parent families the children have more than ample attention. However, the probability is greater, and for that reason teachers should be sensitive and knowledgeable about resources in the school and community that could be called on for assistance.

Culturally Different Parents

Already, in the preceding chapter, in describing the diversity of students in our schools, we reported on cultural and linguistic differences that had an important bearing on school behavior and performance. We continue those themes with an emphasis on cultural differences among parents, and on the implications of those differences when teachers conduct conferences and have other contacts with parents.

In working with parents from diverse social backgrounds it is well to begin with the understanding that *no groups, be they racial, ethnic, or religious, are "culturally deprived."* However, they may be culturally different from you. Learning those differences is a challenge for teachers, but one with a great pay-off. For one thing, we become much more competent in conducting productive conferences with parents from diverse groups; for another, we enrich our lives by acquiring an appreciation of the richness of cultures different from our own.

It is too little known that historical studies of African American families and communities show them as "strong and resilient" (Scott-Jones, 1994). Granted that today's families have problems aplenty, their strength lies, in part, in their extended family networks. Through relatives, especially grandmothers, extended family members in need find emotional and financial support. These relatives, often possessing meager resources themselves, open their homes and their arms to disadvantaged kin (Morris, 1992).

Also too little known is the fact that, like European, Asian, and Hispanic immigrants, African Americans possess a significant cultural legacy. Those who work with African American parents should know that "African Americans who were brought as enslaved persons from Africa had already experienced a rich history of social, cultural, economic, and political development, which began long before many of the civilizations of Western Europe" (Carrasquillo & London, 1993, p. 18).

Several cultural values of Hispanics influence the nature of parent–teacher relationships. Three values in particular are especially powerful: *familism, machismo, and respeto* (Fracasso & Busch-Rossnagel, 1992).

Familism refers to an intense sense of commitment to the family. Family ties are exceedingly close and the major responsibility of an individual is to the family.

Machismo refers to male domination in gender roles. The father is in an authoritarian position. Boys are socialized to follow in the steps of their fathers. Girls are socialized to devote themselves to family, that is, home and children.

Respeto refers to the obedience to the authority of parents and also authorities outside the home. It is the source of children's deferential behavior. Respect is what every parent deserves. With Hispanic parents, this means respecting parental authority, even when it contradicts the teacher's instructions. Recognizing the nature of these roles, teachers will want to win the support of the key figure, the father, as well as the mother, in conferences aimed at helping their children.

Asian American families tend to be stable. This may be due to the fact that on the average they marry at older ages and have fewer marital disruptions than the population at large (Carrasquillo & London, 1993). With child bearing postponed, they have opportunity for higher education and to improve their economic well-being.

Traditionally, Asian Americans have had great respect for education and for authority. With this combination, they are not likely to question educational policies and practices. They believe that teachers are not to be challenged. The teacher who wishes to hear parental views about their child's experiences will have to work at developing trust and demonstrating the acceptability of their input and criticism.

These brief sketches of a few of the cultural differences among three major groups are meant as an introduction for those not already familiar with such differences. Through readings, workshops, discussion, and also conversations with members of minority groups, you can increase your knowledge.

We would like to repeat a point made earlier. These groups are not themselves homogeneous. There are variations in cultural values within each group. Furthermore, time itself brings about change. With each passing generation, some values, attitudes, and practices change, as they get modified by experience.

Parent–Teacher Meetings/Parents' Open House Night

These school events are settings where you are most likely to meet the parents of the students in your classroom. These contacts will probably be brief, perhaps little more than a simple introduction. Nonetheless they can be meaningful, both to you and to the parents.

The parent–teacher introduction at events like these serves an important function for parents. Now they can greet the person who had been but a name spoken by their child and perhaps repeatedly mentioned over the dinner table. Having met the parents once, even briefly, it might be easier to invite them for a conference about their child, should that be necessary, or to solicit their participation in some classroom or extracurricular activity.

In most school systems, parents' open house night is scheduled once each academic year. Parents come to this event to learn about the year's curricula, to visit their youngster's classroom, and to meet the teachers. Because parents will be in the classroom itself, parents' nights call for more preparation than school-wide meetings. If you are fortunate enough to begin student teaching in the fall, when most meetings of this nature are scheduled, carefully observe how your cooperating teacher prepares for this event.

At the elementary school level most teachers decorate their rooms with work produced by the youngsters. Curriculum materials are made available on the children's desks, and the teacher typically presents the curriculum content for the school year, as well as the class rules and expectations.

Frequently teachers give an overview of homework guidelines and projects that will be expected during the school year. Many teachers talk with parents about developmental characteristics of children in their age group (e.g., basic information about interests, bedtimes, and stress, and how to help children develop a positive sense of self).

At middle and high school levels, parents are often given the opportunity to follow (in an abbreviated time frame) their children's daily schedule. A teacher may have only 10 minutes to present to each group of parents. During this time, teachers need to describe curriculum goals, provide information about grading procedures and homework assignments, describe class rules, and so on. To state the obvious, teachers (and student teachers) can make the most of this time by preparing in advance and putting their best foot forward.

Open House night is not the time for individual parent conferences, but it is the time to let parents know you welcome the opportunity to meet with them individually. A brief word to a parent on parents' night may open doors to future opportunities for an in-depth meeting.

Individual Parent–Teacher Conferences

In most school systems, one and frequently two days/evenings of the school year are set aside for individual parent–teacher conferences. Parents are encouraged to come and discuss their youngsters' school progress on an individual basis. Often the success of such a day is dependent on how teachers approach this opportunity. Observe carefully how your cooperating teacher notifies parents of this upcoming event and makes other preparations.

Although preparing the classroom and collecting work samples representative of recent class work and student progress are important, these tasks are relatively easy to carry out. More difficult, and perhaps more important, for both you and your students, is to prepare yourself. That involves giving consideration to each student with respect to progress to date, what you would like to find out about the student from the parents, and the information about the student that you deem appropriate to share with them. To maximize your learning, and to avoid embarrassment or causing harm by saying something that should be left unsaid, in advance share your thoughts as much as possible with your cooperating teacher.

Susi discovered that, by reviewing each of the children with her cooperating teacher, she learned a great deal about them and a great deal about herself:

3/30: Beginning of this week I helped Mrs. C. write out conference slips indicating the strengths and weaknesses for each of the children. I found this to be really enlightening insomuch as I discovered my reactions to the children on a one-to-one basis.

I was hit rather hard by the realization of my own bias regarding each of the children. I discovered in a few cases I have been reacting toward certain children as extremes. One boy, for instance, is a constant discipline problem. I had no trouble listing his numerous weaknesses, so many, in fact, that there wasn't enough room. The surprise part came when I couldn't think of a single strength—not one positive attribute. This was very upsetting to me. I had horrible visions of stereotyping and self-fulfilling prophecies. Not trusting myself to make a mental note, I immediately started an observation sheet on the boy and have listed some positives. Also I have made an effort to provide him with positive experiences.

I also discovered difficulty noting weaknesses for the superlative children. I felt this was also a stagnant attitude inasmuch as it impeded pathways for new exploration. My attitude about them has been something like, they are so fantastic there can't be anything they need to improve on. I think in this case I need to reevaluate just how challenging school is for them.

Consider Susi in a parent conference prior to the insights she reported in this journal entry. Parents would have been misinformed. The parents of the unruly boy would have become defensive ("You just mean you don't like our son?") or worse yet, they would have accepted the version of him as "all bad." The parents of the "superlative children," as Susi called them, would also have been given a distorted portrait of their offspring. Susi's preparation made a big difference for her, as it will for you.

A good way to prepare for a parent conference is by being empathic. By putting yourself in the parents' shoes, you will understand that they want to hear about their child's strengths, weaknesses, progress, and problems. Further, because they want the best for their children, most will be willing—perhaps even delighted—to listen to suggestions you make about homework procedures, supplementary study materials, and so forth.

A difficulty some teachers and student teachers may face in preparing for parents' nights is in mobilizing themselves to overcome their fear of meeting parents. Another problem is in taking the initiative in directing informative and useful discussions with them. Young and inexperienced people, in particular, have difficulty presenting themselves as professionals to parents, who generally are a few years older and perhaps well established in the work world.

If your cooperating teacher provides you with an opportunity to talk to parents, you will see that most parents will take you seriously and will respect your training. More to the point, you have something they value: information about their child. They will appreciate your helpful, constructive appraisal.

In sharing knowledge with parents, remember that you have a right to feel confident (you have been trained as a teacher), and you should remind yourself of that. If an occasional parent is unjustly critical of you, questions your behavior in the classroom, or even gets angry at you without provocation, put that in perspective. Remember that some adults, parents among them, lead lives of great frustration. They may not even be reacting to you personally but rather to their feelings about school, their difficulty in coping with their child, or their own reaction to authority.

After experiencing your first parent conferences, and having assessed what they produced, you, like Laura, will probably be relieved to find the following: the conferences were helpful to you in understanding your students, easier to conduct than you expected (even if you had to deliver bad news), and a boost to your morale when you heard from parents about the positive impact you were having on their children. Laura expresses this in two journal entries:

2/19: The parents I met were concerned about how their children were doing in school. After talking to the parents it became very obvious that the children whose parents worked with them at home were the ones who did best in school.

2/20: There were more parent conferences this afternoon. I had my first and second experience in telling parents that their child was most likely going to have to repeat unless they made tremendous progress by June. Both parents received the news better than I had expected. The conferences have been a very enlightening experience. A few parents complimented me, and some said their children had spoken about something I had taught. It made me feel good hearing that.

Active steps can be taken to increase the likelihood that parent–teacher conferences will achieve their purposes. On the one hand, teachers can get help from experienced teachers or supervisors in conducting such conferences. Judy Daher (1994), a bilingual/bicultural specialist and once a principal, says teachers need help simply in how to improve communication with parents in general and, we would add, especially with parents whose background is different from their own.

Understanding and respecting differences is a first essential to productive communication. Next comes clarity. Daher proposed five rules as a guide to clear, practical communication. These are presented in Figure 6.1. Daher also introduced several guides for use by parents to make the parent–teacher conferences more productive, and also to make clear to them that they were not to be a one-way dialogue, teacher to parents (see Figs. 6.2, 6.3, and 6.4). The first, "Let's Talk," provides parents with a tool to use to obtain information from their child that will enhance the usefulness of the parent–teacher meeting. It also encourages communication between parent and child about school. The second guide, "Before I Go," helps the parent prepare for the conference. The third guide, "Letter to My Child," helps the parent organize her or his thoughts in sharing the content of the conference with the child.

These guides can be useful to you during student teaching in helping you organize your thoughts about conferences. Although these guides were developed for use at the elementary level, as you can see, the principles of communication that they convey are adaptable for any level, college as well as secondary. You may want to use them in their original form or adapt them for use in the years ahead when you have your own classes.

Individual Parent Conferences for Special Needs

There comes a time when a student is so troubled or so troubling in class that a teacher decides to meet with his or her parents. The coming together of the important people from a student's two worlds increases the likelihood that the student will be helped by means of a joint venture.

---

1. Make it practical
2. Layperson's language
3. Use the native language!
4. Be consistent in our communication
5. Present a consistent message

FIG. 6.1.   Five rules to communication.

Parent and child can discuss these questions before the parent–teacher conference.
1. What do you like about school?
2. What is your favorite subject?
3. What would you like to change about school? How would you change it?
4. Name one area that you would like to improve at school. What do you think you could do to improve it?
5. What is one good thing you would like me to tell your teacher about your year so far?

FIG. 6.2. Let's talk.

Take a few minutes to think through these questions before you go to the parent–teacher conference.
1. What do I believe my child does well at school and at home?
2. What concerns do I have about my child's progress?
3. Are there any specific problems or incidents that worry me?
4. What do I need to understand about the way the school or classroom operates?
5. Is there anything the teacher needs to know about my child in order for them both to have a successful year?
6. What is the main thing I would like to communicate to the teacher about my child?

FIG. 6.3. Before I go: Thoughts before the parent–teacher conference.

Your teacher told me that she enjoyed you because . . .
Your teacher says that you were good at . . .
Your teacher says we might work at home on . . .
I promised that we would . . .
The thing I enjoyed most about your teacher was . . .

FIG. 6.4. Letter to my child.

The motivation for conferring with the parents is often to exchange information—to "brainstorm." From this joint venture, new understandings can develop that could assist both parents and teacher in planning a program to aid the student. Such a meeting is often useful in helping teachers understand what is happening to a child outside of school that could be contributing to problem behavior or to recent behavioral changes evident in class. For example, an increased need for attention might be related to an imminent divorce of the student's parents. Mo's comment during an interview is relevant:

> 11/18: I couldn't believe it. Janet fell asleep during my presentation last week in mythology. She's such a great student. I got so angry. Her head kept nodding and finally she put it down on the desk. I tried raising my voice. Finally, I moved right in front of her as I spoke. Only her mom came for the parents' day appointment. It seems that her parents have been having serious marital problems. So Janet's taken on many domestic tasks as well as a part-time job and has not been able to get her usual amount of sleep. I guess that's why she fell asleep in my class.

So far we have noted how information from the parents can aid teachers. There is the other side of the coin. Teachers may feel they can aid a student by making concrete practical suggestions to parents and seeking their cooperation. For example, to encourage confidence in reading aloud, they could recommend that parents and students take turns reading portions of a story to each other every evening for a few minutes.

To aid a student hoping to attend college, the student teacher can assess whether the parents are familiar with the process of choosing schools and preparing applications: speaking to the guidance counselor, writing for information about several possible schools and about financial aid, and studying vocabulary and math formulas before the ACT or SAT tests.

Following are some additional examples of student teachers' involvement in parent conferences. Although the cordiality and results of the conferences varied, as did the extent of the student teachers' involvement, in all cases the student teachers acquired new insights into students' behaviors. They felt better able to devise strategies to help them.

In the first example, Ginny was able to use information acquired during a parent conference in developing a plan aimed at eliminating a problem behavior. First, before creating a behavior change strategy, she had to consider how the boy's home and school environments differed and the kind of treatment he might get in each setting in the future:

> 2/20: I talked to Mrs. M. about Geoffrey today. She said that when she had a conference with his mother she discovered that his mother devotes all her attention to her children. She said that Geoffrey's family has financial problems and his mom feels that the best thing that she can do for her children is to shower them with constant praise and attention. This helps to explain Geoffrey's attention-seeking behavior. So, with this in mind, I tried to reinforce Geoffrey's positive actions today and ignore the negative ones.

As a result of what I did, he was much more at ease and calmer. However, I'm concerned with the end result—I am giving more attention or praise than he will most probably receive in another classroom situation. Although I noticed a change in his behavior today (he was even more sociable with the other children), I really wonder if it is good to do this. Am I just preparing him to be a behavior problem next year? On the other hand, if I continue as is and then gradually taper off the amount of reinforcements, then Geoffrey might adjust. Only time will tell, but this seems reasonable.

Stan, as we see in his journal entries, learned much from a parent conference, but he was not happy with the outcome. His conference with Theresa's mother left him with a greater understanding of a troublesome student's behavior, but also with the knowledge that he would receive little support from the home:

1/10: Mrs. H. told me Theresa has been taught to punch people if they call her a name and that her mother spoils her and stands up for her constantly. Also, Theresa's mother's attitude is belligerent and she lacks warmth and understanding, possibly the understanding and attention Theresa needs.

I saw today that Theresa shows her need for attention by being aggressive, sarcastic, and distracting in the class. I don't know what the best solution would be, whether to ignore her or to keep her busy and make her feel important.

1/14: Today Theresa pushed a book off a boy's desk and cursed. She was also hitting Maria.

1/21: Last week Theresa said she didn't have to answer a teacher "yes" or "no." We had her mom in for a conference today. Her mom didn't smile or extend her hand as I introduced myself. During the conference, she, Mrs. H., and the principal agreed that Theresa should be forced to have respect for her elders. "But I'm still going to tell her, 'If someone kicks you, you kick him back,'" Theresa's mother said at the end. I thought, like mother, like daughter.

Stan looked for civility in Theresa's mother's behavior and found none, except perhaps in the agreement that "Theresa should be forced to have respect for her elders." But that "agreement" solved nothing, as Theresa cannot be "forced" to respect others. In assessing the meeting, Stan realized that to enlist this mother to help change Theresa's behavior would take time. It might also require conferences, dealing first with her mother's negative attitude toward the school. If a problem like this should arise next year, Stan thought, he would develop a year-long plan and enlist the aid of the principal. He would also involve the school counselor in working with the child and the parents.

Mia felt both overwhelmed and excited after attending a conference with her cooperating teacher, Mr. H., and the parents of one of their ninth-grade history students, James. Her experience in this conference left such a powerful impression on her that at seminar the next day she asked the help of her supervisor and fellow students in sorting out her thoughts:

10/20: During our free fourth period today, Mr. H. had scheduled a conference with James' parents. He asked me if I would like to sit in on the conference. I . . . said yes.

Now, for some background info. I really like James. He seems personable, always ready to answer questions in class and to participate in class discussions. But I can't quite figure him out. He seems bright—but he's barely carrying a "C" average. I helped Mr. H. grade the tests from the last unit. James did well enough on section I, true–false. The fill-in-the-blank section was adequate. But he lost the most points on his essays. He never even got to the second essay and I could barely read the first essay. His handwriting was atrocious. He couldn't spell a thing—used the word their instead of there, our for are. You would have thought he was in fourth grade.

Anyway—James' parents arrived, test in hand, as well as a book and pamphlets on the learning disability, dyslexia. They were well prepared—to say the least. They explained that while James was quite bright, he had difficulty reading, taking class notes, and in spelling. I couldn't believe it. They had a copy of his history textbook on tape and James could (and did) listen to the tape as he read along in the text each night. They asked if James could tape our class lectures—in order to help him study, because he had difficulty in note-taking. They didn't want us to "take off" for misspelled words in his essay and explained that James needed "extra" time in taking tests because it took him longer to read and process the questions. They offered us lots of material to read on dyslexia.

Mr. H. seemed almost overwhelmed, but thanked them for the information and said he would take this information into consideration. He would also need to talk with the school's psychologist and the chairman of the history department. He would get back to the parents after that and thanked the parents for coming. We had classes for the rest of the afternoon and didn't have time to discuss it later. Tomorrow in seminar I'd like to discuss this problem. I don't know what to think.

At the seminar, thanks especially to the leader and a classmate who had a brother with dyslexia, Mia began to develop a plan. Aided also by literature that James' parents had brought, she felt confident that she could successfully accommodate James' disability by making minor changes in her lessons.

As in Mia's case, alertness at parent conferences pays off. Sometimes the pay-off is in the form of valuable information given directly. Sometimes, though, such information is not obvious, not direct, and not out in the open because parents are wary of sharing it with you. For example, they may be carrying around with them the feeling that you blame them for their child's problems, groundless as such a feeling may be. If parents feel "accused," it will be difficult for them to work with school personnel.

Student teachers often experience mixed emotions about calling a parent to set up an appointment to discuss a youngster's difficulties. They want to help the student, but a parent–teacher conference seems too grave a step. The mixed emotions sometimes stem from their own feelings of inadequacy because they have not been able to cope effectively with the student. Sometimes they come from the student teachers' hazy and unlabeled feeling that they are "telling on" their students, and that as a result the youngsters would likely undergo harsh punishment at home.

Such feelings typically emerge strongest when student teachers have had problems with a student or if the student's behavior has special meaning.

With her cooperating teacher's permission, after seeing Tanya smoking a cigarette on school grounds, student teacher Denise called Tanya's mother. The telephone call was difficult for Denise because she herself had experimented with cigarettes in school and because, after having trouble with Tanya earlier in the term, Tanya was now responding well to her. After telephoning, Denise felt guilty, but she knew she had taken the right course.

A few days later Tanya began smiling at Denise again. More importantly, she stopped "hanging out" with peers who smoked on school grounds. This reinforced Denise's conviction that she had acted professionally.

Typically, schools have either a formal or informal procedure to be followed when contacting students' parents. They also usually have procedures for completing formal, written discipline reports and for determining whether they are sent to parents. Early in your student teaching, discuss such procedures with your cooperating teacher. You may learn that when a student is involved in a physical dispute, an immediate phone call is placed to the parents in the hope that this early phone contact will prevent a larger, more complex problem.

One useful way to prepare for individual conferences with parents is by acquainting yourself with resources that can be helpful to them. Often, you will find these resources helpful to you, too. Because underachievement is a problem that frequently calls for an individual conference, you may want to read and recommend a book like *Boosting the Underachiever: How Busy Parents Can Unlock Their Child's Potential* (Cogen, 1990). For individual conferences with parents of special-needs students, a book like *Optimizing Special Education: How Parents Can Make a Difference* (Wilson, 1992) may be worth your attention.

Parent Visits During the School Day

Parents visit classrooms on their own initiative and also at the invitation of teachers, as part of programs to familiarize them with their schools. They come to meet the teacher, to see the class in operation and, most of all, to watch their son or daughter in action. Ideally, an orientation to the class activities, like the one described in the following two paragraphs, should be given to parents making a class visit.

With both a student and a cooperating teacher in a room, one of them can take time to welcome an arriving parent and to describe the scheduled activities. This should be done unobtrusively. A parent's orientation should include specifics about the content of the lesson, its objectives, and how they fit into broader goals. A copy of the materials the students are using should be provided parents so they can follow the activities.

After the lesson is explained, parents could be told that in watching the activities they will find it helpful to note (a) how attentive their child is, (b) what his or her work habits are, (c) how he or she follows directions, and (d) how he or she relates to classmates. Parents also should be told that their presence might cause their youngster to act a bit differently than usual. For instance, with a parent present, a youngster may be more or less hesitant to raise his or her hand and answer a teacher's question.

On occasion, you might find yourself presenting a lesson with parents observing. What is that like? Joanna reports what happened to her:

> 3/2: With three parents in the room I knew that the kids would be distracted, but not to the degree that they were. I was very surprised to see . . . [them] act extremely opposite of what they had ever acted before.

The students were not just inattentive; they could not sit still. At first, Joanna was disturbed by the disruption, but quickly regained control of the class. She accomplished this by introducing the parents and then immediately setting the students to work, assigning them material that, although not scheduled, generally held their attention. When she saw the slightest sign of disorder, she firmly redirected their attention to the work.

Joanna's reaction to the unexpected behavior—requiring the same disciplined behavior as on any other day—was sensible. Postponing the scheduled activity and substituting another was also wise. The only other deviation she made from regular classroom procedures was to concentrate on giving the students whose parents were visiting ample opportunity to participate actively. Providing such opportunities makes parents feel good and the youngsters happy, all without harm to classmates.

Besides parents, other adults may visit your class, sometimes unexpectedly. Juanita, near the end of her assignment, was scheduled to teach a difficult social studies assignment the last period of the day. As she was about to begin, the principal and several local political officials entered into the room and asked if they could observe. Juanita's cooperating teacher said sure and privately offered to teach the lesson. Juanita said "no," she was prepared. Much to her surprise the children sat, listened, and then participated in discussion. Later, Juanita said, "they behaved like angels."

Parental Reactions to a Student Teacher

From time to time an action by a student teacher, perhaps an expression of warmth or caring toward a child, will be brought to the attention of a parent and will move the parent to react. Most frequently the student teacher gets an oral compliment or a note of thanks. No matter which, it is a much appreciated boost to the ego and should be enjoyed. Charlene reports the following:

> 2/11: Morris had been a terror at home and at school since his sister was born. That was 4 months ago. I had tried all kinds of ways of dealing with his aggressiveness in class. Taking away privileges failed, the principal's office failed, and behavior modification failed. Then I used role playing to show him that he had been behaving like a 3-year old. We role-played for a week and it made a difference at school and at home. Morris' mother called my cooperating teacher and wrote a beautiful, most flattering letter to the principal.

On rare occasions, the note you receive is not one of thanks. Dorothy shares an example of the infrequent critical messages parents occasionally deliver to student teachers. Negative though it was, it set off a chain of events that ended positively:

2/12: One of the girls handed me a note from Leona, who was waiting in the coat room at the time. The note to me was from Leona's mother threatening that I "better let Leona have the Valentine party." The reason for the note was that on Wednesday, due to discipline problems, I informed the children that if their name occurred on the board with three marks after it, then there would be no party privileges for them.

Well, Leona would not stop talking, therefore, I put her name on the board. But she had no marks after it and didn't lose her privileges. Leona misunderstood and according to her mother she cried all night because I wasn't going to let her share in the party fun and trade Valentines. Well, I got on the phone and explained what had happened. I told her mother Leona would be at the party as would everyone in the class. I also said "I'm sorry that I upset Leona so much." After talking to my cooperating teacher I reported the incident to Mr. R. (the principal). He said I used a poor means of discipline, but to forget it.

The Absence of Parent–Teacher Contact

Parents and teachers should be close allies in the education of youngsters. Between them, they have the information necessary to develop a solid understanding of a learner's needs. Between them, they can plan and carry out effective programs to foster the student's development.

Why does the potential power of a parent–teacher team so often go untapped? And it does. A 1988 national survey by the U.S. Department of Education tells us about parent visits to schools. Parents of eighth graders had the following contacts: 50% attended school meetings; 52% contacted the school about the child's academic performance; 35% contacted the school about academic programs; and 29% visited classrooms.

If we examine those facts in another way, we see that 50% did not attend school meetings and 48% did not contact the school about the child's academic performance. What can we do to encourage contact with those parents?

You will probably learn about parents who shy away from school. Their reasons are varied: Some feel they are too busy; some feel the teacher would be unhappy to receive them; some feel intimidated by the teacher; some feel that school visits are restricted to problem occasions; and some feel anxious in school because of unhappy or frustrating experiences during their own student days or because of their own language limitations. As a group, working-class, minority, and immigrant parents are less likely than others to come to their children's schools.

The reasons for parental absence suggest potential solutions, measures to persuade parents that they are wanted and welcomed. These can take the form of written invitations, coffee hours, and requests for suggestions and advice; in fact, consider any and all approaches that might reduce parents' hesitancies and stimulate positive attitudes in them. Besides the reluctance of some parents, some teachers are hesitant to contact parents, either because of busy personal schedules or out of fear of a bad experience. Those in the last group may be reacting to past episodes in which principals or department heads were upset when an angry parent, perhaps irrationally, accused the school of a perceived injustice to their child or objected to an assigned book. Teachers are also aware that some administrators get disturbed—not simply upset—if the complainer is a powerful figure in the community who threatens to take the problem to a higher authority.

Because one angry parent can injure a teacher's reputation with the principal, perhaps even more than several pleased parents can help it, some teachers steer clear of parents whenever possible. Why risk it? Of course, there is a fallacy in this logic. Parents who have had contact with a teacher are less likely to complain to the principal than those who have not.

If your cooperating teacher has minimal contact with parents, in all probability you will have little opportunity yourself during your student teaching. In any case, next year as a teacher on your own, the job of relating to parents will be yours. Because you may have received no formal training in this area, it will be useful to cultivate whatever opportunities you do have.

THE PRINCIPAL

Your first contact with your school's principal may be the day you visit the school to meet your cooperating teacher. In fact, the principal may show you through the school and introduce you to your cooperating teacher.

As administrator, the principal's role is to maintain the smooth functioning of the school. The job includes supervising and evaluating teaching and related services, playing a major role in hiring teachers and staff, and administering all of the operations in the building. Most principals strive to operate their schools in an unobtrusive manner. They prefer to grant teachers freedom within well-defined limits to conduct their classes as they wish, as long as the curriculum is followed. For the most part, principals operate in the background, at least as far as the day-to-day life of the student teacher is concerned. An important exception to this rule, however, is that student teachers are frequently observed and evaluated by the principal, whom they may call on to write a reference when they are applying for a full-time position.

As Classroom Observer

Many student teachers quiver at the thought of having the principal as an observer. It is comforting for them to recognize that generally the principal is a strong advocate of providing the best possible learning experience for students, including student teachers. That the principal should be concerned about you and your welfare is not surprising. Without his or her support, the school would not be involved in a relationship with your college or department of education and would not offer opportunities for student teachers.

The emotions aroused in some student teachers by a forthcoming observation by their principal are not unlike those associated with an observation by their supervisor. The student teacher can cope with them by preparing in the same way recommended earlier for a college/university supervisor's visit.

Jane, whose school had an autocratic principal, found that teaching during an unexpected observation could evoke uncomfortable feelings. Early one morning, late in her student teaching, the principal walked into the class and saw the children out of their seats. Jane wrote:

> 6/5: Mrs. C. walked in and said, "What are all of you doing out of your seats?" I explained to her about my "senses table" and how the children recorded what sense they used to guess what was hidden daily in a box. She said, "That's a terrible way to start the day. You kids sit down." Then she walked out. I was so mad. If she had a comment to make she could have said it to me in private and she shouldn't have told the kids to sit down when I said they could be standing.

Although Jane was understandably upset, she wisely avoided a confrontation, responding only with her explanation of the children's activities. She recognized that there was nothing to be gained by an argument. Although Jane's experience was negative, many student teachers have positive ones. That is, their principals provide them with insightful critical evaluation and sometimes with innovative ideas and a fresh perspective.

In an interview, Molly reported, "The vice-principal had observed me, but not the principal, Mr. C. I had heard about how harsh he was, so I was glad he hadn't come in. Last week, in the middle of my lesson—in he walked—unannounced. Class went OK and afterwards he congratulated me. Turns out he was a science teacher and he gave me several good ideas. I actually told him that I hope he comes back again."

As School Leader

Both as a student teacher and as a beginning teacher, you should find out as much as you can about the principal, his or her philosophy, and mode of school operation. Ask your cooperating teacher about the principal; tactfully ask other teachers too. If the principal is the kind of person who encourages teachers to talk with him or her, then you should do so. You will enhance your understanding of the school if you find out about the principal's educational beliefs and goals.

It is definitely to your advantage to have a good working relationship with the school principal. For one thing, he or she may be an excellent reference and the source of a letter of recommendation. For another, the principal may have influence in who will be hired by the school system next year or may have friends in other school systems to whom he or she could recommend you.

With your cooperating teacher's approval, when you are doing something that you feel might be of interest, invite your principal to observe. One of us recalls working with a principal who, unlike the cooperating teacher, believed children should have limited opportunities to leave their seats. One day, when the students were making silhouette pictures of themselves, the student teacher invited the principal to have his silhouette drawn. His picture was proudly hung with the others on the classroom wall.

In spite of the differences between this student teacher and principal, they got along because the student teacher did not flaunt her different style and did not try to convert him, and because the principal was tolerant of others and believed that if teachers maintained adequate control over their classes, they were entitled to teach in ways consistent with their philosophies.

Because the school principal is the chief officer in the school and the final authority, he or she is the school's ultimate disciplinarian. A teacher sends a youngster to the principal's office when the teacher has exhausted all possible measures in the classroom and the student's presence is disruptive to the class. As a student teacher, you will learn from your cooperating teacher the practices in your school about the use of the principal for this purpose. Occasionally sending a student to the office may be just the emergency measure you need at a particular moment. If your principal is supportive, do not hesitate to have him or her help you control your class in this way. However, as you may also be told, overuse of this measure is likely to lead the principal to believe you have problems controlling the class.

It is also possible that you may be placed in a school in which the principal is a valuable resource person. For example, he or she may be helpful in the development of a lesson or have specialized knowledge or skills to contribute to a unit. The principal in a school in which one of the authors worked was noted for his knowledge of the plants and wildlife in a park adjacent to the school property. This otherwise conservative, authoritarian principal could easily and most happily be prodded into conducting fascinating nature walks in the park, providing an excellent foundation for a science unit.

Sometimes, as in Bob's case, a principal may set a theme for the school. Bob complained, "I'm not happy spending 3 weeks on the town's anniversary, but the principal insists on it." The principal felt strongly that this date was an important one, to be recognized by the students in all grades. He did not indicate how the teachers were to plan their activities but only instructed them to absorb the students in the upcoming event.

During discussion at the seminar for student teachers, Bob came to see that the principal, as school leader, was in his right to set such a theme. In the seminar meeting Bob also learned an important lesson—important to all teachers but vital to student teachers—that they must operate under constraints of one kind or another in this real world. They must find what those limits are and, within them, come as close as they can to doing what they feel is best.

As you student teach, and when you have your own class, sort out your feelings toward your school's principal. You will help yourself if you do not get caught up in feelings that will prevent you from building a useful working relationship with him or her.

THE OTHER TEACHERS

It is true that most of your hours in school will be spent in the presence of your cooperating teacher and students. However, you will encounter other teachers in the faculty lounge, the cafeteria, and the rest rooms. At the elementary school level you may interact with art, music, and physical education teachers who work with your class on a weekly basis, or with speech or reading specialists who see some of your children.

Many middle schools are organized into teaching teams, in which two teachers are responsible for a major portion of the students' classes (e.g., one in math and science and one in the humanities). At the secondary school level you will meet other teachers in your own department, and also some from other departments, especially at meetings and in the faculty lounge.

At all levels, during your short stint as a student teacher you will have frequent opportunities to build collegiality and to learn from others. Clearly, there are benefits from learning about and experiencing more of the life in your school than that in one classroom in one corner of the building. Try to learn about the educational philosophy and approaches of several of the teachers in your school, perhaps by asking them about their approach to and techniques for handling the problems you find difficult. There are many other ways of using the resources of fellow teachers, such as through an exchange of lesson plans and discussions about them.

One of the lasting results of interactions with the other teachers is the professional identity that it helps develop. Previously, in the courses that preceded your student teaching, yours was the life of the student; your thoughts were about courses, assignments, and grades. That is not the case now that you are a student teacher. Now you discuss matters about students, teaching, and educational philosophy with your cooperating teacher and with others in the teachers' lounge.

The other teachers in your cooperating school may be valuable resources when you begin your search for your first position. They may have information that is not yet public, such as one teacher's plan to leave his position to move to another area in the country or another teacher's plan to take a year-long maternity leave.

Perhaps the greatest benefit of interacting with teachers is that it helps you become a professional. Developing the feeling that you are a teacher does not happen just because you get your diploma and license to teach. The license tells the world you are a teacher. But the deep-seated feeling that you are a teacher is acquired slowly, partly as you teach and partly as you rub elbows with your colleagues.

An interesting paper by Kainan (1994) illustrates how the culture of many schools facilitates this "elbow-rubbing." She did this by comparing the lunch-time behavior of teachers and university researchers. Whereas the researchers came into the cafeteria, ordered their lunch, and rushed back to their offices, the teachers settled in, joining tables together and spending their lunch time talking as a group about students, classes, and other professional matters. Of course, teachers also spend time discussing their family, hobbies, and other interests. If you have opportunities to join in these discussions, you will have opportunities to get better acquainted with other members of the faculty, to learn something about their professional views, and to feel part of the community of teachers.

THE STAFF

Armies, it is said, survive because of the soldiers behind the front lines, and elementary and secondary schools survive, we believe, because of the work of the staff. Although you as a student teacher will probably have infrequent reason to call on the services of the secretaries, it is good to get acquainted with them, if for no other reason than to appreciate the totality of the school's operation.

Although the secretaries do the obvious tasks of an office, such as handling correspondence, phone calls, and supplies, some of their work is unique to a school. For example, they schedule rooms and special events, help check teachers' registers, and make many contacts with parents both by phone and by mail.

There are at least two reasons to develop good working relationships with the school support staff. First, on this as on any job, the work day is more satisfying when one has pleasant relations with co-workers. Compared with most other occupations, this point is in some ways even more crucial to teachers, who need good moments with adults because they spend so much time with children or teenagers. Amy, commenting on her experiences as her student teaching was coming to an end, had this to say: "No matter how bad things were going, I could always be sure of a cheery smile from one of the secretaries in the principal's office and somehow that helped make it easier to go back the next day."

The second reason is a more self-serving one. You may have an occasional need for assistance from the staff. For example, you may need to write or phone a parent or a community resource person and will want the help of one of the secretaries. It is much easier to ask such aid from a friend or acquaintance than from a stranger.

THE CUSTODIAN

Professionals in most fields of endeavor have rare occasion to work with a building custodian. For a teacher, however, the custodian is an important figure. A classroom, even in a senior high school, is more likely to require extensive cleaning than a lawyer's or doctor's office. When your class leaves the room in disarray it is reassuring to have confidence that the custodian is friendly and understanding. Generally, custodians have long tenure on their job and acquire status and influence not usually associated with such a position. Their acquired authority is shown in the following excerpts from Dorothy's journal. We want first, though, to stress that Dorothy's experience is an atypical one. Nevertheless, the report of it shows that the custodian, blue-collar worker though he is, has a quasi-professional standing in the school and often a sensitivity to the needs of the students as well as of the teachers. We want also to stress our consistent point of view that the student-teaching experience is a prologue to your teaching position. This period is a good one in which to practice building relationships with the kinds of workers you want to know on the job next year:

> 3/7: Today I made another mistake. I used enamel paint in the classroom. Well, the children got it on their hands and just a little on some of the desks. Ms. K. had not been in the room all day so she didn't know what was going on. But when she found out I had used enamel paint she wanted to know why in the world I would use that.

> 3/8: A good thing did happen today. Mr. G., the janitor, came in the room during lunch and I was cleaning off the desks. He said, "What are you doing?" I replied, "Clearing off paint." Ms. K. then said, "Enamel paint at that!" I explained the whole thing and said, "I know I should have used my head." Mr. G. looked at Ms. K. and said, "What are you for?" She did not reply, so he then said, "I mean isn't it your job to help her learn and give her guidance?"

> I must admit he picked up my ego and how thankful I was that someone finally told her what her position was supposed to be. All quarter I've wanted to ask what her job as a cooperating teacher meant to her.

> 3/9: Well, Ms. K. has been much nicer since Mr. G. made his comment yesterday. In fact, she even said to me today that it was too bad she wasn't in the room when we started the painting.

A NOTE ON NEXT YEAR

In Part II we have devoted space to the persons in your student-teaching life, very much in accordance with their significance to you. The students, the cooperating teacher, and the college/university supervisor were each given a separate chapter, and most of this chapter has been devoted to the parents and the principal, with lesser portions to other teachers, the staff, and the custodian. When you become a teacher in your own right, the allocations will change. By then, you will have incorporated the valuable guidance provided to you by your cooperating teacher and college/university supervisor. It will be part of you. And you will have a direct and more involved relationship with the parents, principal, and staff members at the school where you will be teaching.

CRITICAL ISSUES
- How will I feel talking to a parent who is much older than I am?
- I'll have no trouble telling parents some positive things about their child. How do I tell them the negatives in a constructive way?
- What suggestions could I pass on to parents about helping their youngsters to enjoy learning, develop good study habits, and be disciplined about doing homework?
- What resources can I draw on from others in the school?

PART III

What and How We Teach

7

Diversity, Inclusion, and Expectations in Teaching

TOPICS

- Important teacher characteristics
  - Being respectful
  - Being a warm, caring person
  - Being aware of your expectations for your students
- Students who may require special attention
  - Students with disabilities
    - Mainstreaming
    - Evaluation of mainstreaming
    - A student teacher's anxieties about mainstreaming
  - The intellectually gifted
  - Students living in poverty
  - Female students and expectations
- Teaching in a multicultural society
- Critical issues

While walking through the streets of today's cities, you'll find restaurants representing dozens of countries in the world. Go into American classrooms and you find the children whose families came from those countries and many others.

On those same streets you see differently-abled people coping in various ways, some guided by seeing-eye dogs, some wearing hearing aids, some riding electric carts, and still others whose learning disabilities and physical and emotional distress are not apparent. Perhaps apparent and perhaps not, is the diversity in socioeconomic class, educational level, sexual orientation, and the language spoken at home of the people you see.

Ours is truly a nation of diverse people, and the challenge of our schools is to educate them all. Besides presenting educators with a challenge, diversity among people is also a blessing. Children and teenagers of such different backgrounds and with such different characteristics can bring interest and excitement into our classes.

IMPORTANT TEACHER CHARACTERISTICS

In this chapter, we examine several different categories of diversity and show what they mean to student teachers. First, though, we want to make some general statements about important teacher characteristics that apply to all of the categories, in fact to all students. We start with respect.

Being Respectful

Treating all students with respect is something every teacher must strive for. That goal is especially important in a society plagued with sexism, racism, and other prejudices, as the news media and our experiences continuously remind us.

Teachers are models. Many students look up to and try to pattern themselves after their teacher. If they see this adult behave in friendly and caring ways to all students, they are likely to follow suit. In other words, you teach more than a grade or a subject. You teach attitude and behavior and, if you are good at it, your students will learn to respect you and each other.

There was a time when school people isolated certain students. To give you a sense of what it meant to the isolated students, we give you the words of someone who experienced it. Asch (1989), a professional who is blind, quoted from personal communication written by B. Davidson, a handicapped person. She wrote the following about schooling prior to the federal legislation of 1975:

> Socially: We were isolated. Symbolically, and appropriate to the prevailing attitudes, the handicapped and retard classrooms were tucked away in a corner of the school basement. . . . Summing it up, the only contact we had with the normal children was visual. On these occasions I can report my own feelings: Envy. Given the loud, clear message that was daily being delivered to them I feel quite confident that I can also report their feelings: Yuch! (Asch, 1989, p. 190).

"Yuch!" This reaction, we believe, is less common, now that fewer students are segregated. Nonetheless, the need to prepare students to feel comfortable with each other is urgent.

One of us was involved in an experiment involving a blind student that had a much happier "ending":

> My principal asked me if I would be willing to be one of two teachers in the state who would take a blind child in my kindergarten. I welcomed the opportunity and welcomed Karen into my class of 22 children. Everything was out in the open. I explained that she was blind but that she would do just about all the activities. They also learned soon that she was a talented pianist who could play a piece after a single

hearing. It wasn't long before Karen was as much a part of the class as any other child. Yes, she was different, but mainly because of her musical talent.

This mainstreaming experiment with Karen dates back more than three decades. There has been much change since then but, unfortunately, not nearly enough. We could fill this book with quotes from countless other published sources about the following: Immigrant, African American, Hispanic, Native American, and other children who were made to feel inferior; gay and lesbian teenagers who felt alienated; poor children, some migrant, some homeless, all below the poverty income level, who felt unwanted.

We cannot use only the past tense. Today, too, large numbers of students require special effort on the part of teachers to make them feel welcome, wanted, and respected. As teachers, we can help them immeasurably. One way is by being warm and caring persons who break down barriers between students. Another is by holding high but achievable expectations of students, to help them attain the academic objectives for which they are capable.

Being a Warm, Caring Person

Most adults have the capacity to be warm and caring. Some need permission to free that human quality. It helps young teachers to learn they can be firm classroom managers and, at the same time, concerned classroom leaders interested in their students' welfare. Such teachers are sensitive to the hardships many students endure, maybe at home, maybe at school, and maybe between home and school. They manage their classes and use instructional techniques that enable students to enjoy and feel comfortable in the school learning environment.

Being Aware of Your Expectations for Your Students

An experienced social worker, who had spent her career working with orphaned children, always said to her young assistants (including two authors at the beginning of their careers), "It's what the children see in your eyes that counts. It's not so much what you say as how you say it that tells them what you think of them—what you think they can do and what they can be. If we really believe they can learn, they will learn." She meant, in her wonderfully insightful way, that youngsters respond to the expectations for them that they sense in others.

She might have added that our expectations of students also shape our behavior with them: If we think they will do well, we tend to do those things that help bring it about. Thus, we help to see that the expectation (or prophecy) becomes fulfilled.

That was the wisdom of a deeply sensitive woman. Her advice is unforgettable to those of us who experienced it personally, but it lacks the controlled observations essential to convince a profession of its significance. Years later, researchers began systematically studying teachers' expectations of children. Some have found that these expectations turn into self-fulfilling prophecies.

In a classic study by Rosenthal and Jacobson (1966), about 20% of the children in 18 elementary school classrooms were randomly selected as experimental subjects. Their teachers were told that these particular children's scores on an IQ test for intellectual blooming indicated they would show unusual intellectual gains during the academic year. In fact, these children differed from others (control subjects) only in that they had been identified to their teachers as "children who would show unusual intellectual gains." And they did! Eight months later all the children were retested, and those in the first and second grades (although not the upper grades) who had been falsely identified as highly promising showed dramatic, statistically significant gains in comparison with the other children.

Hundreds of studies have been conducted since that one, and the results have been somewhat mixed. Educators who do not put much stock in the phenomenon have seized at these results to argue against expectancy. As vocal as the opponents have been, however, there is too much evidence to discount the impact of expectancy. For instance, Rosenthal (1973) reported that 84 of 242 studies conducted showed that the expectancies of teachers (or subjects playing the role) did affect the performance of students (or other subjects playing the role). On the basis of this statistic and other literature, by the mid-1970s it seemed safe to conclude that the self-fulfilling prophecy was at work at least in some classrooms and for some children, and to recommend that teachers be mindful of it.

In being mindful, teachers come to recognize that they base their expectations on students' past performances. They expect much from students who have records of good grades, and they expect less from students with low grades. In other words, we expect future performance to be the same as past achievement.

Some authors have argued that the expectancy effect has little importance because if it does exist, it causes changes that are small in size. "Even though expectancy effects may be relatively small, this does not mean they are unimportant or do not contribute to social problems" (Jussim, 1990, p. 30). Let us be more specific. If the "relatively small" effects were achieved through a change in expectancy, this could amount to a 20% improvement in academic performance (Rosenthal, 1985). In practical terms—in the lives of the students and the teacher—that is anything but "small" (Rosenthal, 1985)!

One important question has not yet been answered: Supposing that high expectations (i.e., higher than past performance, but judged to be realistic for students) were held not just for one year or less, as in many studies, but for many years, what would be the result? In other words, suppose a girl who has been doing D work in arithmetic gets the message year after year that she could do at least B work? It is possible that the quality of her work would improve, because a small effect of self-fulfilling prophecy may accumulate over the years and have a sizeable effect on individuals.

The negative can happen, too, for example, when a teacher in an early grade indicates in a permanent record, or orally informs the next teacher, that a child is disruptive. The child becomes earmarked as a disrupter and teacher after teacher could, in expecting that behavior, act toward the child in such ways as to encourage its fulfillment.

Gender-related self-fulfilling prophecies can also develop early in a student's schooling. The effect of lower expectations may explain certain differences in achievement between the sexes. For example, there is evidence that parents perceive boys as being more competent than girls in math and sports. These perceptions lead some girls (but certainly not all girls) to value these two less and also to be less interested and involved in them. Over time, of course, girls with this history will not be able to function as competently in math and sports as their male peers, whose parents and teachers expected them to achieve in these areas.

It is human to choose activities in which you are expected to have an interest and do well. If your parents and teachers give you the impression that math and sports are not what your gender excels in, you are likely to look elsewhere. For girls, that "elsewhere" is English, in which our society expects females to excel (Eccles, Jacobs, & Harold, 1990).

These differences in the socialization of the two genders can have significant long-term consequences. The self-fulfilling prophecies for girls may lead them to have skills that do not qualify them for the better-rewarded traditionally male occupations (Eccles, 1987). Far fewer women than men are in the high-paying business world or in math-science positions.

Although we as teachers have limited opportunity to influence parents' stereotypes about gender, racial, ethnic, or religious differences, we have an opportunity to be a significant, positive influence on our students in this area. Perhaps most important, we can monitor our behavior to make sure that we do not (in intended or unintended ways) perpetuate the stereotypes. To do such monitoring, we need

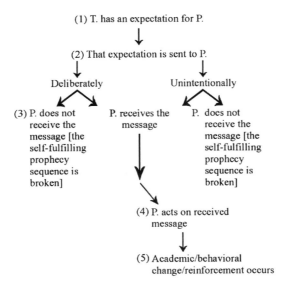

FIG. 7.1. Teacher expectancy and pupil change.

to understand how our expectations can, through a several step process, influence students.

To depict how a teacher's expectancy can affect a child's behavior or academic performance we present Fig. 7.1. It shows that the process begins when a teacher (T.) develops an expectation for a male student (P.). That expectation could be based on a student's past behavior, academic achievement, reputation in the school, dress, body build, gender, name, or other variables.

At Step 4, the student acts on the teacher's message. That could mean he behaves like an angel, assumes a leadership stance with peers, or begins to make rapid growth in reading skills. It seems easier to understand how a student can change his behavior or assume leadership, if he is expected to, than it is to comprehend how he can "decide to make great progress in reading." Nonetheless, research studies have shown that children may "bloom" academically if they are exposed to that expectation and, in part, suggested how the process works.

An ingenious study by Ira Goldenberg (1969), then of Yale University, showed how such unexplainable growth in reading could be fostered. He compared the amount of time, in minutes, that the teachers spent with each first grade reading group, and whether each group was given prime time (early-morning time when the teacher and children were fresh), least prime time (before lunch or dismissal), or neither prime nor least prime time. The results were unequivocal: Unwittingly, the teachers generally spent more and "better" time with the more advanced reading groups. That is, their expectancy was for higher achievement from these children, and the teachers performed in such ways as to have this prophecy fulfilled.

Another study of first- and second-grade reading groups in eight schools showed distinct differences in the ways teachers interacted with low versus high reading groups (Grant & Rothenberg, 1986). Children in the higher groups, but not in the lower ones, were helped to acquire the skills, values, and styles of behavior that gave them advantages in school and in life.

For example, Grant and Rothenberg, who were interested in the personal relationships between teachers and children in these groups, found that one important indicator of closeness was evidence of chats between teachers and students during lessons. They noted that chats made student–teacher relationships less formal, more relaxed, and broke down social distance. To illustrate, children in a higher reading group chatted with the teacher about their homes. The teacher, in turn, talked about national parks and asked if any had been to one. The students then shared their experiences.

Some of this chatting occurred in the low groups, but to a lesser degree. Further, when a child in a low group wanted to talk about his brother's birthday party, for example, the teacher was more likely to cut him short, saying that they had to finish a story and they would talk about his brother's party at another time. The message embedded in the teacher's interruption "told" the child in the low reading group that his comment was a diversion. He, of course, may have earlier observed that when the child in the high reading group described his home, the teacher listened and responded.

Grant and Rothenberg explained that the teacher's chats with the higher-group students contributed to a pleasant, relaxed environment, one that carried over as the group turned its attention to academic work. The investigators also pointed out that other researchers had similarly reported that teachers tend to create a warmer socio-emotional atmosphere for brighter students. Of course, teachers do not deliberately deny children in the lower groups these advantages. For the most part, the teachers are unaware that they, themselves, are responding to their own expectations about slower and more academically advanced students.

The significance of these studies is clear. As a teacher, you have considerable impact on the lives of your students. The influence comes only partly from your effectiveness in helping them master important skills and knowledge. It also comes partly from the fact that when they look at you, often in awe, they see a successful adult figure who has great significance in their lives, and who conveys important information to them about themselves.

Your students look hard at your communications, actively trying to "read" you. They do this by listening to your words, watching your expressions, and noting your body language. You need, therefore, to be conscious of your communications to them to be as sure as possible that you are conveying a positive outlook and the expectation of maximum possible development. It is then incumbent on you to help them fulfill that prophecy through well-planned activity.

An interesting study of elementary school students with learning disabilities bears out the importance of the students' own perceptions of their disabilities. The investigators (Rothman & Cosden, 1995) checked on the relationship between how students viewed being learning disabled and the following perceptions: self-concept, behavioral and intellectual competence, social acceptance, and achievement in mathematics. The results showed that children with less negative perceptions of their learning disability have more positive self concepts and higher assessments of their competence, achievement, and social acceptance.

The study does not tell us that more positive perceptions of a learning disability leads to these more positive outcomes. It says the two are related, but not which is the cause. Nevertheless, it implies that we, as teachers, can profitably intervene by setting positive expectations and modeling acceptance and support; creating a positive and supportive climate in the classroom; and providing learning experiences that help the students realize those expectations.

But how does the teacher "set positive expectations" for a student who has not performed well and who seems unmotivated? That is the challenge. Several researchers (Weinstein, Madison, & Kuklinski, 1995) engaged in an ongoing study of a collaborative team (teachers, administrators, and the researchers themselves). The team's aim was to raise expectations for ninth grade students in an inner-city high school who were at risk for failure.

To set positive expectations, they concluded that teachers and administrators must counteract low expectations of change that are "ingrained in the culture of the school" (p. 152). To do that, the culture needs changing so that all personnel in the school challenge the limiting beliefs. The team believed that the best results would come when the change in outlook about expectations is school-wide. Teachers' own beliefs about their ability to have a positive impact on student learning was vital. Their success in a given school is more likely if there is collaborative work among teachers and genuine support from administrators.

For you as a student teacher, this is the time to be reflective about your attitudes concerning student ability. As a teacher, will you expect your students to perform as they have in the past? Or will you hold the belief that you have the capacity to influence their learning and to raise the level of their performance?

STUDENTS WHO MAY REQUIRE SPECIAL ATTENTION

In this section we focus on students who may require special attention: those with disabilities, the intellectually gifted, those living in poverty, and female students.

Students with Disabilities

The term *special needs* applies to individuals at the two poles of the continuum of learning ability—students who are gifted and students who are developmentally handicapped. It also applies to students with learning disabilities or behavioral disorders as well as those who have sensory, neurological, or other physical disabilities. A 1975 federal law, the Individuals with Disabilities Education Act (IDEA)—formerly called the Education of All Handicapped Children Act, PL94-142—was implemented in 1977. It mandates that a system be introduced into each school district involving the periodic review of each handicapped child for place-ment in the least restrictive setting. Unless the review weighs heavily against it, special needs children are to be placed in regular classes (i.e., "mainstreamed" or "included") and the school provides the necessary specialized personnel, equip-ment, and services on an individual or group basis. However, "least restrictive environment" and "mainstreaming" are not synonymous. For many exceptional students, the appropriate least restrictive environment *is* the regular classroom, but for some, it is not (Schloss, 1992).

Mainstreaming.   The trend is to mainstream special needs students. Under the circumstances, it is probable that you will have one or more mainstreamed students in your student-teaching class. If your knowledge of special needs children is limited, you should seek more information. Your college/university supervisor, cooperating teacher, or campus librarian will probably be able to recommend useful resources to you. Books are available that will help you better understand the handicapped child. In one such book, *Two-Way Talking With Parents of Special Children*, the authors (Chinn, Winn, & Walters, 1978) include a section on the needs of the special child. In this old but still useful book, the authors stressed this important fact: Students with disabilities are, first of all, children. Their needs are those of other children, but the satisfaction of those needs is complicated by the nature of their disability and especially by the ways in which people in their environment react to that condition. We now examine three important needs.

A primary need is for clear, honest communication. Special needs children do not need to be shielded from the realities of their "differentness" and its effects on their lives. They are harmed rather than helped if a teacher, out of pity, sets lower standards of scholastic performance or social behavior for them than for the rest of the class. A second basic need, particularly for the physically challenged, is for acceptance. A teacher, of course, can monitor whether or not this is happening in the classroom and intervene if necessary. A third basic need is for freedom to grow.

One of the ironies about special needs children is that their parents' genuine concern about safety, health, and welfare leads them to inhibit their children's opportunities to "spread their wings and fly." In protecting them, they may also be impairing them psychologically and physically. Teachers also fall victim to such overprotectiveness, so they must reflect on their own feelings and actions as a way of guarding against that. We can remind ourselves that the Special Olympics have shown that people with disabilities can participate in many sports with great satisfaction. Moreover, feature articles and television news stories have shown that students in wheelchairs can play basketball, tennis, and other sports. Teachers who encourage special needs children to participate on the playgrounds and ballfields do need to exercise care; watchfulness is always essential in those settings.

These three basic needs—clear, honest communication, acceptance, and freedom to grow—hardly exhaust the list, whether for special needs or other children. However, they are illustrative of the mindful attention special needs students require, and of the sensitivities that teachers need in order to provide them with a facilitative, health-promoting learning environment.

In an article entitled "Mainstreaming Revisited," Schloss (1992) highlighted the shift in the roles of teachers brought about by IDEA. Teachers must engage in various forms of interventions and assessments before referring a student for special services. They need new skills to work with both the academically and socially disadvantaged, and they may be required to learn new technologies to make the learning environment adaptable for students with various disabilities (ranging from visual to aural to orthopedic to language impairment and learning disabilities). Their methods of disciplining may have to be adapted to the new mix of students, and their efforts at building a community spirit in the class may need to be geared to the social integration of children who may have been formerly rejected by their peers. Finally, to build an effective learning environment for special needs students, teachers may need to participate in planning with professionals from other disciplines.

Evaluation of Mainstreaming.   Educators have paid much attention to the process of mainstreaming in the research literature, conducting studies that have evaluated its effectiveness in the classroom. We discuss some of their findings next, along with influential thinking on this topic.

A first issue of concern was the sensitivities required of teachers who worked with mainstreamed classes. To state the obvious, papers and research on this topic were needed immediately by school people when the important mainstreaming concept was enacted into law. For example, an author in the 1970s wrote that physical education teachers should accept the fact that sooner or later they will have physically challenged students in their regular classes (Jansma, 1977). The article, devoted to in-service training programs, proposed covering many topics to prepare teachers for this new challenge and opportunity.

A related concern given major attention was the attitude of teachers who have never had training about or experience with special needs students in their classes. In the absence of what we would call an open attitude, teachers would be unable to become self-sufficient in serving these students and in providing them with an optimizing learning environment. For instance, an open attitude allows a teacher of diabetic children to recognize that, although there are limitations to be aware of and precautions to follow, students with this disorder can engage in virtually all kinds of physical activities (Engerbretson, 1977). This teacher can also help the student's classmates to understand that he or she may have to pause during physical activity to eat a sweet. The open attitude also benefits teachers who instruct mainstreamed visually impaired or blind students in their classes.

Although successful integration of these students into the classroom requires the assistance of specialists and equipment and instructional materials designed for them, still, effective mainstreaming depends most on the teacher's readiness. Moreover, a teacher with an open attitude is best positioned to help his or her students with the adjustments necessary. By students we mean both sets, the special needs youngsters and their classmates, who must be ready to accept each other.

Another important issue was that of preparing students for mainstreaming. One good technique involves structuring instruction so as to bring the special needs students and their classmates into a close working relationship. Another effective procedure calls for the use of role playing. Carefully planned and sensitively carried out, role playing can help students in the upper elementary and higher grades appreciate the feelings and limitations of being disabled.

Structuring instruction to bring students together was very much part of a study that used a system of cooperative learning known as Cooperative Integrated Reading and Composition (Stevens & Slavin, 1995). About 1300 students in Grades 2 through 6 were divided into a cooperative learning group and a traditional group. Of the academically handicapped among them, 72 were mainstreamed and participated in cooperative learning team activities, whereas 65 were in traditional, non-mainstreamed programs. First, it was found that cooperative learning proved beneficial for the whole group. Second, it was found that the academically handicapped in cooperative learning, mainstreamed classes had significantly higher achievement, compared with the special education students in traditional classes, in the following: language expression, reading vocabulary, and reading comprehension.

Research has progressed to the point where there are enough outcome studies of mainstreaming that an author can look at these studies together and conduct a meta-analysis of them. In conducting a meta-analysis (or a study of studies), a researcher statistically examines the effects of two or more studies and draws conclusions that take into account the results of all of them. A meta-analysis of 11 studies examined how well special education students in mainstream classes compared with those in segregated programs. The overall results suggest that mainstreaming produces the following:

1. Improved performance as measured by achievement in subjects like reading and mathematics;

2. Improved attitudinal outcomes such as students' self-concepts, mainstream and regular students' attitudes toward each other, and parents' and teachers' attitudes towards mainstreaming;

3. Improved process outcomes, such as favorable interactions among students and between students and teachers (Wang & Baker, 1985–1986).

Wang (1989) emphasized the need for more research before concluding that mainstreaming is the answer. While mainstreaming is being evaluated, the fundamental idea of separating any student on any basis is being challenged. There is an inclination among some to oppose the concept of the "least restrictive environment" on the grounds that this maintains segregation for those in other than mainstreamed classes. Once regarded as progressive, some now view the concept as an obstacle to integration for those in great need of that. For example, Lipsky and Gartner (1989) argued, "the current failure to provide quality education to all students, and the perpetuation of segregated settings is morally unsound and educationally unnecessary" (p. 285).

Asch (1989) believed that too many disabled are still getting "crumbs." Yet, in her opinion, "the law provides the right guidelines when thoughtfully applied. Although it works far too little of the time, it does work sometimes, and it can work far better" (p. 204).

Another productive line of research important to teachers is identifying classroom and school features that are related to successful mainstreaming. Through a study of third, fourth, and fifth grade science classes in which students with disabilities were successfully mainstreamed, Scruggs and Mastropiere (1994) found "seven variables which appeared to be meaningfully associated with observed mainstreaming success, across categories of disability and grade level" (p. 794). These seven are:

1. Administrative support
2. Support from special education personnel
3. Accepting, positive classroom atmosphere
4. Appropriate curriculum
5. Effective general teaching skills
6. Peer assistance (i.e., nondisabled students assist their disabled peers)
7. Disability-specific teaching skills (pp. 794–801)

These seven include support of two kinds from the outside (administrator and special education personnel) and five in-class features. Two of the five in-class features (positive classroom atmosphere and effective general teaching skills) are those that any teacher in any class wants to achieve. Two of them (appropriate curriculum and disability-specific teaching skills) are geared to the composition of the class and to the specific disabilities represented. Finally, "peer assistance" is a useful teaching–learning procedure in any class, helpful both to the peer "teacher" and the peer "learner."

As we said, your classes will very likely include students with disabilities. Increasingly, this is the direction American education is taking. In the meantime, educational researchers are working hard at evaluating outcomes of mainstreaming and of other approaches to educating students with disabilities. For example, an entire issue of a journal was devoted to "Educational Outcomes for Students with Disabilities" (Ysseldyke, Thurlow, & Maher, 1995). Of the 17 articles, one discusses how to achieve better outcomes for students with disabilities (Danielson & Malouf, 1995); another is on how the local school level can use the national outcome data collection program to study outcomes at the local level (McGrew, 1995).

A Student Teacher's Anxieties About Mainstreaming.   Teachers' feelings about individuals with disabilities make a vital difference in the climate of their classrooms. Sensing that fact, one student teacher asked the following question:

> 1/8: I'm troubled by something that surprises me. In some of the classes that I'm student-teaching in, a few of the teenagers are mainstreamed. I don't know much about that—but that's not the problem. One boy has trouble walking, uses a crutch and all that. One girl has speech trouble—stammering and halting speech. Also there's a big 15 year-old who is developmentally delayed. I'm bothered by their disabilities, I get distracted. Sometimes I pity them and get upset. I wonder if I'm going to have kids like that in my own classes? I had sort of a problem like this when I came to college. You see, I came from a pretty-much all White town, but after a while I really got used to being friends with African American, Hispanic, and Asian students.

The student teacher's supervisor responded by explaining that one major objective of the Individuals with Disabilities Education Act is to see that students are schooled in the least restrictive environment. That means they should, if at all possible, have the opportunity to learn in regular classes in the company of their nonhandicapped peers. It also means that teachers have to modify their teaching. For example, your teaching strategies may now call for more emphasis on auditory communication for the sake of visually impaired children, or increased repetition and more simplified explanations for developmentally delayed students.

As you have seen from materials in your cooperating classroom, certain teaching decisions are informed by the needs of given students, as spelled out in their Individualized Education Program (IEP). This is prepared for a special needs student by a team, including a representative from the school's special education department, the classroom teacher, and other school personnel. Each school year a student's IEP is revised and a parent conference is held to review the plan.

As you probably observed in your cooperating classroom, when it comes to tests and grading, your cooperating teacher takes into consideration such facts as the poor handwriting of some neurologically impaired students and the need for extra test-taking time for students with certain learning disabilities.

Having said all that, we have still left your important question unanswered. Because your question is so honest, you are already on the road to dealing with your problem. It is not unusual for caring people to be upset in the presence of children or adolescents who have disabling conditions, even if those individuals are accustomed to their disabilities and are well adapted to life.

One way you can help yourself is by getting to know them as individuals. That way you will find that they do not need and do not want pity. You will also find out what you discovered when you came to college and began to mingle with racially and ethnically different people—that they are different and yet the same. They, too, have insecurities and fears, but also strengths, and they, too, enjoy humor and lightness. They do have special needs, and we attend to those needs. Beyond that, we try to interact with them as we do with other students.

In all probability you will be able to do that once you sit and talk with the special needs students in your classes. If the problem persists and you continue to feel uncomfortable, you might want to discuss your reaction with a member of the team that prepares the IEPs, maybe the special education teacher, the school counselor, or psychologist.

You will also find it helpful to call on resources in print. We referred earlier to Nancy Wilson's (1992) book, Optimizing special education: How parents can make a difference, which includes a chapter entitled *"Parent and School: A Winning Combination."* Besides containing a wealth of information about special education, the book also conveys, in very human terms, the emotional impact on parent and child of the child's disability. You will find this useful in learning to accommodate to special needs students in your classes.

Although the law calling for placement in the least restrictive environment became fully effective as long ago as 1978, the results of evaluation studies are by no means conclusive. This is so partly because the job of evaluation is made difficult by the very features that make special education special—special curriculum, materials, methods, and techniques that are not routinely used in regular education settings (Kavale, 1990). With variations in defining which students are disabled, differences in the definitions of the handicaps, and differences in curriculum, materials, and so forth, it is difficult for researchers to obtain clear-cut and reliable results.

Problems in defining "special needs" are substantial. The current system of classifying students and certifying them as disabled has been called into question. For example, the label of "learning disabled" is one of those considered to be vague and ill-defined. Although some students do have neurological problems, when literally millions were found to be classified as having "minimal neurological dysfunction," the label lost its credibility among some specialists (Coles, 1987).

As a result of questioning the diagnostic classification system, some states are moving away from its use. Instead of classifying students in terms of their disorders or disabilities they are categorized in terms of need. For example, some students need close supervision and small-group instruction, others need intensive study of language, and so on. This functional system may become more popular in the future.

The Intellectually Gifted

Thus far we have concentrated on the physically and mentally challenged. Only in our first paragraph have the gifted been mentioned in connection with special needs students, and then only in passing. That we have neglected them up to this point and that we devote much less space to them is not fortuitous. It is, in truth, a sample of the treatment the gifted have received in the professional literature. The limited research has, however, indicated that there is a definite need to identify children who are gifted in order to challenge them and stimulate their intellectual activity.

Among the teaching-learning procedures recommended are some that are equally appropriate for all students. One procedure of that kind, self-directed learning, has been characterized as a priority for the gifted and talented (Treffinger, 1975). The author identified some misunderstandings about that kind of learning: It is not random, disorganized, or unstructured, and it does not "just happen." On the contrary, self-directed learning must be cultivated. Treffinger derived his proposals from research both on the gifted and on programs for stimulating independent thought and learning. He formulated four steps in the process of moving toward self-directed learning: (a) identify goals and objectives, (b) assess the entering behavior of the students, (c) identify and implement instructional procedures, and (d) assess the student's performance.

He then provided four stages within each of the four steps. In each stage the student achieves a little more independence. It is helpful for teachers to note that even gifted children need instruction in how to study if they are to assume ever greater responsibility for their own learning.

Many models for the education of the gifted have been proposed. Various types of curricula are spelled out in Eby and Smutny's (1990) book, *A Thoughtful Overview of Gifted Education*, which also includes chapters on the special needs of both minority students and girls in gifted education.

The various models attempt to enrich the curricula and introduce teaching strategies suitable for talented students. The models are presumably useful whether you are a specialist teacher of the gifted or a regular teacher who has gifted students in class.

The models include such variations from usual procedures as those in content (greater depth and elaboration), in process (such as independent study and research), and in product (such as addressing real-life problems; Maker, 1982). The models proposed strategies like acceleration, creativity training, and use of higher-order thinking skills.

Do teachers of the gifted use these strategies? Do they use them more than regular teachers and pre-service teachers? And if they do not use them, why not?

Starko and Schack (1989) designed a study to get answers to those questions. Their subjects were 57 teachers of the gifted, 85 regular classroom teachers, and 176 pre-service teachers. Through a questionnaire, the teachers indicated "how well the identified strategies met the needs of gifted students, how confident teachers felt in using the strategies (teacher efficacy), and how often they actually used the strategies" (p. 119).

The researchers found that as they went from pre-service to regular teacher to teacher of the gifted, the subjects saw the following: a higher need on the part of the students for those strategies; greater teacher confidence in using the strategies; and greater frequency of use. In other words, the more experience as regular teachers, and the more training and experience teaching the gifted, the greater they saw the need for those strategies and the more they used them.

We believe that a most useful finding for student and beginning teachers is this: The researchers found a much closer relationship between teacher feelings of efficacy and confidence and their use of strategies than between their recognition of need and their use of strategies. In other words, teachers had to be confident and comfortable, it seems, before they used a new strategy. That is hardly surprising, yet often forgotten.

The researchers recommended the following to those responsible for staff development: There is less need to persuade teachers that these strategies are useful than in giving them simulated and real-life practice in using them. Practice leads to feelings of mastery and confidence, and these lead to usage. This year, next year, or some time in the near future, you may be able to get supervised experience in using these strategies. If such opportunities do not arise, you may want to develop your own plan for trying to learn to use these strategies.

Several books written for parents may be helpful to you for two reasons, first, as resources to bring to the attention of parents, and second, for your own further education about the gifted, especially about the interaction of parent and child. These are *Parents' Guide to Raising a Gifted Child: Recognizing and Developing Your Child's Potential* (Alvino & editors of *Gifted Children Monthly*, 1985), and *The Survival Guide for Parents of Gifted Kids: How to Understand, Live With, and Stick Up for Your Gifted Child* (Walker, 1991).

During your student teaching, and especially if you have one or more gifted students in your class(es), you may wonder whether enrichment of their classroom experience makes a difference. Do they progress as a result of such enrichment? Issues about the social/emotional and academic effects of gifted education are discussed by a number of authors, for example, Eby and Smutny (1990) and Southern and Jones (1991).

Students Living in Poverty

The reality of the poverty in which some students live confronts student teachers with a form of culture shock. It is one thing to sit on a comfortable chair in the tranquil surroundings of a university library reading about poverty and oppression; it is quite another to come smack up against it and its consequences in real life. Despite courses in sociology and anthropology in which the problems of poverty were examined, one of us experienced a cultural shock as a student teacher. She wrote in her journal:

> 5/2: We were returning [to the Bronx] by bus from an all-day trip to a nature park in Staten Island. The fifth graders were tired but happy after a very enjoyable day of walking the nature trails, visiting the museum, and picnicking and playing outdoors. The children surrounding me on the bus in this happy atmosphere of the day were conversing in a friendly and trusting way. One girl said she hated to think that her cousin was coming to visit for the weekend. I asked her why, whether she didn't like her cousin. She liked her all right, but the cousin, a girl her own age, was coming with her whole family. That meant, she said, "Us children will have to sleep on the floor."

Very naively I asked what was so terrible about that for a few nights? She looked at me, now a little embarrassed, perhaps at my own innocence, and said, "I can't get myself to fall asleep on the floor because I'm afraid of the big rats." Of course, I had read about poverty and rats and malnutrition and brain damage from lead poisoning in hungry little children who eat the peeling paint off the wall, and more, but I had not connected them with my children, with this girl who I had felt was not much different from me only 10 years before.

Another one of the authors remembers an experience in an inner-city teaching assignment early in her professional career. She and her first graders completed a unit of study in nutrition. The teacher was giving herself a pat on the back. What a success her lessons had been—a trip to the local supermarket, a "tasting" day of new and exotic fruits, an afternoon of making "Stone Soup" with a variety of vegetables the children had brought to school.

On one particular morning the class was reviewing some of the concepts learned. "What vegetable did you have for dinner last night?" Various children responded— french fries, greens, carrots, corn, and so on. Tiffany's response was "tomato soup." How clever—she's really made the connection. For some reason "tomato soup" kept sticking in the teacher's mind that day. As the day was coming to a close, she finally remembered why. A day ago, Tiffany had said her stove was not working. She took Tiffany aside and asked how her mother had cooked her soup. She hadn't. She had opened the can and Tiffany had cold soup for dinner. Tiffany never returned to school after that chat. Two weeks later the teacher was notified she had moved and her new school was requesting school records. Tucked into her records, the teacher placed a note to her new teacher to keep an eye on Tiffany's home situation.

A recent study on academic achievement of middle school students had some useful findings (Mau, 1995). Among the questions asked of the children was whether they go to their teacher for help to improve their academic work in school. In the large, nationally representative sample, 62% of both boys and girls said they went to their teacher for such help. That means 38% did not. The study did not use social class as a variable. However, we can be rather sure that children in poverty, many undernourished, made up a disproportionate share of that group.

Female Students and Expectations

Teachers treat male and female students differently. They interact more with boys; they give more approval to high-achieving boys than to high-achieving girls; they ask boys more questions than girls; and they give more recognition to boys' ideas. Also, boys evoke more and harsher punishment and receive more negative communication from teachers than do girls (Seiler, Schuelke, & Lieb-Brilhart, 1984).

Those findings led the investigators to recommend practices that would help eliminate automatic, out-of-awareness biased responses. Combining their recommendations with ours, we propose the following:

1. Make a serious, ongoing effort to identify your own attitudes about the two genders.
2. For your own use, observe and describe your behavior in mixed gender groups.
3. Reflect on your attitudes toward students of the two genders in your class.
4. Examine your behavior toward students of the two genders in your class.
5. Use praise and disciplinary action in a gender-blind way, basing them only on students' behaviors.
6. Use language and voice tone appropriate to the situation, not to the gender of the person addressed.
7. Maximize interaction between the genders by integrating study groups and teams as well as seating arrangements.
8. In assigning roles such as distributing work sheets, reading aloud, writing on chalkboards or serving as messenger, avoid "typical" male and female stereotyping.
9. In recitations and discussions, be aware of both the teacher tendency to call on boys and the female tendency to be less assertive than boys (e.g., wild hand-waving to get the teacher's attention).

The gender gap shows up in surprising areas. Who would have expected that it would show up in the National Geographic Society's National Geographic Bee? Yet, of 18,000 winners, 14,000 were boys; of the 57 state winners, 55 were boys; and of the finalists in recent years, usually all have been boys. Lynn Liben (1995) and her associates, in an ongoing series of studies, have found thus far that the boy–girl differences "reflect students' knowledge of and interest in geography" (p. 9). This says to teachers that if you want to narrow the gender gap, encourage girls to have greater exposure to geography, and do that under circumstances that give them enjoyment. Help them to like geography.

The gender differences that will appear in classroom behavior begin before children go to kindergarten. Studies of children aged 1.5 to 4 years tell us that gender identity starts early. At those early ages, when children organize their own groups they tend to choose to be in same-sex groups. However, teachers can influence group membership. For example, when teachers organize an interest group and participate in it as well, then boys will join it even if it is composed more of girls than boys (Lloyd & Duveen, 1992). It seems that teaching style affects the "gender culture," that is, how we teach and organize groups determines the time and the experience the two sexes have together and separately.

Young children have a bipolar conception of male and female—the two are distinct and opposite. They hold fast to that simplistic view because of their level of cognitive development. The fact that the two genders have much in common, while also being different, is too complex for them to understand. In time, they can go beyond that, partly as a result of their further cognitive development and partly as a result of their experiences in our classrooms.

TEACHING IN A MULTICULTURAL SOCIETY

Many Americans travel abroad to enjoy the "difference." They find pleasure in diversity—different foods, different expressions, different practices. In our multicultural society we are blessed with some of that diversity right here at home. Such cultural differences can be used by teachers to great advantage. They can be used to liven a class by exposing students to new and interesting views of life.

Before this can be accomplished, however, many teachers must help their students overcome stereotyped thinking about people. Such thinking stems from an ethnocentric view of the world—from seeing the world only through the eyes of one's own group. People who think this way usually are not deliberately narrow-minded; they just have not had the opportunity to correct the stereotypes they learned. Here, in Irene's journal, is an example of stereotyped thinking and its consequences:

> 2/21: Today I tried to do some "teaching" in the teacher's room. Quite unexpected. I was all alone having coffee in my free period when Jim [another student teacher] came in. One class he teaches is algebra. We got talking about our classes. He has an odd classification system: "These kids are good in basketball, these others in putting on nail polish and doing their hair and those in working a grill, so I don't expect much from them in algebra." He said it with a straight face and really believes it. He said he has good classes, no problems, because he "knows their nature." He doesn't put any demands on them.
>
> When I started to point out some social reasons for concentrating on sports or appearance, he cut me off. That's when a couple of teachers came in and changed the subject.

People like Jim can retain such stereotypes as long as they avoid and deny information that challenges their beliefs. That kind of thinking makes it easy for teachers in one sense: If students are not learning, it's due to their "ethnic or racial genes." Teachers do not have to challenge themselves by setting higher expectations and trying every means possible to encourage the students to aspire to and to achieve higher goals.

Ordinarily, as we said earlier, when we travel abroad we enjoy the national and ethnic cultural differences. Whether we find them "quaint" or "colorful," we usually take pleasure in describing them to our friends. "You should have seen them in that village on the sea! You should have seen how they eat (or talk, dance, greet each other, etc.)!" Yet, when we "live" with those "different" practices, we are not so comfortable, partly because we do not recognize them as such. Here is an example.

A high school in Stockton, California had a school population composed of about one third each of Hispanics, Blacks, and Asians. Because of racial tensions and the outbreak of fights, the Community Relations Service of the U.S. Department of Justice offered its services to introduce a problem-solving strategy. That involved a series of meetings with parents, teachers, administrators, and staff. It began with 2 full days of student sessions (Hule, 1989). On the first day, students met only with their own race/ethnic group, on the second, in mixed groups. The effort was well worthwhile. For example, within 1 year, the suspension rate during a quarter dropped from 147 to 47.

The student discussions revealed ignorance about each other's practices. For example, it became apparent that the Asian students felt intimidated by the Black students. How were they intimidated? The Black students, they said, stood in the middle of the hall and talked loudly. The Asian students, having freely shared their concern, now learned a helpful principle about culture: Cultures differ in many ways and one of these is in their style of speech; some differ, for example, in how loudly or softly people speak. Knowing this, students are less likely to be frightened by a loud-spoken person or group, or to attribute shyness or submissiveness to a soft-spoken person or group.

The strategy of the Community Relations Service was to bring the differences—uniqueness—to the surface in the interest of solving problems of group relationships. As teacher, we can bring them to the surface for this purpose and for other reasons, too, like making our teaching more interesting. Cultures relate to every subject we teach. They are obviously related to literature and history. Virtually every culture has given something of value to the arts. And members of many different cultures contributed to knowledge in mathematics and the physical sciences.

We can bring cultures into our classes, either by indicating their contributions to the topic under discussion or by having representatives of cultures make presentations, depict native dress, or share distinct foods, authentic speech, and unique customs. Often our aim in doing this is to bring concepts to life and to add spice to classroom experience. One way to test the potential benefit in doing this is to run through your own experiences as a student. Rewind the mental videotape of your elementary and secondary school history, so to speak. See where your teachers might have added cultural examples to enrich and enliven your learning experiences. Could it have made a difference?

In summary, when you walk into the classroom as a teacher, for the most part you carry with you the identity of a single culture. The challenge you face as a true professional is to serve students who together may be identified with as many as a dozen cultures. To serve them well means keeping your expectations deservedly high. You cannot know the distinct meanings for all events for all the cultures in our country, but you can become aware of the meaning of differences, as the students in the California high school did.

Racial and ethnic differences in our country are no longer submerged and denied. In reaction to the years of glorifying and imitating the White Anglo Saxon status type (or really a stereotyped version of it), other groups are now strongly identifying with their past and proudly and publicly displaying their present image of themselves. Probably because of years of oppression, some act in ways that exaggerate their separateness.

Dorothy, a White student teacher, was assigned to an elementary school in a poor neighborhood. In her second-grade class about 25% of the children were African American. One of them, Thomas, concerned Dorothy because she felt that he was much more capable than he showed in his work and that he lacked self-confidence. Her expectations were higher than his own; her problem was how to get him to aim higher. Dorothy's excitement about the possibility of helping Thomas is shown in the first of two journal entries that were written on 2 successive days:

1/10: When Thomas came back from the testing (by the school psychologist) Ms. K. was assigning math to be done before the lunch bell. For the first time Thomas did all the problems. He came up to me saying, "Look, I finished just as the bell rang!" I replied, "Thomas I'm so excited for you—you have the problems all done. May I check them?" Thomas: "Yes." I continued to examine his paper. When I found a problem wrong I would ask him to recheck the problem. Thomas would and then bring it back to me. It appeared that the psychologist showing interest in him motivated Thomas to work. I'm very pleased with the math problems Thomas did.

1/11: Still having a tremendous discipline problem. Felt it's due to the lack of stimulating the children's interest plus the fact of someone new in the classroom and they are testing how far they can go. During reading groups Thomas continued hitting other students, causing confusion and disturbance. I asked Thomas to sit at the experience table to finish the work Ms. K. had assigned the class. It appears that the daily English, spelling, and writing assignments do not hold his attention. Thomas continued jumping up out of his seat, hitting other children, and they then started shouting, "Thomas is bothering me."

He got Keith and Horace siding with him, and then when Horace's reading group came back to work with me, Horace refused to do anything. So I moved Keith to a desk by the reading group and he began to do work. I told Horace to read. I did not give him a choice—he read but grumbled. I now had become very upset with Thomas, so I took hold of his arm and told him to sit in his seat. Thomas shook his arm loose and said, "Don't ever grab me again." I replied, "Thomas, I'm wrong for grabbing you, but you must get in your seat and do your work." Thomas did sit down and start working.

Next day in seminar, after being complimented by the other student teachers for the effective way she reacted to Thomas's complaint, Dorothy explained that she was taken aback by his reaction. Because he grabbed and hit other children it seemed so ironic, she said, that that kind of complaint should come from him.

An African American student teacher helped Dorothy and the rest of the group understand what it means to many African Americans to be physically restrained or controlled, and how jealously many African American parents restrict the right to use physical means to discipline their children, granting it only to those whom they believe do have the children's interest at heart.

African American students are very conscious of that attitude, having been well trained in it. The African American student teachers were the first to point out that despite her ignorance about that cultural fact, Dorothy had respected the child's feelings while insisting that he do as she demanded.

Another illustration of lack of knowledge about or insensitivity to cultural variations was observed by Eleanor, a student teacher:

1/28: Mrs. B. wasn't there today and we had a substitute teacher. She and Marshall had problems from the beginning. Marshall was out of his seat and she told him to sit down. As usual Marshall did not respond. She grabbed him by the arm and said, "Now listen here, boy, you get in your seat and don't let me catch you out of it again." Marshall replied by declaring that he is not a boy, he is a person, and she was not his mother or father and he didn't have to do anything that she said.

Marshall is African American, and as with many African American males he objects to being called "boy." Eleanor did not report the substitute teacher's response. We would have said, "I will not call you 'boy' again because you don't like it. I'm not your mother or father, but I am your teacher today and I will tell you what to do whenever I have to. Now I tell you that you are to stay in your seat and do your work. If I can help you with it, I'd like to do that."

The words we used are not special. What is important is to convey understanding and respect combined with unwavering firmness about our expectation of the student's behavior. However, these are not easily achieved if we are not in touch with lives that may be very different from our own. Being aware of these differences alerts us to the substantial need for anthropological–sociological input in teacher training and for the need for student teachers to try to appreciate the students' perspectives and how they differ from their own world view.

Jeff's experience as a social studies student teacher shows that an ethnocentric outlook is counterproductive, if not destructive. Jeff's cooperating teacher, Mr. Y., had asked the 11th-grade students to write a paper about a significant historical character, indicating the reasons for their choice. He gave Jeff the first opportunity to read the papers and write comments on them, which Mr. Y. then reviewed.

During a free period, Mr. Y. praised Jeff for the worthwhile questions he posed in his comments and the positive reinforcement he gave to many students. Then he added that he was surprised by comments on two papers. One African American student, who wrote about Malcolm X, agreed with the latter's argument that African Americans must stand strong "as a nation." Jeff's comment was: "I thought we were all Americans!" An Hispanic student chose Cesar Chavez, the head of the Farm Workers Union of America who organized a consumer boycott against grapes. Jeff wrote, "Couldn't you find a more significant person than Chavez?" Jeff did not yet understand that by attacking role models, he was undermining his students' confidence and their self-expectations. Here is Jeff's delayed reaction:

3/13: A week ago, when Mr. Y. pointed these things out, I knew immediately that I had blundered. I wished the earth would open up under me. But I grew up in the suburbs as an "all-American boy." When I got to college and mixed with other people, I guess I learned about their ideas and values. But I put that knowledge in a separate compartment. I still sort of believe that we're all Americans, who all have the same opportunity, but the other part of me knows it's not 100% true. I must reconcile the two different ones. I owe a lot to Mr. Y.

At various points during your student-teaching experience, and next year when you have your own class, go through your roster and ask yourself about each student, "What are my expectations about him or her? Are they realistic and will they promote maximum growth and development?" And think about your behavior toward each individual. Ask whether it conveys your caring, support, and belief in them. Does it lead them to know that you expect them to learn and to grow?

As you ask yourself these questions about individual students, you will be crossing the whole spectrum of group diversity in our schools—diversity in gender, race, ethnicity, culture, special needs, and social class. You will be examining ways to include all children in your educational objectives and plans. You are likely to find this process both difficult and challenging.

As you engage in this process, be mindful and try to identify any conclusions you might have otherwise drawn, almost automatically and based on stereotypes. Consider what Barbara and Danielle learned as a result of a conversation they had about student teaching. Barbara was student teaching at an inner-city school in an extremely poor area while Danielle taught at a private school that served affluent families. Barbara was lamenting about how her students arrived each day hungry and half asleep. Danielle empathized and shared her observation that much of her class arrived hungry, pushed out of their home without breakfast by their two-career parents who put their careers first. Further, Danielle explained, her students went home to caretakers who often provided inadequate or no supervision and who could not provide the love and support that the children needed from their parents. Barbara and Danielle discussed the issue further and recognized that although their students came from different worlds and were as diverse as they could be in some ways, the students were much alike in many ways and had similar needs. Thoughtful teachers in both schools can help these youngsters work toward fulfilling those needs.

CRITICAL ISSUES

- Think of three different students in your student teaching class(es) and decide on the level of performance that you expect of each of them. What are your reasons for your decision in each of the three cases?
- What can you do to help students raise their own levels of expectation?
- What steps can you take to help you "see" students as individuals and not as members of particular groups (e.g., a learning disabled group, or an ethnic group).
- Identify some of the benefits of teaching a class in which several or more cultural groups are represented. Are those benefits found in your student teaching class(es)?
- What qualities in a teacher do you consider so fundamental to good teaching that they apply whether the class is mainstreamed, or limited to special needs students who are either emotionally disturbed, retarded, or gifted?

8

Curriculum and Teaching: Becoming Competent and Confident in the Classroom

TOPICS

- Curriculum guide/course of study
- Textbooks and the curriculum
- The computer and the curriculum
  Computer-related issues in cooperating classrooms
- Observation of the curriculum at work
- When you begin to teach
- Using the arts
- Resources
- Using technology in your teaching
- How much individualization?
- Cooperative learning
- Assessment
- Teaching the whole class the first time
- Next year
- Critical issues

By the time you begin your student-teaching assignment, you will have studied the principles of curriculum, observed in a classroom, and perhaps participated in an early field experience program. During your student teaching, your readings and studies will come to life—in your very own hands, so to speak, with you as the central figure.

Our objective in this chapter is to examine the curriculum from the point of view of the student teacher.

CURRICULUM GUIDE/COURSE OF STUDY

You may recall from your studies that the word "curriculum" is derived from the Latin verb *currere*, meaning "to run." The noun *cursis* in Latin means "race" or a "course." In essence, we as teachers conduct a group of children or adolescents on a course; we head them down one pathway or another.

Those using a pathway or road generally have a destination. True, we could wander aimlessly, selecting roadways quite randomly. That can be an appropriate choice during a vacation, especially when we want to be totally carefree and can afford to arrive wherever the path leads. Obviously, it is totally unacceptable when we are responsible for the education of our students.

No dallying? But of course. We can dally only after we have chosen our objective (e.g., the basic concepts of decimals or the causes of the American Revolution), made the important decision about the route we will traverse to get to our destination (e.g., readings, chalkboard demonstration, drills, worksheets, laboratory experiments, games, drama), and set ourselves a reasonable timetable, taking into consideration all of our destinations during the term or year.

Then we will have a clear idea about how much time we have to dally. And dally we must, at least if by that we mean spending some time following the interests that arise quite naturally (and sometimes unexpectedly) out of the planned and scheduled work.

You will not be involved in selecting the curriculum objectives for your student teaching class. That will already have been accomplished, probably carried out by a team of teachers and administrators, maybe under the aegis of the school district's curriculum council. These individuals look at a curriculum in its totality and build continuity in material from one year to the next.

Once you are established as a regular teacher, you can play an active role in reviewing and revising the curriculum and in selecting textbooks. But for now, as a student teacher, the course of study that you are to be guided by is fixed. Still, that allows you considerable imagination in leading your students through it.

The curriculum objectives you must work toward are spelled out in detail in the school's curriculum guide. Typically, these guides explain the significance of a particular subject to the total educational experience of the student, and also detail the specific importance of each particular concept and skill.

After specifying the subject's importance, guides move right to the heart of the matter, to the measurable, behavioral objectives, such as the specific skills to be learned in connection with decimals or the concepts to be understood in connection with radiation. Those objectives must be clear and concrete if by the end of a unit's work we are to reliably determine whether or not our students have mastered them, which is another way of seeing the extent to which our instructional plan has been effective.

To illustrate, one fifth-grade course of study in mathematics includes the following among its objectives: reducing fractions to the lowest term, defining *equilateral triangle* and *right triangle*, rounding decimal numbers to the nearest whole numbers, 10ths, or 100ths, and then 70 other objectives. In the next section of the guide these objectives are cross-referenced to the textbook selected for use in the fifth grade. Then suggestions are given for resource aids and materials on the given objectives.

Videos, audio recordings, instructional kits, instruments, books, computer software, and other educational aids, as well as suggestions of field trips, resources in the community, television programs, and other educational experiences, are listed. Also included is a section on lessons and exercises that the teacher may use to reinforce the learning of the concepts.

Finally, in some guides, there are tests that can be given periodically to evaluate learning during the study of a given unit. Preferably these are tests that are diagnostic in nature, enabling you to pinpoint the particular concept or skill that each student has or has not mastered. With that valuable information you will be in a position to provide very targeted instruction.

College students in education, appropriately excited by the prospect of conducting a class as a student teacher, have a large supply of creative ideas. On seeing the school's curriculum guide, some of them become resentful, as if an overwhelming power were at work to force them into a lock-step kind of teaching. This is not so. The curriculum guide is intended to be just that, a guide, or a map. It will select a road for you to take and provide many helpful signposts and resources to use as you wish. But what you "see" on the road, at what stream or wild flower you pause, what berry you taste, what hare or fawn you photograph en route is for you and the interest shown by your students to decide.

The course of study or curriculum guide is an extremely useful resource. In all probability you will find sample course of study/curriculum guides in your college/university library. If you are not yet acquainted with them through assignments made in your education courses (and if you have not yet begun student teaching), you may wish to familiarize yourself with their contents now. See how they are written, their general format, their valuable content, and the ways in which they can be helpful to you in your teaching.

We would like to stress an extraordinarily important principle: The curriculum objectives and the methods of instruction are determined by a number of decision makers. These include the public, the media, school boards, political leaders, test publishers, teachers groups, and others (Clark, 1988). That truism, however, must not obscure another equally important truism: Teachers and their students also create the curriculum (Clandinin & Connelly, 1992).

Persons outside your classroom decide on the objectives and write the guides, but your cooperating teacher (and you) and the students will determine what learning goes on in the classroom. The teacher is not just a conduit, like a telephone wire through which a curriculum is piped into the ears of the students. This year, to some extent, and certainly next year, your creative ideas and the responses and participation of your students will shape the curriculum. For although the curriculum guide provides the potential for what occurs in the classroom, the teacher plays a major role in determining what that potential will be. So, when we think about curriculum development, we need to consider teacher development as being as important as material development.

To learn what teachers and students, in the privacy of their classrooms, do to "create" the curriculum, talk to teachers and hear their stories. In a landmark book called *Life in Classrooms*, Philip Jackson (1990) took a tack very different from the questionnaire/statistical type of study of large groups of teachers. He listened to a small number of teachers and reported their stories. Teaching came alive in the pages of his book, as it does when teachers are encouraged to talk freely about their lives in the classroom.

Is there an overarching aim of the curriculum? According to two educators who have studied the field for many years (Tanner & Tanner, 1995), the curriculum is the means for learners to reconstruct for themselves the accumulated human knowledge and experience, enabling them "to grow in exercising intelligent control of subsequent knowledge and experience"(p. 191). They go on to say:

> Educators have no way of knowing the exact nature of the subsequent experience of the learner in life. But if the process of education and that thing we call curriculum are successful here and now, the learner will be enabled to grow in social power and insight throughout life. (p. 191)

It is not a coincidence that the aim of the curriculum for your students in a basic sense is the same as the aim of student teaching: to enable you "to grow in exercising intelligent control of subsequent knowledge and experience."

TEXTBOOKS AND THE CURRICULUM

If your cooperating teacher has not shown you the teacher's editions to the textbooks for your class during the first week of your student teaching, ask to see them. Also ask how much your cooperating teacher uses them, refers to them, and deviates from them. You will also want to know the teacher's expectations about your use of them. Request the opportunity to examine the complete set of textbooks used during the year and their accompanying teacher's editions. Take special note of the objectives as you study the volumes. Familiarity with these textbooks will help you become better informed about the program at your school and better prepared to teach.

The teachers' editions usually include the entire content of the textbook and more. Usually they contain information similar to that in a curriculum guide, although in greater detail. In addition to an overall description of the material and a list of objectives, you will find information on the specific objectives of individual chapters or units, the instructional materials and vocabulary needed for each unit, estimates of how much time should be devoted to each lesson, and suggestions for handling evaluations.

Within each lesson of the unit there are detailed suggestions on ways of introducing concepts and instructing students in the material at hand. Frequently follow-up activities, evaluative tests, remedial measures and enrichment activities, and references for further study are also included.

Considering the need for large amounts of lesson preparations during the course of student teaching (not to mention during a full school year), commercially prepared textbooks and the accompanying teachers' editions are of great value. With their use you need not devise every single exercise, assignment, and test; you can use those that are provided, in the original or an adapted form, altered to serve your specific purposes.

THE COMPUTER AND THE CURRICULUM

Student teachers today are likely to be more comfortable using a computer than are their cooperating teachers, especially if the teachers are at mid-career or beyond. When they were trained, computers for instructional purposes were unavailable in most schools. If you are knowledgeable, your cooperating teacher might ask you to do a large share of teaching that involves the computer.

Computers were named for the primary purpose for which they were intended, to efficiently compute mathematical operations. Now they are used for many other purposes. You have seen your airline agent check on your reservation and print your ticket by use of a computer, and perhaps you yourself have been writing your term papers on a computer. Rapid advances in hardware (machinery, electronic equipment) and software (computer programs) have led to the mass production of affordable and powerful personal computers (PCs). These are now in use by millions of people, including increasing numbers of elementary and secondary students.

Through the Internet, an electronic network that connects computer users around the world, anyone with proper equipment can communicate with people everywhere on the globe, obtain vast amounts of information on virtually any subject, and leave information for other computer users around the world to obtain.

Computer-Related Issues in Cooperating Classrooms

Enormously important fast-paced changes are occurring in computers and computer technology. Although one cannot predict specific developments, we do know that advances in several areas will continue to interest teachers.

- Increasing amounts of information will be readily available to students for classroom and home use. As a result, teachers' roles will shift, with less emphasis placed on disseminating information and more on facilitating student's ability to acquire and process information.
- The computer will become a powerful teaching tool, well-integrated into classroom life. How effectively it is used will depend a great deal on teachers' understanding of computer basics and their ability to use them creatively.
- School administrators will be asking teachers in the near future to complete report cards and other paper work on the computer. That will facilitate the administrators' tasks of record keeping and storage.

- In the world in which your students will live as adults, computers will be an increasingly important tool in their occupational and personal lives. You are helping prepare them for that time. In teaching them to use computers, however, you may find that you have to deal with obstacles that go beyond the machines themselves. Computers can be intimidating. Consider the child who says to himself, "I'm not smart enough to learn about computers," and the girl who thinks, "Learning about computer programs is not feminine." People's attitudes play a major role in facilitating or hindering computer literacy.

Student Teachers Who Believe, "I Can't."   Unfortunately, some student teachers have the attitude: "I'm ill-equipped to help students learn about computers because I'm weak and a poor learner in that area." With that attitude combined with knowledge that computers are here to stay, they are bound to feel that they are falling behind. We advise such people to help themselves in several ways.

Develop and follow a plan to master the computer. On an early visit to your assigned school, ask to borrow computer and software user's guides. Also, check your college computer center for helpful material.

Tell yourself, "I'll master computers, just as I mastered other material during college, a step at a time." Remind yourself that you are not alone. Many student teachers enter schools with little knowledge about computers.

Remember that you teach students by means of deeds as well as words. If they know you are studying computer use, you will serve as a model of an adult who values that learning.

You May Learn Much About Computers While Student Teaching.   In an interview, Larry shared how much he had learned during his first weeks of student teaching:

> Larry: I began with minimal knowledge of computers. As I jokingly told my friends, all I could do was find the on-off switch. My supervising teacher was understanding and gave me a few brief lessons, manuals to read, and free time during the day to "play" with the programs. Within 10 days, a new world opened to me through the computer. In time I grew comfortable enough to be able to share my computer knowledge with my students.

> Interviewer: How have you been using the computer with your students?

> Larry: In many ways. First of all, half the students have e-mail "pen-pals." Second, I've used the computer in a geography lesson. I used a program on CD-Rom to show the value of maps and map reading skills. This program allowed me to display maps of every country, city, and town in North America including my home town, Cranston, Rhode Island. I was even able to show the cross-street intersection closest to my parents' house.

> In a second lesson, I used the program to "visit" several Caribbean islands. We saw pictures of major points of interest and priced the best hotels. Later that week I continued the lesson by forming groups and having the students pick where they would vacation if they had ample funds for a week in the sun. They even phoned the airlines for prices.

Interviewer: What was your assessment of your geography lessons?

Larry: I was pleased. It met my objectives and accomplished much more. Also, because students asked me to show them how to search the Internet, my cooperating teacher suggested that I build on the enthusiasm and teach other lessons on computers.

Interviewer: How did you prepare yourself to teach the next lessons?

Larry: First, over several nights I read as much as I could. Each morning I'd come to school early and try the techniques on the computer that I had read about the night before.

Interviewer: What else have you done with the students?

Larry: Following my supervisor's suggestion, I made myself available during the second half of lunch hour and after school twice a week for those who wanted to learn more about computers.

On the first day, we found a list of "discussion groups" made up of people around the world who have a common interest. Members of the discussion groups write in questions, comments, or their thoughts on the topic of the list. Everyone on the list receives a copy of what this member wrote, and can respond to that person or to the entire list. The "discussions," it is said, are held in cyberspace, that is, in the world-wide computer connections that run to and from each member's personal computers through major hub computers, often located at universities.

The students voted to join a discussion group made up of people interested in our hometown ball team. We sent a message to the given e-mail address, and before we knew it we had mail back from the "list owner," the person who takes charge of coordinating the list. Every day since then we have received several letters from list members, and three times we sent a message into the list.

Interviewer: I suppose while the students were searching through the discussion list titles, you saw several interesting groups that discussed teaching, educational philosophy, and so forth.

Larry: I did, and next year I'll be able to afford my own computer. I'll set it up at home and will join several education-oriented lists.

Interviewer: Is there anything else you want to mention?

Larry: I've taught the students how to connect to external resources where they can find census data, job listings, and computer programs. Most important, I taught them to have a healthy attitude about computers. After all, I'm living proof that with commitment, anybody can learn to use the computer.

Oh, let me also mention that I've learned to use the computer to conduct library research and, believe it or not, to ask for and receive help through the Internet in planning lessons and handling class problems and research.

Teaching The Computer Whiz. If not during your student teaching, sometime during your first years you may have a computer genius in class with great talent (far beyond yours) in working with computers. How will you react to this student?

We know how you will want to react. You will want to think of this youngster in the same way as you think of the other students; that is, as a member of the class who, like everybody else, has unique learning needs and strengths.

Because we recognize that having a remarkably skilled student computer whiz in class can be stressful to student teachers who are teaching their first lessons on the computer, we offer this advice:

As always, prepare thoroughly for every lesson.

Remind yourself that eventually (and many times during your career), you will be asked questions by students for which you do not know the answer. The computer whiz may be the first to do so. Think about how you will respond. You might decide to turn this situation into a healthy learning experience for everybody in the room by saying, "I don't know the answer to that question. There is always more to learn, to know, and to discover. That is why we have libraries, laboratories, schools, and universities. I want to find out the answer to your question, and here is how I will go about doing the research."

Monitor "automatic" thoughts that you have as you prepare for the lesson, particularly those that "wander" through your mind. Research shows that these thoughts, called "self-talk," affect your feelings and your behavior. For example, you might experience self-talk that says, "I'm the teacher. I should know more than the kids." If you don't "catch yourself" when you have this thought, you will feel bad when asked a question you cannot answer, and not know why you feel that way. You feel bad because, outside of your full awareness, you compared yourself to an arbitrary standard (teacher must know the answers to everything students ask), and found yourself lacking. In actuality, however, it is the standard that is lacking and not you, yourself.

By regularly monitoring your self talk, you will catch yourself more often and then ask yourself what is it about a student knowing more that disturbs you. Are you imagining that the student who knows more will embarrass you? If so, ask yourself what circumstances would allow that to happen. Then remind yourself that you will be in control of the class so that you can direct the flow of events in ways that avoid such embarrassment.

Whether you are preparing or teaching computer lessons, answering questions, or engaged in other teacher activity, it is always useful to monitor your self-talk. Through monitoring and active efforts on your part, you can reject unhelpful self-talk and encourage yourself to make more positive self-talk.

Student Attitudes Toward Computers. Regardless of your skill level, your students' attitudes toward computers will vary greatly, presenting you with a teaching challenge. There are many ways to help them develop positive attitudes.

- By your words: You might begin a discussion about computers, and attitudes toward them, by writing on the board a message that was printed on a U.S. commemorative postage stamp some years ago: *Learning Never Ends.* Then you could have them discuss what this means in the realm of computer hardware and software where advances are made almost daily.

- By being a good model: You teach through both verbal and non-verbal communication. Using both modes, you can use your enthusiasm for computers, and the high value you place on them, to shape positive attitudes in your students toward mastering computer skills.

You know that the thoughtful use of technology, including computers, audiovisual aids, and other instructional equipment makes teachers more effective, whether they are working with kindergartners, graduate students, exceptional children, or those in any other classrooms. Developing your skills with instructional equipment is like any other task that you face during student teaching. If you want to maximize your chances of being successful, you need to analyze the situation and determine what steps you can take to lead you toward your goal.

Now (or as early as possible as you begin your student teacher assignment) and when you have your own classroom, conduct an equipment survey. Identify every teaching aid available (from the school, your home, your university, friends' loans) that could help you accomplish your teaching goals. This list should include chalkboards, bulletin boards, tape recorders, special books, phonographs, CD players, radios, slide projectors and filmstrip machines, bookbinders, office machinery (photocopying machines, laminators), VCRs and cameras, overhead and opaque projectors, televisions, and computers (including CD-ROMs, Internet, etc.).

When your teaching aid list is complete, do the following:

1. Place a check mark next to every item you know how to use.
2. Conduct a self-assessment to determine whether you find any of the items or equipment intimidating. Put a double check next to any item so identified.
3. Next to items without checks, put a target date by which you will want to have read the directions for the use of that item, and tried to use it.
4. Next indicate the target date by which you want to identify and work with a resource person who will help you master the items with double checks.

Paste a copy of your master list of resources in your appointment book or somewhere else where it will be easily available to you. Each school day, after you identify the objectives of the lessons you will be teaching, think about the best ways to get your points across. Consult the list of the resource aids that are at your disposal.

OBSERVATION OF THE CURRICULUM AT WORK

Observation, as you have surely heard many times, is more than simply looking or watching. It is purposeful and focused.

There are few skills that will be as useful to you as observation in so many different ways throughout your career. Observation can be used for the purpose of learning your cooperating teacher's implicit objectives in a given lesson, the subject matter he or she teaches, the methods and techniques he or she uses, his or her own personal behavior (both initiatory and reactive), the reaction of the students, and the evidences of the success or failure of a lesson.

And observation can be used to help you gain a fuller understanding of your students and the learning process in which they are engaged. You learn a great deal by observing them in different settings, such as in the homeroom before activities begin, in the corridors between periods, or at certain transition points in a lesson. There are other uses, a great many in fact, that you might want to apply in order to acquire insights about the students—all in the interest of understanding and, therefore, teaching them more effectively.

We have several examples of observations made by Linda Kozusko, a fulltime secretary who was attending evening college prior to her student–teaching assignment. Although the quality of her presentation of her observations is enhanced by her literary talent, one need not be an English major, as she was, or possess her facility in composition, to train oneself to make keen observations.

The first is a report of her observations in the school cafeteria, beginning at 8:30 a.m. We present Linda's journal entry as an example of purposeful observation that leads to a deeper understanding of the students and of the learning environment provided by this school:

5/22: The room was enormous, especially with the added space of external landscape provided by the floor-to-ceiling windows that composed one entire wall of the room.

It was very quiet; students moved to seats and either just sat, or pulled out frazzled looking notebooks and small books to peruse. No one seemed in a hurry, either to talk or to study. The day was beginning for these students who had the pleasant expectation of a soon-to-open kitchen where breakfast would be available.

The students were all White in that room. They were as friendly as half-awake people can be expected to be, and they seemed not unhappy with the fact that it was Wednesday. They were in school and the books in front of them had to be read. This sense of contentment was present throughout my day at Franklin High School.

Lunch hour was more hurried, laughter and calling replaced the silence and shuffling of the morning, but the lack of consternation, the smiling and the eating remained constant. Teachers ate among the students, talking with them, stopping on their way to tables to follow up on plans for some project, basketball news, play problems, etc. The classroom was not a set of walls; teachers and students coexisted on easy terms throughout the day's schedule (even during the fire drill in the afternoon) and in every hall and room that I entered.

It was nice seeing that school could be so open, so cheerful. I went away kind of happy that there are kids lucky enough to be in a free atmosphere in which to learn. I also went away feeling that the school was somewhat unreal—too White, too friendly, too campus-like, too disruptive-free. Perhaps this is an overreaction, but I can't help feeling that Franklin High may be just a little too "West" of cities of hatred, of dirt. All that contentment may not be functional in the future world of these kids. I hope that this feeling is wrong and that the school is not so much an incubator or isolation ward as it appeared in a one-way glance.

This report and those that follow show the quality of observation that penetrates beyond the obvious. It shows what you as student teacher should look for. One notes physical attributes ("the floor-to-ceiling windows") and more so the human attributes ("friendly as half-awake people"). Going deeper, Linda generalized about relationships ("teachers and students coexisted on easy terms throughout the day's schedule"). Even further, she weighed what she had seen and speculated about its meaning ("all that contentment may not be functional"). Now after having made these wide-ranging observations, and after checking their validity, she would be in a better position to develop and teach lessons for these students. The same qualities, interpretive as well as descriptive, are evident in the following report:

5/23: The cold remains of what was at one time a form of ravioli sat on the cabinet. Next to it, a young man sat with a teacher, Ms. P., to whom he had come for advice on a project for another class. She was very informal with him, her language was that of an adult talking off-handedly with a kid, no pompousness, no "let me tell you how." They were talking about music, about themes present in the songs on a new album of folk music, and she was throwing in some names of appropriate research sources for a paper on one theme. They were involved with one another, eager to talk through the idea, eager to understand each other's feelings about the singers, the theme, music in general. It was good talk, profitable, I felt, for both. I didn't have any sense that Ms. P. had given up her free period to help a kid who was not her own student—all of which, in fact, she had done.

On several occasions during the day, teachers in the department of English identified their goal as being a "Renaissance Person." The creative drama teacher is a musician; he has studied dance. Ms. P.'s off-time activity revealed how thoroughly open to new ideas, new avenues of art and knowledge the teacher should be ready to pursue, how thoroughly open to interruption and brain-picking a teacher must be. I felt so very challenged: my 10 years of staunch secretarial avoidance of questions and interruption hung in the air of that room like tight-lipped gauze that will have to be torn down if I'm ever to teach successfully. All my narrow studies in literature cracked under me—what else do I know, am interested in? Ugh! What a challenge.

Linda's observations brought her face-to-face with a problem a good many student teachers eventually confront: Even after all my courses, do I know enough to teach a meaningful lesson? Will I be asked a question I cannot answer? These natural doubts are usually soon overcome. Moving on now to observations more directly related to curriculum, we have Linda's report on the behavior of a teacher in a course on fiction. The course was designed to encourage an interest in and habit of reading:

5/22: It is second period of the day and I hurry along a laughter-filled students' corridor toward Room 303 where I am to witness Franklin High's answer to the "uninterested reader disease." On my way, I note a shortish teacher, zooming along with an enormous cart of books, stopping here and there to talk with students. I eavesdrop long enough to learn that the topic of one of his chats is girls' basketball scores. Upon entering Room 303 I find the energetic cart pusher is the man I've come to observe,

Mr. W. His zeal for basketball news is immediately redirected into the students in his room, "What book you reading? Who needs a new book? Got a great one on . . ." I'm reminded of the hospital aide who turns the inertia of illness into active interest through the appeal of a seemingly innocuous Milky Way [candy bar]. It's salesmanship I'm witnessing, high class, very sophisticated, salesmanship.

The buyers are ordinary-looking teens. Males predominate, and I'm told by Mr. W. that the course's appeal is that a free period in which to read is an opportunity valued by the blue-collar sons who spend post-school hours pumping gas or loading supermarket shelves. T.V. has become a drag for most of these guys, and the day's long hours of school and work make a second-period breather for silence and reading a pleasure to be sought. The students are not college bound. The goal for the course, one with which Mr. W. is enormously in tune, is to make reading a free, happy, and worthwhile experience.

He succeeds. A slight girl passes in two index cards (one is required after completion of each book) on which she has written her concise appraisal of the books she has read. Pinned to the cards is a poem, unexpected creative writing from a student moved to write her thoughts on the theme of one work. A huge, young football-type senior rolls over to our section of the room (desks and tables are in wonderful disorder; Mr. W. and I are sharing two seats dead center of the room near the cart) to display with great displeasure a large paperback. "It's boring." "Why?" "Same stuff all the time." "Why not write a parody on it?" "What's that?" "Mock it." Mr. W. uses every student comment and yawn to teach something—and it's so painless, this teaching.

He and I chatted at length. Kids inspire Mr. W. He loves their energy, their zest. I'm afraid it's catching—9 a.m. is a ridiculous hour for zeal. A dedicated teacher, Mr. W. is working on his doctorate in education. His most important task as teacher: Make them write. He expects very little of each student: Read and respect the right of others to read; write a critique of each book, and whenever possible, write some original stuff on the works—a different ending to a novel. A better dialogue within a scene. The course is an elective; within this elective is complete choice of material. His cart is not the world—anything the student chooses to read is acceptable. He sees the writing of the students improving every week. He also brings films to class. *Of Mice and Men* is on the cart, and he will bring the film in soon for the students to see.

All the while that he and I chat, students read, write, approach the cart, bring a problem or thought to Mr. W. for straightening and also at times for simple sharing. Silence and sun prevail. My initial fear that Mr. W.'s zeal might overpower, making him the sole motivator for activity, dissipates as I realize that he's only an arm to the cart. The students are using him. I'm excited to see this—a human teaching machine—push a button and your next novel is suggested, your misunderstanding of a word is sent to *Roget's* for qualification, your disgust with pornography's repetition is shared. I wonder how this happens. I hated the class I had in high school whose purpose was similar. Perhaps the difference was that silence was mandatory; or perhaps it was the want of choice of material. More likely, though, is the fact that we never "did" anything with our reading. You read *Jane Eyre* and that was that. The requirement to place the reading experience on the page surely is an important character in this course's success. I'm excited by this realization. I share it with Mr. W.—he agrees.

My first observation is worth coming here for—I've learned something. Translate an inactive, receiving experience into a communication, out of solitude into sharing, active writing from inactive reading, unconscious reaction to conscious, specified feelings. Read and write.

In the next report Linda relates what she witnessed and experienced in a course on creative dramatics. Her observations are worth taking note of, no matter what grade or subject you teach:

5/22: The course is open to juniors and seniors and is an elective. In its description (which is available to students when registering), the following focus is identified:

"In addition to a study of the structure and types of drama, the course provides acting experience, critical judgment, and a deeper enjoyment of drama through the total development of the student in a group activity that demands constant adjustment to other people."

The period which I spent with the class certainly demonstrated the characteristics identified in this description. In the first place, I was not permitted to observe—students and teacher hoisted me on stage and initiated my creative drama career right there in Franklin High School!! Did I fail, succeed? No. No one either fails or succeeds. We had fun, and that fact is something of a phenomenon in the face of stifling heat in the room and the lateness of the hour (it was nearly time for the close of school).

The teacher was there, but not there. Mr. S. focused our thoughts on a task and then withdrew, after a demonstration, to sit—all attention—on top of a couch to observe the class in the act of carrying through the task. For example, after assigning us into groups of three or four, he quickly identified to each group an activity to perform as a group (one of ours was to move a set of living room furniture into an awaiting moving van), and then become a member of the audience—the remaining class members to attempt to guess what we were doing.

During our act, he called out changes, "it's a piano"—to which we had to adapt and respond appropriately. This teacher's physical and mental agility, performed with ease and a cheerful manner, had no aggressiveness in it and surely moved this tired old student to find a new relationship with space, students, and objects. Bravo! My group changed three times during the period; in each new set of students, I found the students warm, happy, and as excited about the class as I. Discipline problems? No way. The kids supported each other through teasing, suggested improvements of activity, and applause. One devastating way that creativity came into play was through the presence of a student in a wheelchair. When this group was playing with the ball, the ball (imaginary) had a way of getting caught in the spokes of the chair, and he and the others had the devil's time freeing their "toy" for action.

Does the course "provide . . . the total development of the student in a group activity that demands constant adjustment to other people?"—you bet it does. And through such a freeing, happy method!

The final observation took place in an atypical class, in that it was composed of only five students. We have included it, however, because of the characterization of the teacher, so different from Mr. W. and Mr. S. and yet excellent in achieving the curriculum goals. There is, as you know, no one correct way to be an effective teacher, or to teach content effectively:

> 5/23: By the time I had reached Ms. P.'s room, the heat and newness of the day had won. The class (in home economics) was tiny, five students, I believe, in all. The room was a combination lab and study; this day the students were at desks (large tables shared by more than one student) attempting to plan a menu. They also seemed a bit dried out and tired. Lethargy smacked from each of us in the brightly lit, pink and white cooking lab. All of us, of course, except Ms. P. She was as bright and comfortable-looking as the room. I saw my grandmother in her, so quiet was her way as she moved next to the students to encourage each one's search for recipes. No mean task apparently, since the young girls are terribly diet conscious and planning meals to be eaten is a struggle against calories.

> Of those teachers whom I had observed during the day, Ms. P. seemed the most at ease with her students. The "grandmother" image I think was not peculiar to me. She was genuine in her interest in why I was there, and I felt that sincerity. I'm sure others, for example, these hot, tired kids, also feel that sincerity. She worked the entire period, always aware of what each was doing (not doing), turning her attention to each of them to help. Watching her competent, friendly manner turn a dull period into a nice experience was, in a way, the highlight of my day.

Linda's experiences in the classrooms, lunchroom, and halls of Franklin High yielded profound insights about students and teachers. She especially valued the opportunities to observe three different teachers using very different styles of teaching to achieve the curriculum objectives of their respective courses.

It is true that some courses are more amenable to certain methods than to others (e.g., the controlled experiment in the physical sciences and role playing in the humanities, rather than vice versa). However, the differences among these three teachers were not due just to the subjects they were teaching but also to their general styles of relating to their students, their temperament as people, and the particular teaching strategies they employed—individual reading and critique writing by the first teacher, participatory dramatics (role play) by the second, and encouragement and support combined with an individualized research approach by the third.

As we said before, there is no one correct or effective way to implement the curriculum. As you become skillful in observing, you will be able to analyze the styles of different teachers. The best time to start doing that is when you observe your own cooperating teacher.

Answer questions like these in your journal: How does this teacher introduce a new unit? In what ways does he or she make the topic relate to the lives of the students? What else is done to make it interesting? What activities does the teacher initiate? How does he or she get the students involved in activity? What resources are used? Diagnostic tests? Follow-up instructional methods?

If you were a student in this class, would you have found a particular lesson interesting? Would you have learned? If you were the teacher, what would you have done differently? What assessment would you make of the effectiveness of the unit? After you have answered these questions, list issues you want to discuss with your cooperating teacher in order to get fullest benefit from your observations of his or her teaching.

WHEN YOU BEGIN TO TEACH

When you first go to your student-teaching class, locate the points in the course of study/curriculum guide(s) and the textbooks where the class is working. Scan the prior sections to get sufficient background, then read beyond.

Because your teacher might give you the option of teaching the unit or units of your preference, review the guide and the appropriate textbooks with that in mind. When you begin to prepare for the lessons you will teach, study the relevant sections of the course of study and textbooks. Reflect on the objectives so that beyond question you understand what is meant by each of them. Thereafter, while referring to the textbook, you can begin to set your plans for each one:

- How you will introduce it in such a way as to capture the interest of the students,
- What activities you will initiate to make the concepts meaningful, given the conceptual level of the students,
- What exercises you will employ to give them experience in using the skills connected with the objectives,
- At what point you will begin your assessment of their mastery of the work and your diagnosis of weak areas that need strengthening,
- What you will do about those weak areas, and
- What your part will be, along with your cooperating teacher and college supervisor, in evaluating your unit of work.

As you think through these issues, remind yourself of five basic principles, discussed next, which you probably studied in your previous courses.

Be Aware of Different Objectives, Affective as Well as Cognitive

At any given time a variety of objectives are implicit in the activities of the teacher and the students, not just the explicit one connected with a unit. While we set our goal, let us say, to raise the reading level of the students in certain specified directions (i.e., educational objectives in the *cognitive* domain), we are simultaneously involving the values and feelings of the students (i.e, educational objectives in the *affective* domain). (See Bloom, 1956; Krathwohl, Bloom, & Masia, 1964.)

To illustrate, as young students are learning through newly acquired phonetic skills to read more difficult words in a story about a family, they are having reactions about the family portrayed in the story. It may give them positive feelings because it is like their family or negative ones because theirs (perhaps a single parent family) seems inferior by comparison. Or, as a result of rapid-paced learning, the able student's self-confidence and satisfaction with school is reinforced while that of a slower child is diminished.

Negative affective outcomes are not inevitable. The sensitive teacher learns to anticipate them and to take measures to prevent or overcome them. For instance, in the case of the slower learner, diagnostic tests enable the teacher to aid that student by pinpointing areas that require further study. In the case of the child from the single-parent family, the teacher can make certain that such a family is not ignored in discussion of the story but is treated in the positive and constructive way it deserves.

Be Aware That Thinking Ability Changes With Age

The thinking ability of humans of different ages, at least prior to adulthood, varies widely. Jean Piaget (Piaget & Inhelder, 1969) identified four major stages of cognitive development, each of which can be broken down into substages. Although the stage theory is still open to question—whether the stages follow strictly in the order given, whether one can be in more than a single stage at a time, whether the movement from one to another can be accelerated, and whether these stages are found in all cultures—there is considerable agreement that individuals' minds tend to follow a general pattern of development.

We briefly describe the stages here to refresh your memory or to acquaint you, if you are not familiar with them. We do it particularly to highlight the qualitative differences in thinking at the different stages.

The sensory-motor stage extends from birth to about age 2, when the child starts to acquire language.

The preoperational stage, which runs from about age 2 to 7, includes preschool and the first years in school. During this time the child can focus on only one dimension at a time.

The classic example used to illustrate this point involves showing a child a round ball of clay. Then right in front of the child, the clay is rolled into a long "sausage." The child thinks the sausage is bigger and therefore is made of more clay. He or she cannot coordinate the two dimensions—thickness and length. Because it is longer it is bigger to the child; he or she does not consider the fact that the sausage is also thinner.

The meaning for the teacher is that this child should not be expected to be able to work out problems that require simultaneous manipulation of two or more dimensions. When one encounters a child in this age group who is unable to understand (and most are unable) that a mother, at one and the same time, is also someone's daughter (two different dimensions!!), this child is not backward or dull, but simply at the preoperational stage of development.

The stage of concrete operations extends from about age 7 to 11. Although students in this age group are noticeably different from their younger counterparts in their mental abilities, they still have limitations in their thinking when compared with adults. They are rigid and dependent on a concrete form of thinking, thinking that is tied to what they know through their senses or through manipulation. This means that they are unable yet to work out problems that require them to consider systematically a variety of possible solutions to problems. They are not yet capable of thinking in terms of hypotheses.

In teaching children through the age of 11 or 12, working with concrete materials is of exceedingly great value. Symbols, whether words or numbers, get their meaning from the world of concrete objects. One way to reduce the number of vacant stares during lessons and of failing test scores is to give concrete examples. For instance, help the children learn the concept of subtraction by letting them see the result of "taking away" some pebbles or marbles or pennies.

The stage of formal operations typically begins at about age 12. It is at this stage (which not all people achieve) that individuals acquire the ability to conduct the most advanced form of thinking. They can engage in hypothetical thinking; that is, they can consider a variety of solutions to problems, including those that are not available to their senses.

Having general knowledge about cognitive development, and being sensitive to the cognitive level of your students, will help you plan your lessons. Still another advantage in knowing how we humans develop our learning and thinking abilities is that it can help us, as teachers, accelerate the growth of those abilities in our students. Although there has been considerable controversy about the possibility of "accelerating growth," the best judgment now is that the kind of teaching that encourages active thinking (and not just memorizing and drill) does facilitate that development (Schwebel, Maher, & Fagley, 1990).

Be Aware of the Importance of Questions in Teaching and Learning

There are distinctly different kinds of questions that a teacher can use, and the teacher should choose the type in accordance with the educational objectives to be met. Questions can be thought of as being at different levels in a hierarchy. Students must be able to answer questions at a lower level before they are able to deal with those at the next higher level. The levels are derived from the taxonomy of educational objectives (Bloom, 1956).

At the *knowledge (or information) level,* we seek to know if the student has possession of essential facts, for example, whether the student knows what a state legislature is. Next we are interested in the student's *comprehension level*; that is, whether the student can explain in a meaningful way, in his or her own words, what a state legislature is. At the *application level* the student is asked to explain the services that a legislature performs and the products that emanate from it.

The *analysis level* may be assessed by questions that break down material into its component parts and show relationships among the parts, such as questions that get at committee structure, party control, and lobbies. The *synthesis level*—the ability to put it all together—is tapped by asking for a description of the situation in the state if there were no legislature. Finally, at the *evaluation level* students use their own standards and values to critically assess state legislatures, maybe considering such standards as efficiency or speed and such values as fairness to all constituents and the influence of lobbies. Here, the questions are clearly not to get "right" answers but the students' own thinking and reasoning.

As teachers, our aim is to raise the level of questions so that students will have practice in thinking and reasoning at the highest levels of their capability, or we might say, in the deepest ways. For your purposes during student teaching, it is enough for you to be aware of the differences and to use questions that challenge the students.

In virtually all situations you will surely want to tap the knowledge and comprehension levels of the students (Do they know and do they understand?). The application level is important not only because it is further evidence that they understand what they are studying, but also because students are likely to be more interested in class when they see usefulness in what they are learning. In the long run, the aim of our education system is to help students develop to the point at which they can field any level of question. In other words, through questions we take the material apart, to understand each part. Then we put it together and have a deeper meaning of it.

To get the deeper meaning of material (e.g., the U.S. Constitution, the process of photosynthesis, or Keats' "Ode to a Grecian Urn"), it is essential to analyze and, subsequently, to synthesize it. In the illustrations just given, it is obvious that these critical approaches are necessary; however, even in dealing with more prosaic problems like why clothing fashions change so often, such intellectual strategies are invaluable. Teachers can give their students the opportunity to gain deeper understanding through the use of questioning (oral and written) at the analysis and synthesis levels.

As you prepare a unit for your student teaching, remember that the evaluative process is essential to life. Students need practice in establishing a set of values (e.g., democracy) and determining how closely the set of ideas (e.g., the Constitution) come to those values. Therefore, if possible, you will want to develop questions at the evaluation level. In brief, you will find that students enjoy the challenge of trying to answer probing questions, provided they are compatible with the approximate stage of their conceptual development.

One other interesting way to think of questioning is to break it down into the following two types: convergent and divergent. Convergent questions have answers on which most people generally agree, that is, they "converge." These questions can be as simple as, "What is the capital of the United States?" or as complex as, "What is the derivation of Einstein's theory of relativity?"

Divergent questions, as you would expect, have answers on which people differ or "diverge." Here is one: "Supposing we were choosing a new capital for our nation, what would you choose and why?" As you can see, such questions—and you can introduce comparable ones even at the kindergarten level—force us to think. Many students enjoy the discussions that follow such questions.

Some teachers encourage questioning to go both ways, teacher to students and students to teacher. When students get good experience in having all types of questions directed at them, they themselves may learn to ask varied types of questions. Teachers open the door to curiosity and reflection even more when they encourage students to share those questions with the class. Although there is great value in asking thought-provoking questions, studies show that teachers tend to ask students too many questions (e.g., 40–150 in a 40-minute class) and students rarely ask any (about 2 in a 40-minute class; Sarason, 1990).

Tim shows that it does not have to be that way:

> 4/19: I made a discovery today! Well, it wasn't a real discovery because Pat (university supervisor) has talked about it a lot lately. For me, it was a great step. First, instead of asking a whole slew of little questions, like "How does the blood stream handle oxygen?" I asked, "Supposing you didn't have a heart, what would be missing?" At first they laughed and said, "Your life." Then they started thinking and debating. I had them hooked. With this one question we got into more than half the reading assignment. And before class was over one boy asked what smoking did to the heart. I felt good.

Tim's experience gave him confidence. Children and teenagers do not want to be bored any more than college students. They respond to a teacher who respects and encourages their thinking ability, and who is not afraid to have them ask questions.

Be Aware That Students Are More Interested in Material and Efficient in Problem-Solving if They Understand What They Are Doing

Test out this principle on yourself. Think of how helpful some of your college instructors were when they explained how to go about doing particular assignments. They were even more helpful if they taught you to step back and look at your own ways of thinking about particular problems—in other words, how to be your own critic, such as in critiquing your own papers.

This process of examining our own thinking and the products of our thinking, as you probably learned, is called *metacognition*. It involves such activities as awareness (e.g., awareness that I don't understand what I'm reading and I want to find out why), monitoring (e.g., setting a goal in what I'm studying, checking along the way that I'm working toward my goal by asking myself questions), regulating (e.g., when monitoring shows that I do not understand what I'm reading, I reread, or search for meaning in some sections, or draw on past knowledge to make sense of the text; Haller, Child, & Walberg, 1988).

Similarly, when we prepare a lesson plan, we know what we are about and why we include particular content, student exercises, and homework. However, our students may not have the slightest idea how this particular material fits into understanding the lesson. So, they go through the boring process of rote learning, or of trying to memorize material they do not see as connected to the lesson. One of the easiest jobs in teaching is often neglected, that is, explaining what we are doing and how it is connected to broader learning objectives. The following study shows the value of doing that.

The study involved children and teachers in 22 fifth grades in 13 elementary schools (Book, Duffy, Roehler, Meloth, & Vavrus, 1985). The study focused on teaching reading. Using a good system of controls, about half of the teachers (the treatment group) were trained in the explanation model. The model, which they used in developing and teaching reading lessons, included (a) an introduction of the skill to be taught (what, how, and why), (b) an explanation of the skill which includes the thinking process modeled aloud by the teacher, (c) teacher interaction with students during which students practice the skill and explain their thinking, and the teacher corrects mistakes and tries to get students to think through the use of the skill on their own, (d) practice in using the skill (e.g., on worksheets), and (e) application of the skill in connected text (Book et al., 1985, pp. 30–31).

Besides learning about these components, the treatment group teachers were shown how to analyze the tasks involved in the skills they wish to teach, and how to put that thinking into the introduction of their lessons. They also were taught to check their success in teaching the lesson by having the students answer the questions: "What was learned?," "Why is it important?," and "How do I do the task?" (Book et al., 1985, p. 32).

The results were very positive. They showed that if teachers are trained to use explicit explanations of what they are teaching, students are more aware of what was taught, how they would use the skill that was taught, and why it is important. Students in the control groups showed no such progress. The further "happy news" from this study is that the results were positive for students in the low reading groups.

As teachers, the more we try to put ourselves "in the shoes" of our students and try to understand what they are experiencing in our classes, the more likely we are to follow the example of the treatment group of teachers. We help them understand what the lessons are all about so that they can monitor and regulate their part in it.

Be Aware That What You Teach and How You Teach Are Linked to Students' Behavior

Curriculum and the maintenance of discipline in the classroom are finely intertwined. The fact that an appropriate, well-executed curriculum can have a great impact on students' in-class behavior is discussed in chapter 9. Here we want only to say that the planning of a lesson can be thought of as a combined logical and psychological process. Your thoughts may be, "The students in my class, no matter how homogeneous they seem, are bound to be different in their past experiences, in current state of knowledge, in interests, and inclination to attend to class activities. True, I am not a psychologist and my job is not to analyze them, but I will be better able to teach if, as I prepare my lesson plan, I think of particular students. That way my plan will be directed to the faster as well as the slower students, the quieter as well as the more vocal, the girls as well as the boys, the educationally disadvantaged as well as the advantaged, the children of racial and

ethnic minority groups as well as of the majority. My questions, my illustrations—yes, even my physical positions in the classroom when I teach—will be
attuned to these differences and will enable me to capture most of the children's
attention for most of the time. With this in mind, the process of planning a unit of
instruction is straightforward: my objective; the road to get there; the time available;
the dallying we will do en route; additional enriching material or activities to
introduce if the lesson is completed sooner than I anticipated; additional time that
can be added if, as a result of class interest or need, I decide that the lesson should
be extended; and finally, the method that I will use to check out, both en route and
at the end, how well I did in teaching to my destination."

We, the authors, are also engaged in a logical and psychological process as we
present these ideas to you, a member of a diverse group of student–teacher readers.
We are considering the questions and concerns that might arise in your mind, like:
How in the world am I going to keep all these ideas in my head while I am teaching?
Answer: Do not try to. The suggestions we have given are intended for your use
primarily while you are planning lessons. By incorporating these ideas into your
plans, you will immediately increase the likelihood of a better lesson. In any event,
you should not try to juggle dozens of ideas in your head in class. We pass them on
to you in the same spirit as a coach advises the players to remember the basics,
before they begin a game. For us teachers, "the basics" mean thorough knowledge
of the substance of our unit, a solid plan, and a clear link between our plan and the
composition of our class.

And another question we are sensitive to: How can I be prepared for the
unexpected? Answer: No matter how well you plan, the unexpected could arise in
any given lesson. And, on the basis of the laws of probability, over a long period
of time it is likely to arise. However, you can lower the probability by anticipating
"the unexpected."

Consider the different questions students might ask. Answer them now, in
advance. If a new one arises and you do not know or are not sure of how to answer
it, be straightforward. Explain that you will find the solution by the next day. On
the next day you would explain just what steps you took to obtain the answer, for
you will be sharing with them the invaluable knowledge about the process of
investigating and problem solving. Only then would you give them the solution.
An alternative approach to that difficult question would be to make the search for
a solution a joint one. Whichever you choose, it need not in any way detract from
your status as teacher.

We have a final point in connection with this section on teaching and the
curriculum. Many student and beginning teachers have a tendency to prepare
lengthy lesson plans. That can be a valuable exercise. However, it is no
substitute for a concise plan with which you are so familiar that you hardly need
consult it during class. Effective teachers proceed through their lessons
smoothly, keeping an open eye on student attentiveness and response, and
shifting emphasis as needed.

In the remainder of this chapter we examine the use of the arts and technology
in the curriculum and then discuss the role of individualization and assessment.

USING THE ARTS

The arts belong in education and not only in their own right, as courses in the arts. Why? They have special appeal to people of all ages. Besides, they can be helpful in virtually any subject you might teach. Notice the excitement when you tell your students that you are going to present a movie. They will show similar reactions about putting on a play, doing dances, playing music, singing, or painting.

The arts usually involve attributes that attract young people:

1. Human feelings, as in the play "Romeo and Juliet," the movie musical *West Side Story*, the painting "Mona Lisa," the song "Yellow Submarine," and the novel *Tom Sawyer*;
2. Activity, such as painting, sculpting, dancing, singing, performing a role, composing;
3. Applications, or seeing theoretical topics made more concrete, as when kindergarteners and first graders learn arithmetic by "going shopping" in the make-believe store; fourth and fifth graders learn about similarities and differences in ethnic cultures by experiencing their dances; and high school students learn history through mock conversations between Jefferson and Hamilton, through listening to and comparing the music of northerners and southerners in 1860, and by examining the fiction, drama, and poetry produced during the depression of the 1930s.

In the book called *Academic Preparation for College*, the College Board (1983) included the arts along with English, mathematics, science, social studies, and foreign languages as basic areas of study. Then, in *Academic Preparation in the Arts*, the College Board (1985) showed how the arts help develop the following basic academic competencies: reading, writing, speaking and listening, mathematics, reasoning and studying, and also such basic skills as observing and computer competency.

Role playing has special merit because it requires no equipment and particularly because it catches the attention of children, teenagers, and adults. It can be used in virtually any subject, on any topic. For example, you could set up an imaginary conversation between Pasteur and those who ridiculed his germ theory in 19th-century France, or a confrontation between two imaginary friends to show how to resolve an argument.

RESOURCES

It is no exaggeration to say that teachers' resources are unlimited. They have access to the universe. However, we restrict our discussion here, looking to materials close at hand to you as a teacher and to your students. For almost every subject in the elementary and secondary school, there are teaching aids or other useful stimuli accessible without cost. Through the school window or in a walk around the block, teacher and students can find pictures to paint, objects to sculpt, and themes for poems, stories, essays, plays or narratives.

For early childhood and primary school arithmetic, there are the pebbles to provide the concreteness so important to learning number concepts and arithmetical skills. For science, there are birds to see and hear, trees to study, a collection of random items picked up from the sidewalk to classify or to analyze in a laboratory, and clouds and the wind to observe and study. For sociology and economics, there often is diversity of population in the area (if not in the classroom) and indications of historical change in the buildings in the surrounding blocks. Granted that in some suburban and rural areas, some of these resources are absent. To compensate there are probably others not available in a city school district.

Our emphasis on what is in front of our eyes, if we will but see it, is not intended to discourage the use of materials especially designed for the classroom. We favor their use. We believe, however, that you will be a more effective teacher, and a more confident and independent professional, if you can rely on your own imagination in choosing additional materials to incorporate in your teaching.

Essentially, we are asserting that resource usage should not be limited to what is listed in an attractive catalog (and then ordered) or by what is available in the school's storeroom. Usage should be based, first and last, on what kinds of concrete and illustrative or stimulating or provocative resources or experiences you think will help your students learn.

Once you set goals and identify your resource needs, by all means use the storeroom and the colorful catalog and any commercial materials available to you, but choose them to serve your purposes, by which we mean the needs of the children. The following are some resources you could draw upon in your school system:

1. Central library with accompanying borrowing privileges and the services of a reference librarian.

2. Central resource center (with accompanying borrowing privileges for specialized curriculum materials).

3. Specialized personnel including the services of a drug and alcoholism prevention specialist, psychologist, speech therapist, and teacher specialists for physically, emotionally and learning special needs students.

4. Specialized equipment for teaching science, mathematics, art, geography, music, physical education, etc.

5. Central office curriculum departments (i.e., math, science, reading) to aid with advice and in acquiring needed teaching equipment and materials including computers and software packages and audiovisual aids (e.g, opaque, film strip, slide, overhead and movie projectors, videotape cameras and machines and a library of materials to be used with them).

6. Buses for approved school trips.

Of special long-term benefit to you during your student teaching will be developing the habit of reading one or two professional periodicals, in which you are likely to find timely and practical suggestions about curriculum and the use of various resources.

USING TECHNOLOGY IN YOUR TEACHING

Welcomed or not, the era of "high tech" has arrived in America's classrooms. Look in any urban, suburban, or rural school and you will find computers and various other pieces of high-tech equipment. When you started kindergarten, teachers could get by if they had working knowledge of only a few machines—maybe a phonograph, a tape recorder, a ditto machine, a film strip projector, and a movie projector. You will have much more machinery to master, but then you will have many more tools at your disposal.

Most of us need help in using the many resources of the high tech era. Fortunately, help is available through various sources. Among them is the Office of Educational Research and Improvement (OERI) of the U.S. Department of Education. For example, we know that electronic access to information will open new opportunities for teaching and learning. For teachers to obtain the latest information, they can call the toll free telephone number of OERI's National Library of Education, which provides public access to information on education through electronic networks.

What thoughts come to your mind when you hear the words "Technology in the classroom"? Amy, a high school foreign language student teacher, made these entries in her journal:

9/7: On my way to my cooperating school today, my first day, every fear I ever had crossed my mind. Would I get lost on the freeway or on the roads through town to the school? No, I practiced the route on Sunday. Would I get nervous when I walked into the classroom and saw Mrs. G., my cooperating teacher? No, I met her last month. She's nice and she'll help me. Would I put a Spanish verb in a French sentence during my first chance talking to the French 2 class? No, I'll be fine.

But a worry I never considered turned out to be the biggest one. The classroom computers. After all, I spent time and money in college to steer clear of computers. I mean I wrote my papers out in long hand and hired people to type them, etc.

Who expected you'd need to know how to operate computers to teach foreign languages? Well, Mrs. G. loves computers and worse yet, there's a bunch of computer whizzes in our classes. I'll have to admit to them that I don't even know how to turn those machines on. What will they think of me?

9/10: I stayed after school today. Just me, THE MACHINE, and a computer-tutoring program. Getting started was difficult. I'm 10 thumbs when there's mechanical and electronic stuff involved. But, with Mrs. G.'s help, but mostly by myself, I came to terms with this high tech thing. I'm a teacher and I'm proud to be one. I have to be a model, a good model for the kids. I tell them they can learn irregular verbs if they try hard enough, I'll have to do the same with the machine. Besides, I have to face REALITY. We are living in a high tech world, and my time and effort will go further if I use computers in my teaching. Reality can be painful.

11/11: I developed learning materials for my kids on the computer. IBM beware— here I come.

12/18: I went with my dad to pick up my own Christmas present. You'll never guess what Santa is going to be bringing me. Yup. My own computer.

By the end of her student teaching experience, Amy had become a "high-tech nut," a convert from the world of the computer-phobic. Under Mrs. G.'s guidance she learned how a teacher can harness the power of a machine and use it to enhance her students' learning. Ironically, during a farewell dinner that Mrs. G. hosted for Amy, Mrs. G. said to her:

"Beware, Amy, computers and other high-tech teaching equipment are seductive. Don't be lured by their gloss. They are tools, just plain tools. And you are the craftsperson. You will find that for many of your teaching tasks the good, old-fashion, 'low-tech tools' like the chalkboard and the pen and paper, do a better job than 100 computers would.

"One other point, please don't fall victim to thinking that new material delivered on a VCR tape or CD can provide a magical cure for a student's learning problem. You, the teacher, help the child solve the problem, perhaps by deciding to use a machine. In other words, don't let the availability of a new machine or a new tape tempt you to wonder, how can I shoehorn this stuff into my lesson, when the questions you want to ask are, what material should my students be taught and what is the most effective way to deliver it."

HOW MUCH INDIVIDUALIZATION?

You are probably wondering why such a question should be asked. After all, individualizing instruction is a keystone in American education. However, another keystone complicates matters—ensuring that students spend a high percentage of time in academic learning activities, rather than in conversational asides or staring out the window. Unfortunately, these two important instructional principles collide. With about 25 children or teenagers in a room, it is difficult to work with one individual or a group of four and at the same time monitor the rest of the students (Copeland, 1987).

Some educators have characterized teachers as "decision makers." According to this model, teachers carry out routines watchful for cues about how instruction is proceeding. If a cue tells you it is not going as planned, you decide whether the situation is beyond your tolerance. If so, you decide what move to make (Shavelson & Stern, 1981).

For example, you asked a question about Tom Sawyer's behavior with his aunt. After several student comments, boys in the back start their own conversations, laughing loudly. That behavior is beyond tolerance, so you interrupt the general discussion and tell the disruptive boys that they may talk in their turn and their comments would be welcome.

Every day, every class period presents challenges like these, and you must react almost instantaneously. For example, in the lower grades, one child is crying, another must go to the bathroom, and a third is pushing a fourth. In an eighth grade class, one is cursing another, a third has her head on the desk, a fourth is launching a spitball at a fifth. As Doyle (1986) said, teachers face very complicated sets of cues of different kinds and many of them come at the same time.

When you individualize, you focus your attention in one direction, and not in other directions. As much as you can help those students you are working with, you lose touch with the others. The fact that you cannot monitor the behavior of the others explains why individualized instruction is so difficult, unless a class has few students or the teacher has well-trained aides.

COOPERATIVE LEARNING

Chances are you will be doing your student teaching in a traditionally oriented class. If that is so, we are not proposing that you experiment with another approach, or that you try to persuade the cooperating teacher to choose another way. Nevertheless, knowing the *principles* of cooperative education can be helpful even in a traditional class.

Cooperative learning is a fundamentally different approach to learning. Instead of a teacher verbally imparting information to the class for long periods of time, students ask questions and work together to answer the questions and solve problems by drawing on many resources. In one sense, they are young researchers and scholars investigating problems while working together for a common purpose.

The arguments in favor of cooperative learning are that it stimulates and involves students, encourages them to learn, and inspires a spirit of cooperation and community. It fosters academic achievement and positive interactions among students, two primary purposes of education.

One of the best known and most extensively researched cooperative learning methods is that created by Robert Slavin (1994; Slavin & Shaw, 1992) and known as the Student Teams Achievement Divisions (STAD). It has been used from Grade 2 upward into the college years, and adapted for science, social studies, English, math and numerous other subjects.

The idea is a simple one. As Slavin (1994) described it, you, the teacher, present a lesson. Your students will be attentive because their individual scores and *their team scores* depend on listening carefully. Then all the four-member learning teams already organized in your class—each made up of a student mix in sex, ethnicity, and performance level—get to work. Their job is to see to it that all team members master the lesson. They help each other in the interest of the team, and they do this by studying worksheets, discussing problems, comparing answers, and correcting misconceptions and mistakes. Then they take individual tests, during which students are strictly on their own. Individuals win points if they equal or exceed their own past averages. They are not compared with other students.

You have probably played on some team or participated in a musical, drama, or dance group. If so, you know how important it is to do your best for the team, and also how much the team is helpful and supportive because your doing well is so important to every one else. Who wants to see a teammate strike out all the time, or play a note during a rest period, or take a misstep during a dance performance? Slavin said: "The team provides the peer support for academic performance that is important for effects on learning, but it also provides the mutual concern and respect that are important for effects on such outcomes as intergroup relations, self-esteem, and acceptance of mainstreamed students" (1994, pp. 6–7).

STAD is one of many forms of cooperative instruction. Some, like STAD, and the Learning Together approach developed by David Johnson and Roger Johnson (1989), are curriculum-free and meant to be applicable to many subjects and grade levels. Others, like Team Assisted Individualization in Mathematics and Cooperative Integrated Reading and Composition (CIRC), were developed to apply the principles of cooperative learning to domain-specific (i.e., different subject) learning (Slavin, 1994). The results of the use of these methods show that achievement could be increased in all students in heterogeneous classes. In fact, as we indicated earlier in discussing students with disabilities, CIRC proved very effective for academically handicapped students who were mainstreamed. They achieved at significantly higher levels than their nonmainstreamed counterparts who did not have the advantage of this cooperative learning approach (Stevens & Slavin, 1995).

The basic elements of cooperative learning have been defined by Johnson and Johnson (1991). These are:

1. Positive Interdependence. Students realize that they depend on each other to complete the group's assigned task.
2. Face-to-Face Promotive Interaction. Students help, encourage, and teach each other, and they share resources.
3. Individual Accountability. The teacher assesses the performance of each student and shares the results with the student and the group.
4. Collaborative Skills. Teachers instruct students in the essential skills such as trust building, communication, leadership, decision making, and conflict management.
5. Group Processing. Groups spend some time discussing their progress in achieving goals. Teachers also give feedback on the groups' performance, to the groups and the whole class.

What can student teachers learn from the cooperative learning movement? They can learn that student involvement makes learning more exciting; that student team-work, or cooperation in any form, brings students closer together; and, especially important, that team work leads to higher achievement.

ASSESSMENT

Let us assume that you have completed your first unit of teaching, and you come now to a salient feature of student teaching or, to be more accurate, of teaching in general—assessment of progress during the course of the unit. This is not the easiest or most comfortable process teachers face.

For the most part, we are bound in retrospect to find some flaws in our lesson plan, our mode of instruction, our interaction with the students, and so forth. For this reason, we tend to put off criticism and self-criticism until tomorrow. Yet when things are fresh, it is of extraordinary value to review the entire process of planning and conducting the class through the unit, recognizing what parts of it went well, what activities, experiments, drills, performances, and the like were and were not effective and with what kinds of students.

You want to consider the interactions with and between students and your handling of the unexpected. Then come your findings from your interim diagnosis of progress, your change in plans resulting from that, and finally your end-of-unit evaluation of student progress. How well did your students fare?

Ideally, you should do this type of critique prior to receiving evaluation from your cooperating teacher or college supervisor, so that you have practice at doing this independently. Even if circumstances do not permit that, you will find it to your professional advantage to engage in self-criticism.

Another critical step is to ask yourself about the future: What will you do differently, and what the same, the next time? To what extent will you change the proportion of whole-class to small-group teaching? Will there be more or less student participation? Will you again use the same reading materials, exercises, workbooks, illustrations, poetry, role playing, experiments, instruments, outside consultants? Will you plan to use the same kinds of questions? Were the questions that were representative of more than one level of questioning appropriate to the cognitive levels of your students?

If you record the critiques, yours and others, in your journal or elsewhere, you will be able to evaluate your professional growth as you progress through student teaching and your first year as a regular teacher. You will also have a record of the resources, aids, techniques, methods, questions, and personal styles of your own that worked for you and that you might want to use in the future.

There is still another useful way to evaluate your professional development, now and in the future. Using a guide introduced by Tanner and Tanner (1995) you can determine at what level you are presenting the curriculum to the students in your class(es). You may find that your mode of bringing it to life is reflected by one of the following descriptions (taken from Tanner and Tanner, 1995, pp. 630–631):

1. Level I, Imitative-Maintenance: Teachers at this level slavishly follow the curriculum guide, using only ready made materials, like workbooks and textbooks, without evaluation of their appropriateness or effectiveness. They show no imagination and seem to feel no freedom to introduce activities or create materials that would strengthen the curriculum.

2. Level II, Mediative: Teachers at this level "are aware of the need to integrate the curriculum and deal with emergent conditions," like students' questions about things that concern and interest them. They are aware of the need for a curriculum that integrates and does not fragment knowledge, and they evaluate the materials they use, not using them blindly. However, for the most part, they remain "at the level of refining existing practice" (p. 630).

3. Level III, Creative-Generative: At this level teachers act collaboratively with other teachers to create and generate an improved version of the curriculum and ongoing assessments and revisions of it. At the same time, they are engaged in their own classroom in evaluating and improving their own teaching. They identify their teaching problems and use problem solving methods to overcome them. They experiment with different teaching modes and share their experiences with other teachers.

As the Tanners pointed out, one does not have to pass through the first two levels to reach the third. Level III does not require years of experience. Teachers can attain that level early in their careers, depending in all probability on the professional role models they have had and on their personal and professional values. The more teachers that function at Level III, the greater the likelihood that the curriculum will be a living experience, responsive to changes in knowledge and society.

TEACHING THE WHOLE CLASS THE FIRST TIME

The bulk of this book is meant to help you prepare to teach. Because the first time one teaches the whole class is very much on the minds of student teachers, we are setting out some general guidelines for your consideration.

- Begin to plan the lesson a week before the assigned date.
- Be clear about the objectives of the lesson as spelled out in the curriculum guide or given by your cooperating teacher.
- Master the content of the lesson.
- Prepare print and/or audio and/or audio–visual material.
- Check that material is in the sequence you will use it, and that all equipment is in good working order.
- Consider ways of engaging students ("getting them hooked"), maybe by having them involved in activity.
- Prepare "filler" material and activity to be used in the event that the lesson is completed earlier than expected.
- In your mind, picture the class before you, with the cooperating teacher sitting in the back row.
- Direct your attention to each part of the classroom, looking at each student at some point during the lesson.
- Picture the lesson going along well.
- Prepare for the possibility that a student who is occasionally disruptive disturbs the class.
- Picture yourself talking to the class and leading a discussion.
- Encourage many students to participate; don't be controlled by the wild hand-wavers.
- Prepare an interesting closure to the lesson.
- Picture your satisfaction at a well-taught lesson.

- Start rehearsing the lesson, from beginning to end, a few days before you teach.
- Having prepared so well, go to class that day feeling competent and confident.
- Afterward, evaluate the extent to which the objectives were achieved.
- Evaluate the quality of your teaching, looking at strengths and areas that need improvement.
- Welcome and be open to the cooperating teacher's critique, and use it to improve your teaching.

NEXT YEAR

Lo and behold, your student–teaching experience will be behind you and the new school year will be upon you much more quickly than you anticipated. The summer is a time for preparation. Like a squirrel collecting food for the snow-covered winter months—that is the way you should occupy some of your available hours.

Get acquainted with the neighborhoods in the school district and the student composition that is likely to be represented in your class or classes. With that information and the curriculum guide and textbooks, you will be in a good position to prepare for your work next year.

Build a collection of resources for the units, at least those scheduled for the first part of the school year. Review all the possible sources of materials; for example, your former cooperating teacher and college supervisor, other teachers in the school where you student taught, your student–teacher peers, friends, and acquaintances who teach.

This is a time, too, to collect a set of materials that interest and excite students of the age group you will be teaching. These could take the form of quiz shows, cartoons, anecdotes, games, experiments, and how-to activities (repairing cars or baking). High school students will welcome illustrations and materials that are representative of teen-age culture.

We conclude the chapter by noting that, beginning next year, you will possess the power to plan your own role as a teacher. You will not be dependent on others to tell you how to teach and manage the class or what materials to use. Advice is different. You will find it useful to receive and you may even seek it out. But you will be free to choose from it what you consider helpful and to incorporate that, as you see fit.

CRITICAL ISSUES

- In what ways can the curriculum guide be helpful to you?
- Through your teaching, how will you help achieve the objectives?
- What are a dozen or so resources (human and other) that you can draw upon to help achieve those objectives?
- What have you learned so far about the class's curriculum that will help you in your student teaching? In your teaching career?

9

Classroom Management
and Discipline

TOPICS

- The different meanings of "discipline"
- Seven principles of successful management
    1. Functioning as the adult leader
    2. Managing time—Managing ourselves
    3. Developing your own theory of management and discipline
    4. Problem solving
    5. Planning
    6. Assessing progress
    7. Preventing problems
- Critical issues

Discipline! The word captures every teacher's attention. Everyone knows that keeping order is top priority in today's schools.

We take it for granted that discipline is very much on the minds of student teachers. What about "old hands" in teaching? Problems of discipline can be so difficult that they are on the minds of experienced teachers as well, as you see in the following words, reported by Clapp (1989):

> Discipline and classroom management were my biggest fears as I entered teaching. After 19 years of teaching (though I am considered by others to have very good classroom management—my principal always recommends that visitors observe my classroom), each summer before school starts I still have nightmares featuring my class in an out-of-control situation. (p. 32)

This teacher was one of 1,388 respondents to a questionnaire study of 10 educational issues by the education magazine *Instructor* in 1989. Discipline was ranked first of the 10 issues by 69% of the teachers who responded. It ranked ahead of such issues as teacher salaries, teacher preparation, and teacher empowerment.

Note another important finding. Almost 80% of the responding teachers were in Grades K–6. They ranked discipline at the top even though they were not teaching teenagers.

Two positive findings are worth considering. First, the teachers did not blame themselves or the children. They saw discipline problems as the result of larger social issues. For example, 38% attributed class disruption and the other assorted discipline concerns to changes in the American family. One teacher said, "It's hard to punish a child for misbehaving . . . the breakdown of families causes poor self-esteem and results in discipline problems" (p. 32). Another teacher said, "Hunger, abuse—physical and sexual, neglect, etc—are issues in the suburban public school I teach in" (p. 32). The behavioral problems, these teachers say, are evident in the children, but they were caused by social problems over which teachers have no control.

The other positive finding is that teachers try very hard to be more effective in coping with problems of classroom management. Most of them seek help from other teachers. This survey indicated that they also sought help from school administrators, college professors, supervisors or mentor teachers, and support staff. Student teachers got help from their cooperating teachers and their college supervisors. When they were asked which was most valuable of all the resources they used in the area of discipline, almost one third cited Lee Canter's Assertive Discipline program. That program is discussed later in this chapter. First, we turn to the meaning of discipline.

THE DIFFERENT MEANINGS OF "DISCIPLINE"

The word *discipline* has several meanings. A common one, often applied to education, is the punishing of students for the sake of maintaining order. Less common, but of greater importance, discipline also denotes a positive approach to education, the kind of order that enables a class to achieve its objectives and, therefore, enables students to become competent and more confident. Used in that way, discipline means good classroom management.

In general, we speak of a disciplined way of life as one that follows a consistent pattern. The reason people organize life that way is to help them fulfill themselves, to accomplish what they set out to do in their professional and personal lives. The same may be said about a disciplined way of teaching; that is, it allows you to accomplish your teaching objectives. In a disciplined class you have plans for meeting learning goals and built-in policies to bring your students along with you. The perfect marriage of teacher and students comes when class members experience you as a person interested in strengthening them. If they recognize you as such, they will accept as appropriate almost any form of classroom management. They will accept as required whatever measures you consider necessary to maintain a disciplined class.

Order

A disciplined class can be more or less structured, more or less permissive. Your crucial objective is to be consistent and to keep the kind of order needed for your method of instruction. Order is as necessary in a classroom as it is in a family, and in both settings youngsters prefer orderly situations and orderly lives, even if circumstances lead some of them to behave as if they did not. They like it, want it, and need it, as much in a permissive or open classroom as in a traditional one.

Without some order, there can be no teaching and very little learning. Consequently, the student teacher's priority is to maintain his or her kind of order. Psychotherapists believe that resistance to therapy must be dealt with before anything else: If the client persists in fending off the therapist, the two engage in a struggle of wills and nothing worthwhile is accomplished. The same struggle can take place in the classroom, and it is the teacher's role to circumvent it and to build order in the classroom environment. Here is an example taken from Steve's journal, reporting on the problems of his cooperating teacher, whom he regards as a good teacher:

> 1/15: The children do not listen to the teacher when she is presenting a lesson. They are doing a thousand other things. Some children were playing tic-tac-toe, others were playing cards, some were coloring, while still others were doing homework. She is a good teacher, but none of the children were listening, so they don't even realize that she is a good teacher. While Mrs. S. was giving the language arts lesson, only about 7 or 8 students out of 30 were listening.
>
> What have I learned from this observation? I have learned that I must have the children's complete attention in order to really teach. It doesn't matter if I'm a good teacher if nobody is listening. One of the things that I am going to demand from my students is that their desks be cleared off—as many distractions as possible must be eliminated. That is not to say that I will have their complete attention, but at least it will be a start.

By no stretch of the imagination could Mrs. S. be classified as a good teacher on the basis of this observation. Perhaps what Steve was reacting to was a well-organized presentation of valuable language-arts material. That is of no value whatsoever if, as he himself said, "nobody is listening." Facing this kind of situation, teachers must give up their present method of discipline and experiment with others until they find one suitable to the students in their classes.

With other students who, from experiences at home and in school became accustomed to listening, this teacher might have been well received. And it is possible that her current mode of discipline and presentation would be usable at a later time in the year. However, if she is to be able to use this method successfully, these students must first be taught through experience that when the teacher presents a lesson to the whole class, it is a time to listen, watch, raise a hand for permission to participate, and so on. As Steve came to see, when Mrs. S. "finally exploded and scolded all over the place," it silenced the students temporarily, but "hollering" and scolding usually are not effective as long-run solutions.

When a teacher relies on loud scolding to curb disorder, inevitably disruptions will recur and escalate, and the class will not come under control until the teacher again scolds loudly. It is better by far to introduce the ultimate means of control when your voice and demeanor, although firm, have not reached your upper decibel limit. For your sake and that of your students, condition the students to expect that, after a second warning, for example, there are no more, and that the disturbing students are given immediate punishment.

Bear in mind that you have double responsibility to function this way. First, you owe it to the class to lead (you are the leader) in such a way that they will get a disciplined education, one that perfects and strengthens them. They deserve your help in gaining mastery over the skills and content in the curriculum. Second, the most effective way for children and adolescents to learn good citizenship is by living it, not by reading or hearing lectures about it.

Obviously, maintaining order in the classroom is essential to effective teaching. In the *Instructor* survey, 69% of the respondents saw discipline as the most crucial of 10 issues in teaching. About 50% said the biggest discipline problem was disruptive students, those who interrupt, are rude, leave their seats, are sarcastic, and who seek attention (Clapp, 1989, p. 32). Similar concerns about disciplining disruptive students were expressed by teachers studied by Corcoran, Walker, and White (1988), and reported in their book, *Working in Urban Schools*.

How can you, as a student teacher, maintain order and manage disruptive students? We propose seven important principles for successful discipline and classroom management. Note that these principles depend on action you take both inside and outside the classroom.

SEVEN PRINCIPLES OF SUCCESSFUL MANAGEMENT

Functioning As the Adult Leader

The first important step you can take toward being an effective class manager and disciplinarian is to accept the fact that you are on the other side of the desk. You must function as an adult leader.

As teachers, we are responsible for a major portion of the education of our students. As the only adult in the classroom, we are responsible for establishing the kind of environment that is conducive to learning. We are not complete adults in class if still in a corner of our brain there lurks the consciousness of being one of "them," or the desire to want to be one of "them." If you find such thoughts in your mind, explain to yourself why you must rid yourself of these outdated notions.

Amy, in telling of her problem with Randy, explains her "shock" that the child followed her instructions. Amy had not yet thought of herself as an "adult leader," a necessary step for being effective with discipline:

> 4/25: I have noticed that I have to be firm with some of the children and I definitely have to follow through with what I say. Although I always knew this was true, seeing the children react to my behavior provided evidence of my beliefs.

Amy reported in her journal that when she had a few of the children outside, Randy was disobedient, threw stones, and refused to go inside as she had directed. She warned him that if he didn't go inside as ordered, he would not be allowed to go out later in the day. Randy disobeyed Amy, and so she told him he had lost his afternoon recess privileges. That afternoon, Amy was on the playground with the other children and Randy wandered out of the building. Amy reminded Randy of his punishment and Randy returned to the classroom quietly and without protest. Amy entered this in her journal, "He followed my instructions. I was really shocked!"

Remember that all the Randys in your classroom view you differently from the way you view yourself. Although Amy may think of herself as somebody just a few years out of adolescence and as a learner in the classroom, to Randy she is an adult, a teacher. At various points during your student–teaching experience, assess how you think the students perceive you. Then check your perceptions by noting how students actually do react to you.

Functioning as the adult leader means asserting oneself as a teacher, being strong and effective. Often, this can be done in thoughtful and quiet ways. As we said earlier, problems can be avoided by such means as minimizing boredom for students, keeping the class lively, listening attentively to students as they express concerns, and rewarding good behavior, usually by praise. Using CONTROL-C to disentangle the causes of some ongoing discipline problems is also a "quiet" approach.

Managing Time—Managing Ourselves

People are paying more attention to time management, largely because so many of us feel overwhelmed by the demands of our jobs and our personal lives. During your student teaching stint, you too will probably feel you don't have enough time to meet your responsibilities at your assigned school and at your college/university and also to manage to enjoy your personal life.

In coping with such a heavy schedule, it helps to realize that the idea of time management, though catchy, is misdirected. It sounds as if we had to manage *time*, when in fact, we have to manage *ourselves*. Managing our time really calls for self-management.

Our aim is for you to be more aware of how you use time and better able to manage the time available to you, so that you will be in a position to develop schedules that allow you to invest time in ways consistent with your goals.

Tess was faced with a self-management problem. She liked her student teaching assignment in science at a high school that had recently won the women's tennis state championship. Besides student teaching, she volunteered to be an assistant tennis coach. She thought that the coaching would make her more competitive in the job market.

Two weeks into the term she found that she was overloaded. Besides spending after-school hours with the tennis team, she used her evening hours to prepare for her science classes. Her friends called Tess "the shadow," because she was here for a moment and then gone.

Fortunately for Tess, a speaker at a faculty meeting discussed the topic of efficiency. Three related points the speaker made hit home for Tess and led her to take action:

- Identify, in writing, all the tasks you need to accomplish for the time period under consideration. That could be tomorrow's classes, or the full week ahead, or the remainder of the semester. (The speaker humorously suggested that once they are on paper, the brain cells in our heads that were working to remember those tasks are freed for other uses.)
- Rank each item according to its importance. Use three categories: "must do," tasks that have direct impact on you and your teaching; "important but not essential," tasks that may offer indirect or lesser benefits; and "useful but not essential," tasks that have potentially desirable benefits, but fewer than the previous categories.

  When you make a laundry list, items do not need to be ranked because every garment needs to be washed and it doesn't matter in what order. However, with your "to do" list, the items always have different levels of importance.
- Within rankings, prioritize your tasks, giving yourself a push to do the least pleasing tasks first. Doing them first reduces your tension about having to face those unpleasant tasks later.

Most of us resist applying this advice. We're accustomed to tackling the simplest, quickest tasks first and then, with pleasure, crossing "to do" items off the list. For maximum payoff, we should be crossing out the most essential tasks first.

Applying these guidelines to your student teaching experience, here are some questions to consider:

- In the coming week, what are the most important challenges? Rank order them.
- Considering each one, what must I do to prepare for it, and how much time is needed for that preparation?
- Taking into account the time slotted for class(es), including supervision, at my college/university, and the time for essential personal appointments or tasks (including recreation), how many hours are available for preparation?
- If those hours are not sufficient, what can I cut out this week to give me more time?
- Having entered the necessary hours for each important challenge in my weekly calendar, am I psychologically ready to tackle the least pleasing tasks first?

These guidelines apply also to the in-class experience: setting priorities for each unit and estimating time for each one. However, as a teacher interacting with students, although a schedule (class plan) is essential, it needs to be flexible. Experienced teachers will not suddenly terminate discussion of a topic that has their students thoroughly engaged. They will wait for a good closure point, say "We can return to this topic at another time," and go on to the next scheduled unit.

Time management is a subject you could discuss with your cooperating teacher. How does he or she manage time? The same topic is an appropriate one to raise at your weekly meeting with your supervisor and other student teachers.

Next year, as a full-time teacher, hopefully with a rich and satisfying personal life, managing your time effectively will be essential. There is no better time than during student teaching to develop the habit of monitoring and regulating your use of your time.

Developing Your Own Theory of Management and Discipline

This is the third principle of successful management and discipline. In your education courses you probably became familiar with several different approaches that would allow you to manage a class effectively. It is good to get acquainted with a variety of approaches while you are still developing your own theory of management and discipline.

Two educators (Tompkins & Tompkins-McGill, 1993) proposed a variety of methods to manage students' behavior. They tell about one boy, Eddie, whose humorous antics started a painful cycle: He joked, other students laughed, the teacher (a series of them!) got furious, he joked more, then more teacher anger, etc. Finally, one teacher reacted by enjoying Eddie's humor and joined in the laughter with Eddie and his classmates. It didn't take Eddie long to learn that it was all right to be funny once in a while and at appropriate times.

The practice used by this teacher is called "tension decontamination through humor." Among many other methods proposed by the two educators are the following: "planned ignoring" (useful if you believe that by not giving attention to it the unacceptable behavior will stop); "signaling unacceptability of behavior" (a useful first step by getting eye contact with the student and giving a stern look); "time-out" (useful when the student is out of control or disturbing a group, and when there are physical dangers to the self or others).

Time-out is most productive when teachers can calm down students and speak to them for the purpose of helping them "learn about themselves, see how they contributed to their difficulty, and how they might have done something differently" (Tompkins & Tompkins-McGill, 1993, p. 58).

In developing your own approach, it will be helpful to consider four different discipline models proposed by Balch and Balch (1987):

Behavior Modification.   Encourage favorable behavior mainly by giving positive reinforcement (like praise) to that kind of behavior. The teacher controls the class by conditioning the students through the use of commands and rewards and, when necessary, punishments. The teacher does not look for the causes of the behavior. This general approach is described by Madsen and Madsen (1974).

Assertive Discipline.   Assertively communicate disapproval of the behavior. Explain what behavior is acceptable and the consequences of misbehavior. Canter and Canter (1976), leading proponents of this method, give special weight to spelling out the class rules. The consequences of breaking a rule, which are given equal prominence to the rules themselves, should be acceptable, even comfortable, for the teacher and respectful of student rights. The third part of the Canter model is composed of the motivational strategies the teacher will employ as positive reinforcement for appropriate behavior.

Reality Therapy. With responsible behavior as a prime goal, use class discussions to help students become responsible for their behavior and also find problems that are barriers to their responsible conduct. According to Glasser (1969), the teacher is an enforcer who confronts disruptive students with their misbehavior. He or she shows how the student is irresponsible in violating the rights and disregarding the needs of others. Punishment is not considered to be effective and, for the most part, is limited to removing privileges or isolating the student, but even then not as punishment, rather as an opportunity for the student to consider how others have been injured by the misbehavior.

Low Profile Classroom Control. Focus attention on content, avoiding the distraction of calling out to an inattentive student. Instead use students' names to keep them involved in lessons. The point is not to make mountains out of mole hills, but to distinguish between classroom problems that are teacher-made versus those that are student-made. As Gordon (1974) said, the teacher does not seek to control, enforce, or punish, but rather is an enabler, one who listens, supports, and facilitates. The teacher does not exert his or her power over the child or teenager.

One author, himself a teacher, finds pluses and minuses in the methods just described. Seeman (1988) claimed that the books we have cited are useful resources but have weaknesses that he sought to correct by adding the following points. We think these are important:

- When does a situation or a problem deserve to be called a "disciplinary problem?" Because teachers differ among themselves, and even within themselves from time to time, this question is not easy to answer. Sometimes teachers transform a non-problem (like a joke a student cracks) into a disciplinary problem. Sometimes, Seeman said, a mishandled difference about a grade or about a student's motivation unnecessarily turns into a discipline problem. In his definition of a discipline problem, note especially what he puts in parentheses:

  a behavior (not merely the expression of a feeling) that disrupts (or is potentially disruptive to) the learning of the rest of the class (not just the learning of the disrupter), or disrupts the role responsibilities of the teacher (not just the personal feelings of the teacher). (Seeman, 1988, p. 42)

- In order to prevent discipline problems, we ask, what are their sources and what events precipitate them? In a study he conducted, Seeman found, for example, that some problems originate outside the school, some inside the school (but not in the classroom), and some inside the classroom. Those in the last group could be due to classroom climate, student interactions with each other or teacher–student interactions. There is a big payoff to teachers who, early in their careers, learn to classify the origins of problems and introduce ways to prevent them.

- Why does one technique work for one teacher yet not for another who is in virtually the same situation? Ms. Doe calls for order and the class is silent; Ms. Roe does the same and you would think no one had heard her. Seeman's study revealed the important concept of congruence: How students react to directions, assignments, and reprimands depends on how believable they evaluate the teacher to be. If they regard the teacher as credible, they respect and obey him or her. If they see the teacher as a "phony," they do not. "Sincere" and "genuine" are apt terms to describe the way students perceive teachers who command respect.
- Why limit oneself to a reward and punishment system? That could result in ignoring the sources of the problems as well as the feelings of the students. In Seeman's view, classroom discipline should be based on a good relationship between student and teacher as well as on the teacher's power, and not just on the latter.
- Why limit oneself solely to nurturing and empathic relationships or to the use only of reason? Such limited approaches neglect the value of reward and punishment (hopefully exercised by a respected and respecting teacher). They also tend to be applied to the needs of the individual at a cost to the class as a whole.

An eclectic approach, one that draws on whatever strategies you find useful, seems most desirable. An effective approach must fit with your personal values and personality—you should feel comfortable with it. Besides suiting you, the approach should give your students the feeling that you mean what you say, whether you are talking in caring and supportive or demanding and critical ways.

Think about your own theory of management and discipline. Try to define it. Compare it with those previously given. Be open to change as a result of knowing other theories and approaches and as a result of your ongoing experience.

Problem Solving

A third important principle for successful classroom management and discipline is to routinely use a logical problem-solving process, such as the CONTROL-C method described in chapter 2. Even for the experienced teacher, effective management practices and procedures for handling disruptive situations come with careful thought. After reviewing and analyzing the day's events, a teacher is in a better position to handle whatever difficulties might develop tomorrow. The following two sections illustrate how much better student teachers usually fare when they use effective problem-solving approaches to student teaching, in contrast to an approach marked by "impulsive problem solving and inconsistent behavior."

Effective Problem Solving.   The entries here, written by Janet, show how she used her journal to actively analyze what was happening in her class and to plan for the days ahead. Although her wrestling with problems was sometimes frantic, Janet battled like a young "pro" determined to master her craft:

3/11: Some days are good and some days are just awful. Today was awful. When it comes to a group activity I lose so many of them and I don't think it's me; it seems to be because a couple of children disturb the rest, and when I'm trying to take care of them the others start talking and I can't blame them. When I say some children disturb the others, it's a physical disturbance that has to be dealt with. I guess I have to try and keep things going at a faster pace to try and eliminate any "time" for them to hit. Even though the rest of the day went fine, that small part discourages me.

Janet engaged in an important problem-solving process: She diagnosed the onset of problems as resulting from a couple of children who, by drawing her attention, lead her to neglect the rest of the class. Further, she proposed a way to go about dealing with the problem, that is, by keeping the students involved in learning activity. A few days later Janet was pleased to see some signs of progress:

3/15: Things went better today, I had my head together and things went a lot more smoothly. I still have trouble keeping everyone's attention, but I think it's because I don't use Andrea's techniques; as a result they keep testing me. I don't mind, because I know they don't mean it personally and it's not taken as such. We started a new subject today, the circus. I'm excited and am looking forward to it.

Janet had one of those good days, the kind that make you feel you are gaining mastery. As she put it, "I had my head together." That sounds like a Wimbledon tennis champion talking about the need to concentrate on the game and to have confidence. Having our heads together while teaching means not getting rattled (essential to good problem solving) and remembering that we are teacher/adult in the presence of student/child or student/adolescent. A month later Janet wrote:

4/15: The day was crazy. Talking about it in seminar made it sound worse than it was. It's just an incredible feeling of frustration—having so much I want to accomplish and to have the children do, that I get hung up in "management" problems. It's more than that. It's that I'm getting hung up in my idealism and how things seem to be. I know I'm making progress, but it's so slow; maybe I just need more positive rewards by immediately seeing what I'm trying to accomplish. I don't know. It's hard to be your own teacher when you're constantly in someone else's shadow.

Something else bothers me: my supervisor's idealism—I guess it holds for the seminar leaders too. All of you come up with good suggestions, but most of the time it's impossible to implement them to the fullest. I come up with so many ideas and suggestions, activities, etc., but I'm only one person with a class full of active children so I can't always be with all of them, meeting every need all of the time.

By the next day, especially after the seminar, Janet was again allowing herself to feel overwhelmed by the work. She sensed that she was imaginative like her supervisor and seminar leaders, but she compared herself with them, a beginner with three pros, and she found herself wanting. She did not compare herself with them as they were or could have been as beginners, which might have been more valid and reassuring. At least, however, she was near recognizing that it was not they who were setting inordinate demands on her but she herself, and that those demands were creating some of her problems in managing the class:

> 4/17: The day went a lot better. Things went smoother and the children were somewhat more responsive. I'm trying to get them to pick out "worthwhile" activities by making suggestions. It just takes time, I guess. I also seem to plan more than I can accomplish. My mistake, I guess, was trying to pack in too much, like two days' work in one.

In the April 15 journal entry, Janet wrote that her frustration was due to her wanting to accomplish so much that she got caught up in management problems. But management is part of a disciplined class and the hallmark of a master teacher. Good management calls for setting realizable goals and organizing the day in such a way as to be sure the goals are realized.

Janet, in her April 17 journal entry, showed that she recognized that she defeated herself by trying to accomplish too much. She had now gotten a clearer idea of her role as teacher. If she learned nothing more in her student teaching, she learned one of the vital lessons. The classroom is no place for superwomen (or supermen). Real people do much better. They do not demand of themselves or of their students more than humans can accomplish.

Janet developed as a teacher because, as we noted, she regarded her difficulties as problems and she went about working them out in a thoughtful, problem-solving way. On a regular nightly basis she used the CONTROL-C method to define problems, to understand her relationship to them, and to test out different hypotheses. She dealt with her own problems, the kind she called "hang-ups," with courage. Her reward was success as a student teacher.

Impulsive Problem Solving and Inconsistent Behavior. Joyce, by comparison, was not functioning as a good problem solver. Instead of using her journal for systematic problem solving, she simply recorded the day's events.

Because Joyce did not think ahead, when she had difficulties with her class, she had to make important decisions on the spot. As a result, she acted impulsively: she acted first and thought about it only after she had recognized that her actions had not worked. Obviously, such an approach tends to be ineffective, as her journal entries suggest:

> 1/19: I sat Frankie next to Michael to see what effect Michael would have on Frankie. Michael is a bully and he started punching out Frankie. He defies any type of authority. I kept him after school to talk to him, and he sat there and looked at me as if I were crazy. This has really upset me. I've got to reach him somehow, but nothing seems to work.

> 1/20: Susan was a real problem. But some of the fault lies with me. I changed seating arrangements. [I put] Susan . . . next to Eva. Major mistake. She talked, talked, talked.

Within 2 days, Joyce had rearranged the seating of two difficult students and in each instance, almost immediately after doing so, realized her mistake. Joyce became very disturbed over her inability to cope with the situation, and no wonder. When she kept Michael, the "bully," after school and he "looked at me as if I were crazy," she became very upset. This fifth grader raised doubts in a young adult about whether her own behavior was "crazy."

Joyce is distressed by the behavior of her class and wants to understand the students better. However, instead of analyzing the situation, defining the problem, and developing a plan of action, Joyce behaved like the proverbial chicken with its head cut off. Her difficulties were not due to a lack of talent, as she began to think they were, or to a lack of concern for the children. Rather, her problems were largely due to what she was not doing outside of the classroom: logical problem solving.

George, like Joyce, also had a difficult student teaching assignment. His was by choice, however. He wanted to teach science in an urban high school. In his words, "The first week was a disaster."

Mr. L. had him work with a slow group of six students. To George's dismay, after listening to his lesson for a few minutes, they just ignored him. They conversed among themselves, or fiddled with a pencil, or just sat there turned off. By the end of the week George was in crisis: "Do I ask for a transfer to a nice well-behaved suburban school? Do I change my career? Or do I follow my fantasy and go away to a sunny beach?"

Although he fumbled during the first week, trying this and trying that, a talk with his supervisor on Friday afternoon helped him get back on track. She warned him about impulsive and inconsistent behavior, and encouraged him to spend the weekend thinking about the situation, critically and logically. He concluded that he had been too idealistic in expecting the teenagers "to bloom," in the hands of a caring, permissive teacher. And, he decided he could only maintain his sanity and his commitment to urban schools by experimenting with different structured approaches and by setting realistic expectations. He remembered what he had studied in class earlier this year and told himself that he needed to follow the "three mores": More structure in his lessons, more patience, and more realistic expectations. After 3 weeks of reminding himself of the "three mores," and after several conversations with his supervisor, this is what he said:

> 2/12: I feel that some of the kids see me as being on their side—that I'm really interested in them. They're listening a little more and some of them know I mean it when I say, "Let's get down to business." Most important, they're beginning to see that what we are studying does have something to do with their lives. I've got to keep reminding myself to be patient.

George's experience reflects the principle that a teacher's style of management has to be adapted to the circumstances in the school, and doing that calls for effective problem solving. Children and teenagers who see little if any connection between school and their lives are different in their classroom attitudes and behavior from those who see a close connection.

You as a student teacher, like your classmates, supervisor, and cooperating teacher, were motivated by a career goal to succeed in school. We have to put ourselves in the shoes of George's students to understand their experiences so that we can choose the most appropriate teaching approaches for them.

In recent years, new instructional approaches have been developed for students who have missed out on learning essential skills. These approaches were designed to give students the important knowledge and skills that other children acquire in the preschool years and in the elementary and secondary school years (Feuerstein, 1980; Feuerstein & Hoffman, 1990; Haywood & Brooks, 1990). Depending on your assignment, you may want to use these resources in planning your lessons.

Planning

The fifth factor in effective classroom management and discipline includes thoroughly planning a day, preparing for contingencies, and being mindful of the needs and interests of the students.

Sheryl's journals show that she is developing into a "pro." Already she plans a balanced program (which is itself a problem-preventer) and in class reveals a combination of firm control and intellectual stimulation. In her journal she described her preparation for giving her students opportunities to work out problems and receive appropriate rewards:

> 1/27: I had the kids by myself the whole day. I had a chart on liquid measurement, and I asked them very simple questions and we went from cups into quarts, and pints into gallons. Then they did board work and had an exercise in math, which for the most part they did very well. I would check their answers with the book and check the wrong ones and let them try again. When they got it wrong the second time, I would write in the answer and tell them to figure out why it was right. When they could explain it to me, I gave them a "100" and many were eager to explain why the answers were right. After math, we had health. Our health discussion was excellent. It was very mature. Everyone participated, and many interesting questions were raised. There are a lot of things to learn about bacteria, and we discussed the topic until 10:20.

Besides content, Sheryl also had thought through and decided that she would demand the kind of behavior that was necessary for the children to profit from the activities. Also, as the journal shows, her careful planning provided for flexibility:

> 1/27 [continued]: Then we had film strips, and the children were so talkative and inattentive that I turned off the machine. I told them they didn't want to watch it, so they could watch a blank wall if they didn't want to pay attention. They got quiet after 5 minutes, and I told them they could make it up. . . . They had been working pretty hard, so in the afternoon all I had planned for them was music and then working on their masks. There was no scheduled recess and I let them vote if they wanted an early recess or get to work on their masks. They voted to work on their masks.
>
> Since they got restless, I took them down to the rest room about 25 minutes early. We took 20 minutes because they cannot behave in the halls and we started all over every

time I heard them talk. I plan on doing this every time, no matter how long it takes. I keep insisting that they can talk quietly in class but not in the halls. Of all the kids, mine are by far the worst. In a way, I think they appreciated it because they knew I was tired too and wanted perfection. For the rest of the afternoon, I let them work on their masks and they played music. At 3:00 they began clean-up and had it done in about 8 minutes, which was quite an improvement. I read *Charlotte's Web* and the kids really listened. That was a good day for me.

Sheryl's day was successful because she planned well. All the children participated in the health discussion and mask making. She reacted immediately to disruptions and required orderliness both in the class and in the hallway. One senses in reading her report that the children felt she was setting requirements as much in their interest as in her own. Most children respond favorably to rational authority, that is, to a leader whose demands make sense to them.

Sheryl's next reports were positive: Most of her plans worked perfectly; the class was becoming a cohesive group enjoying the exercises, activities, and discussion. However, Sheryl's journal entries also contained the inevitable ups and downs. A few days later Sheryl wrote she was "just miserable," because she had yet to find a way to cope with the few disruptive youngsters. She did not have a solution, but would not surrender to the situation. Sheryl was a determined and proactive problem solver who learned from her successes and mistakes and those of her cooperating teacher. She learned to plan activities that appealed to the class as a whole. She developed the self-control necessary to avoid becoming angry and being drawn into bitter battles with students who had serious problems. Being mindful of her goals and what it took to reach them, Sheryl never yielded to the easy temptation simply to blame the children. She liked them, struggled to understand them, and sought to plan the school days in ways to make the lessons more interesting for them. Here is her final report:

3/18: This will be the last time I write. My class is getting better and they are controlling themselves more. They still are fighting and arguing, but it's more verbal, more reasonable and less physical. Frances and Mindy will have trouble for the rest of their lives. Things frustrate them so easily. Steve is a pain but a smart one and is a leader and salesman.

The kids still get away with more with me than with Mrs. R., but when it counts, they are with me. It will be sad leaving.

The choice of content and method (what and how we teach) is important in preventing and correcting discipline problems. In planning specific class material, one can do much to enhance the likelihood of order simply by taking into account the needs and likes of the learners. Earlier in this chapter when Steve referred to his cooperating teacher as a good teacher, you probably wondered why we included his statement in a chapter on discipline. Most of the students talked, played, and did anything but follow her lesson. You probably thought there must be something wrong with a lesson plan that fails to hold even some of the attention of 75% of the class. You were right.

Discipline and curriculum are inseparable in some very important respects, and noticeably so when most of the class is unruly. Any time such disruptiveness occurs the effective teacher asks, "What is wrong with my objectives or my plans to carry them out?"

In many cases the students have no personal interest in the content being presented. This problem sometimes can be dealt with by combining unappealing subject matter with appealing illustrations. For instance, fractions can be taught using pies, football fields, coins; geography by following the road trips of major-league baseball teams; literature, like Shakespeare's "Romeo and Juliet," by referring to popular music favored by teenagers. The effects of the choice of content cannot be underestimated, as illustrated by the case presented here.

One of the authors taught a ninth-grade English class for boys, in which the behavior of the teenagers was almost uncontrollable. This was the lowest-rated section in a homogeneously grouped system, and some of the students, having been kept back during their schooling, were big mid-teenagers. With the consent of the chairperson of the department, the teacher brought in books that he thought would interest the students—sports, adventure, mystery, mechanics, and science fiction. He encouraged the students to bring in anything they preferred.

Many class periods were devoted to silent reading of a book or magazine of the student's choice. This was followed by discussion about the reading or about a personal experience that the reading brought to mind. Sometimes small groups of three or four would be organized for reading aloud and small-group discussion. When this approach was well established and all students were participating (and most of them eagerly), they were then asked to write a few sentences, then a few paragraphs, and later still a few pages about their readings.

Was this a mysterious, almost miraculous transformation in behavior? Not at all. The students had viewed school as a place where they were forced to go to study topics that did not interest them.

It is easier to compel children to attend school than to compel them to study. Real learning is an active process, and no one can force anybody into it. These ninth-grade English students resisted not because they were mean or recalcitrant, but because education had no meaning to them and made no sense. The teacher said, "Look, you have to be in school. I'm not requiring it, but the state does. As long as you are here you can either waste your time, get into trouble, or make the best possible use of it. I'll help you find whatever you'd like to read—whatever you'll enjoy reading—whatever you'd want to read to learn something for your use—not my use but yours."

When they heard that, not once but repeatedly in words and actions, they came to believe it, and they made better use of the time. Instead of chalk throwing, foot tapping, and outright fist fighting, they were reading, discussing, and writing about repairing cars, baseball, whether the heavyweight champ was as great a fighter as he was supposed to be, how to finish a basement with recycled materials, and some easy ways to estimate the charge for various handyman repair jobs.

As the weeks passed, they took to discussing characters in some stories, and even the way these characters dealt with problems not unlike some of theirs. These students learned, perhaps for the first time in their lives, that reading could be enjoyable and useful, and that school could be in their interest and for their benefit.

Contrast that English teacher's perspective with Nicole's, who wrote: "I feel that . . . [the students in her cooperating class] *are working for me* when we are working on something." We added italics to emphasize a point of view that is not helpful. Indeed, learners do behave in positive ways to please their parents and other adults whose approval they wish. However, education cannot be sustained on that kind of external motivation alone. Much more important is their sense that school is an agent for their own developing strength as individuals.

Assessing Progress

Psychology has given us methods to assess many human characteristics, among them personality, intelligence, sensory acuity, oral language and perceptual–motor skills. Of special interest to teachers are the achievement tests that assess progress in reading, mathematics, and written language, among others. Some of these are standardized achievement tests, sold commercially, in given subjects like arithmetic, reading, English, or chemistry, that can be used to compare the performance of your students with that of a national sample of students. Other achievement tests are those constructed for use in connection with particular textbooks and sold along with the textbooks.

The most common of all achievement measures are those which teachers themselves construct, like quizzes, tests, and examinations. For your purposes, teacher-made tests have advantages over commercial tests. Why? Because you know exactly what your instructional objectives are. Your tests are designed to ascertain whether those objectives were met.

Teachers assess their students regularly and for a variety of reasons (Salvia & Ysseldyke, 1991). In particular, teachers want to know how much and how well their students have learned the content covered in class. This knowledge enables them to make important decisions such as whether the teaching approach should be maintained or modified, whether the objectives should be maintained or modified, how students should be grouped within the class, for example, either for special assistance on the one hand, or for enrichment or an accelerated pace of instruction and, finally, whether referral to a specialist (e.g., in reading or mathematics) is desirable.

You want to know if Jane and John have learned last week's lesson. On a commercial achievement test your last week's lesson might be covered by only a single item. That is not enough. You will use 10, 20, or more items to more precisely pin-point what they learned and what they did not learn. Having that information, you can prepare experiences that will help them fill the gaps in their learning. After all, your purpose is to assess the instructional needs of each student.

From your own experience as a student you know that there are different types of teacher-made tests. Now that you are on the other side of the desk, you will find it helpful to be familiar with more details about the two major formats of such tests and the types under each format. The two are *Select* formats and *Supply* formats.

Select formats are those in which the answer is among the possible responses presented to the subject, who is asked to select one response. The Select format includes three types of tests: true–false, matching, and multiple-choice. The last of the three is the most useful and the true–false is the least because, by chance, students will make the correct choice 50% of the time, even if they do not know the information or concept you taught. Select formats are used to assess knowledge, comprehension, and the application of skills.

Supply formats do not present the answer. The student must supply it in a written (or oral) response. The two types of such tests are fill-in (e.g., The capital of France is _____) and extended response (e.g., Explain the benefits of student participation in class discussion.). The supply format, especially the extended response, is the preferred mode when assessing more than knowledge, in particular, when assessing the ability to analyze, synthesize, and evaluate knowledge (e.g., The testee is told, "Here is a student's record of performance this year and a report on family changes during the year. See what connection, if any, there is between the two.").

In developing tests, teachers need to make them dependable. In the language of test makers, the tests should be *reliable*. An important characteristic of reliable tests is that they are so clearly written and thoughtfully constructed that students taking them again tomorrow would get about the same scores they obtained today.

To be dependable the tests must also be *valid*. Valid tests accurately measure what you intended them to measure (e.g., verb tenses, division of fractions, or the main themes in *Hamlet*). For purposes of classroom use, the tests should have what is called "content validity." To determine whether your test has content validity, ask yourself: Do these test items really measure what we have been studying? Are these items broad enough to cover the area studied? Do the items cover the material at the level of comprehension that was my objective?

For further assistance in constructing and using teacher-made tests, see Salvia and Ysseldyke's (1991), *Assessment*, 5th Edition, published by Houghton-Mifflin. Pay special attention to the chapter on teacher-made tests of achievement.

Preventing Problems

How often teachers will end the school day by saying, "If only I had done so-and so," by which they mean, "If I had done so-and-so, I would have *prevented* the awful problem I'm faced with now."

It is impossible to overstress the importance of prevention. For us teachers, prevention can spare us problems and heartaches of many kinds and by the dozens. That is why, in one sense, this entire book is devoted to prevention: Preparing for student teaching, building good relationships, stimulating interest in learning, to cite a few chapter headings, are all about prevention. In this section, we approach it head on and by name.

Among the many ways teachers can prevent problems in their classrooms is by paying attention to these four important dimensions of classroom instruction, identified by Garland and Shippy (1995): classroom management and discipline, asking questions, motivation, and communication.

Classroom Management and Discipline.   This dimension involves:

- Planning for the start of the school year.
- Using time effectively. High priority units are not hurried. Topics are no longer discussed when students have lost interest and may become bored and potentially disruptive.
- Applying group management strategies, in small or large groups. These techniques encourage student involvement and prevent discipline problems.
- Engaging students in learning, getting them actively interested and involved. This keeps students on target for learning objectives, avoids wasted time (looking out a window) and tends to prevent disruptive behavior.
- Communicating in the clearest and firmest way the rules of student participation.
- Using mediation to resolve conflicts peacefully. This procedure, often conducted by peers (students trained in mediation), is being widely introduced because of its apparent effectiveness.

Asking Questions.   The second important dimension in instruction serves many purposes:

- Stimulates thinking.
- Initiates discussion.
- Encourages creative thinking.
- Reviews material studied.

The question you ask should be matched to the purpose you want to achieve. An excellent question intended to stimulate thinking (e.g., In what way is life different for a child living in the southwest part of the country from one in the northeast?) may be inappropriate as a review of material studied.

After you pose certain kinds of questions to your class, you want to encourage the students to think before responding. Besides encouraging each individual to work hard on formulating answers, this strategy also gives students who are slower responders more opportunity to participate.

Your responses to the students' answers are very important. They can serve as stimulants to continued discussion and, through encouragement, as a boost to student participation. In the meantime, you will be reacting in still other ways. If you lead the class in an objective informational domain, your question might be, "What happens to Jim in Huckleberry Finn?" In that domain you will also be evaluating the correctness of the response. In the subjective domain the question might be, "What is your opinion about any one of Mark Twain's characters?" The answer could be followed by your asking the reasons for the choice, compelling the students to think more deeply.

Teachers want their students to understand a lesson. It is not enough that students give correct answers. These could be memorized responses which, if we investigated, could turn out to be meaningless to the students. Do they understand the difference between top and bottom, heavier and lighter? Do they understand the meaning of gravity, democracy, a verb form, a square root? If they do not *understand*, they have not learned.

Gardner and Boix-Mansilla (1994) pointed out that asking questions is basic to teaching for understanding. Some questions, useful for that purpose, seem to be universal. Gardner and Boix-Mansilla make an interesting connection by saying that certain basic questions are articulated both by children and by philosophers. These same questions are addressed by the various disciplines, the arts, poetry, and religion, and so are applicable to all classes and subjects.

More important for us as teachers is the fact that these questions, which are so important to teaching for understanding, are also excellent tools for teachers. In our collective experience of teaching at all levels, from preschool to graduate, we have found that lessons built around these questions stir the interest of students and set them thinking.

Following are eight categories of such questions and a sample of questions in each category, most of them from Gardner and Boix-Mansilla (1994). These questions, and the countless ones that are derived from them, form the very core of teaching for understanding. In connection with each question, the teacher decides on *what* the students are to understand (goals) and *how* they are to demonstrate their understanding (performance). Through the "how," teachers are able to assess the effectiveness of their teaching for understanding.

- Identity and history: Who am I? What group do I belong to? What is the story of my group?
- Other people, other groups: Who are they, those around me and elsewhere in the world? How do they handle conflicts?
- Relations to others: How do we treat other people? What is fair? How do we handle conflicts?
- My place in the world: Where do I live? How does it relate to other parts of the world?
- The psychological world: What is my mind? How does it operate?
- The biological world: What about other creatures?
- The physical world: What is it made up of?
- Forms, patterns, size: What regularities (or laws) are there in the world? What aids are there to make sense of the world?

Motivation. The third important dimension in instruction is important in its own right, because students wanting to learn make teaching a sheer pleasure, and also because students motivated to learn are less inclined (and have less time) to be disruptive. The happy news from research is that students can be motivated to work, and work harder, when they become convinced that their performance (whether an F, D, C, B, or A grade) is not due to fixed intelligence (Dweck, 1986). When they believe that no matter what their mental aptitude, disciplined study under the guidance of their teachers can lead them to better performance, they will likely work harder and develop more self-confidence.

Communication. The fourth important dimension in instruction, communication, is at the heart of teaching. *How* and *with whom* the teacher communicates has a lot of bearing on the classroom climate and the attitude of students to the teacher. Fair and equal treatment is important to students. So is a respectful attitude toward them.

Giving each student recognition, by name, builds morale. It tells the class you are aware of each of them as individuals. This could be done during recitation or discussion, or at any time, even in saying hello and goodbye.

The research literature on teacher behavior shows that teachers (by no means all of them) treat different groups differently. For example, boys are called on more than girls, and lower achieving students get less attention than others.

Observe what and how your cooperating teacher communicates to the class. Even more important, take note of yourself in this regard. Once you know what your communication behavior is like (perhaps by requesting feedback from your cooperating teacher and supervisor, or possibly by arranging to have a video recording made of a lesson you teach), you can change it, if that is called for. Remember, too, what the literature on expectations says: What you think of your students gets communicated to them by your attitudes and behavior and, in turn, affects their attitudes about themselves and their behavior.

How their teachers make them feel is crucial to students. A recent report from the U.S. Department of Education (1994) speaks about that indirectly. It indicates that 43 percent of students who left school between the 10th and 12th grades did so, they said, because they did not like school. There are many reasons for "not liking school," one of them being that teenagers didn't feel wanted, another that they found classes boring and unrelated to their lives.

So far, we have said that teachers can prevent problems by attending to classroom management and discipline, asking appropriate questions, stimulating motivation, and engaging in supportive communication. We propose another preventive measure. Somewhere down the road of your career you may begin thinking about how to maintain vitality in your classroom. It may be helpful to think about that now. For the sake of your students, not to mention yours, you will not want boredom or a lackadaisical attitude toward class. You want you, yourself, and your students to find interest and even some excitement each day.

An article written to help college teachers of psychology maintain vitality in their classes can be helpful to other teachers as well. Here are some points made by Margaret Lloyd (1994):

- Be willing to experiment. Do something different. Maybe include more dem-onstrations and activities, improve your discussion leadership skills (we're not born with them), or consider using cooperative learning strategies.
- Keep a written record of what works and what doesn't. Write notes to yourself as you get new ideas.
- Look for new ideas about teaching, from your teacher publications, from conferences and workshops, and from books.
- Watch yourself in action. Have a class videotaped and get a unique perspective on your teaching.
- Stay in touch with your students. You are of a different generation from them. If you refer to some TV programs you enjoyed as a child, you might get a

vacant stare because they never heard of them. As you get older, work at knowing the culture of the younger generations.
- Cultivate a positive attitude. Maintain your enthusiasm. Your enthusiasm and your interest in reading, studying, and thinking may infect them.

One final point about prevention affects you directly. You will, of course, be evaluated by your cooperating teacher and your supervisor. You want to be prepared for that evaluation. Bear in mind that you will be assessed about your effectiveness in planning, implementing your plans, managing the classroom, evaluating your students and, finally, your professionalism. The last refers to such items as your attitude and commitment to teaching, dependability and promptness, initiative and self-direction, and your enthusiasm and interest in teaching and in your students.

Before turning to how to cope with specific discipline problems in the next chapter, we want to highlight the seven principles discussed here:

1. Functioning as the adult leader
2. Managing time—Managing ourselves
3. Developing your own theory of management and discipline
4. Problem solving
5. Planning
6. Assessing progress
7. Preventing problems

Think of these seven as equivalent to prerequisites to career success. We believe that by using these principles as guidelines, teachers are likely to build self-confidence and feel in control.

CRITICAL ISSUES
- What can you do to engage students in class activity and hold their interest?
- What is *your* theory of classroom management and how it provides healthy conditions for learning?
- What do you have in mind when you think of *discipline*?
- What problem of classroom management have you faced and how did you deal with it? Would you act differently now? Why?
- What kind of planning is necessary for successful classroom management?

10

Coping With Tough Problems

TOPICS

- Meeting both individual and class needs
- The defiant student
- The intimidating student
- The student with low self-esteem
- The abused and neglected student
- Sexual issues
- The disruptive student
- The student who steals
- Expecting the unexpected
- Growth in coping
- Critical issues

During your classroom observations, you probably noticed the teacher's attention turn from whole class to individuals to whole class, or perhaps whole class to groups to individuals, or vice versa. As teachers, we relate to each of these entities: class as a whole, small working groups, individual students. We also find ourselves in the position many times a day of having to decide which entity to attend to.

How we divide our attention among these entities is worth considering. Of course, the welfare of the whole class is our first priority. For this reason we guard against the demands of one student distracting us from this prime responsibility and leading us to give him or her so much attention that the class suffers as a result. On the other hand, we want to maximize each student's learning, and sometimes, to do that, individual attention is a benefit. As you can see, teaching is a balancing act.

As we examine some of the tough problems that teachers find in relation to individual students, let us keep the class as a whole always in the foreground.

MEETING BOTH INDIVIDUAL AND CLASS NEEDS

This section focuses on behavioral problems of individual students and methods teachers can use to resolve them. We begin with Kate, who discussed discipline with a substitute teacher and gained new insights:

> 2/9: As I thought about it later, I decided that I need to learn to be a little firmer with the children. At times I tend to sacrifice the needs of the group for individuals because I am afraid of hurting their feelings. Consequently when a child begins a monologue completely sidetracking us from the group's discussion, I will usually let the child continue his/her story. But, meanwhile, the rest of the class becomes bored and fidgety. As I get to know the children better I am beginning to realize that children's feelings do not bruise that easily. For example, today I asked Glenn to go on an errand for me. Cindy asked to accompany him, but I told Cindy that I only needed one person for this job. Much to my surprise I got a cheerful "OK" and she went back to what she was doing.

Kate had the good experience of being an effective leader for the children. More important was her recognition that concern about the feelings of a particular child should not stand in the way of what is important to the welfare of the class. Kate was correct about the principle involved, even if her example was a very tame one compared to many reported in the journals. Before we turn to the very difficult ones, read how Julie dealt with a student who frequently spoke out in class, this time during the vice-principal's observation visit:

> 3/15: Mr. R., the vice-principal came in to observe me this morning. I was surprised that I wasn't more nervous. As a matter of fact I was very calm, I thought. I was in the middle of a lesson on the concept of "more and less." The children were all attending to what was going on—their participation helped to keep them all interested. Mr. R. told me later that he thought I did a fine job so I was glad it worked out well.
>
> As I was doing my lesson, Crystal began blurting out all kinds of things, including asking me why I wore glasses. This is not unusual for Crystal: Her attention span is not as long as that of some of the other kids. Of course when you're being observed you want everything to run smoothly, but when my patience was wearing thin concerning Crystal's outbursts I stopped momentarily and asked myself, "Are you trying to look good in front of the vice-principal and forget Crystal, or are you trying to do a good job of teaching?" I knew instantly that I had to stop Crystal from disturbing the class. I did, and I feel good about it.

The day before the scheduled observation, Julie had discussed Crystal with her cooperating teacher and had planned how she would handle her. Julie, knowing that Crystal was an impulsive child who had not yet internalized the social controls necessary for concentrating on a lesson, provided the control externally. She accomplished this by walking close to Crystal and saying something like: "Crystal, I want you to listen—to listen very carefully—and I don't want you to talk again until I call on you. Do you understand?" Crystal responded both to Julie's words and to the tone of her voice.

After Julie had called on several of the children to answer questions or to give an example to help illustrate the lesson, she called on Crystal. That step is an important one in the process of helping a child incorporate controls. It rewards the children for the control they have exercised, no matter how briefly, and informs them that with such self-control they will still get attention from the teacher and have their turn.

THE DEFIANT STUDENT

Steve recognized very early in his assignment that the children were undisciplined and that the cooperating teacher's practices contributed to their behavior. For example, Mrs. S. would pass out two worksheets at once, with the result that as she was giving directions on the second, the children were working on the first. She would also inform the children which worksheets would not be collected and graded by her, a strong incentive to resistive children to ignore them.

Steve was not thrown by the situation. In his third day as a student teacher, "several of the boys were chewing grape gum. I would ask them to throw it away and they would fake throwing it away. I finally ended up taking a piece of paper and telling them to put it on the paper and then throwing it away myself. The children have no self-discipline."

His statement was not that of a teacher in panic. He knew that the "gum" misbehavior was directed at him, a test of the new teacher, and he took it in stride. When his first attempt did not work, he shifted gears and succeeded in passing the test: He maintained his authority as teacher and enabled the group to do the work of the day. Thereafter, with the same spirit, Steve searched successfully for activities and larger projects that won the active participation of all students some days and most of them on other days.

Steve did not have an easy time with John, who is typical of a type of student who challenges teaching professionalism. Sometimes youngsters arouse the animosity of the teacher, a situation that often leads to a battle for power and an almost total preoccupation with how to subdue the student. Such a reaction, although understandable under provocative circumstances, denies the teacher the chance to understand and resolve the problem. Also, the preoccupation with this struggle gradually erodes the teacher's effectiveness with the class.

If the student teacher gets caught up in such a contest, he or she will have less time and energy to concentrate on the class as a whole. Steve's experiences, reported in his journal entries, give examples of what a student teacher must do to avoid getting caught up in such problems:

1/28: Today John was totally obnoxious. It is spelling test day. I gave the children about 10 minutes to study. John just sat there and wrote about five words on a little piece of paper—a cheat sheet. Right before the test I took it away. Then I gave the first spelling word—he spelled it out loud—I ignored it. I, however, reminded the whole class that they must be silent. John shouted out the spelling of the next word. I crushed his paper. Then when we were in line to go to the rest room, he pushed a girl down. Mrs. S. saw it and scolded him harshly. He had been performing for Mrs. S. all week too. He then acted like the scolding was the greatest thing that ever happened to him.

Steve recognized that John's actions were not directed against him personally, for Mrs. S. had trouble with John earlier in the week. For whatever reasons in his personal life, John, at this point in the school year, had a need to get attention, defy adult authority, and attack a female classmate. We may not know what provoked him. Nevertheless, as effective teachers we convey the attitude and behavior of rational authority that says to John the following, but in simplified form:

> John, you have your reasons for doing what you are doing. We know you are not doing it as your preference, because no one chooses to get into trouble and be a failure and a loser. But whatever the unfortunate needs that drive you to it, your behavior is disruptive to others and destructive to you. It is unacceptable and will not be permitted. I will use every means available to me to prevent it, preferably the most humane and least humiliating. While I recognize that ultimately you are not now responsible for what you have become and how you behave, that will not in the least cause me to equivocate. In your interest too, I must act decisively to prevent you from further damaging your self-concept and from further alienating yourself from members of the class.

Steve handled the cheating encounter relatively well. However, when John defied him by spelling aloud the first word he gave on the spelling test, Steve might have said, "I know that you are looking for attention. I can't allow you to get it this way because you are disturbing the class."

Steve also could have said, "I know you're trying to get our attention by doing something you know is wrong. But you can't do that—you can't get our attention by doing something that keeps us all from our recess." Another alternate method would lead Steve to discuss John's behavior with the class and allow the children to tell him that it was foolish or silly or stupid, as they would, thus having his own peers reject his behavior (not him).

Because Steve had handled the incident with John so effectively, in subsequent journal entries John's name linked with trouble appeared only once more. Whether the situation at home (or whatever else had precipitated his outbreak of rebelliousness) had improved, we do not know. We only know that Steve was infrequently faced with disruptive problems from John or others.

Student teachers often ask about effective measures to cope with the disruptive behavior of one or two students who use too much time and energy of the student teacher, leaving too little for the rest of the class. Studies have shown that, fortunately, teachers have a great deal of power to influence the behavior of their students.

It is common for teachers to ignore the children who are working steadily, while being occupied and sometimes entirely preoccupied with the pupil who is disruptive, or to ignore that same pupil when he or she is actually beginning to do class work. Unfortunately, the whole class gets the message: "If you want to be noticed, stop working or, better yet, cause trouble."

As we indicated earlier, the practice of giving attention primarily to the troublesome pupil is self-defeating. In contrast with the habit of noting primarily negative behavior is that of praising positive behavior for the purpose of reinforcing it. Here is a study that shows how teachers can introduce custom-made methods of changing behavior.

The investigators (Madsen, Becker, Thomas, Kosen, & Plager, 1972) sought an effective way for teachers to correct the behavior of first-grade children who were standing when they should have been working. Typically, the teacher directs the offender to sit down and get on with the work. The researchers found that when teachers concentrated on the violations of the children by telling them to sit down (their voices sometimes increasing in intensity), the misbehavior continued, and when they increased the commands to sit down, standing up behaviors actually increased. However, when the teachers turned their attention to praising behavior that was incompatible with standing up (i.e., sitting and working properly), the standing up declined.

A successful approach was this: The teachers "caught the child being good," giving praise, attention, or a smile when a child was seated and at work. When teachers saw a child standing and walking unnecessarily, they ignored the child and instead went to a neighboring child and praised him or her for being seated and working.

The success of this approach may be seen in this finding: In a class of 45 children and 2 teachers, there was a decline of 100 standing-ups per 20 minutes, a substantial difference in the functioning of any class.

Anna tried various techniques in an effort to stop a group of several adolescent girls from talking and/or giggling when she was presenting material. Anna explains:

> 11/4: I reprimanded the girls since Day 1. It didn't work, so Ms. C. suggested our putting some teeth into my discipline. I had them stay after, write lines, clean the chalkboard. Nothing worked. Then I gave a quiz after one lesson. They all failed—but that didn't seem to change them. Then Ms. C. and I re-thought things. I lecture. The girls talk or giggle. I yell at them. The boys think it's great—I'm yelling at the girls, and so on. This week I stopped yelling at them and let them talk. Instead I praised kids that answered my questions. The girls came around. They are definitely listening longer now—last time there were no flare ups.

We become accustomed from our experiences growing up at home and in school to focus primarily on misbehavior. Shifting our gears to a new way of functioning is not easy, but it is worth accomplishing because it enables us to be more effective teachers.

No one should be left with the impression that this procedure means being "soft" on students who violate rules, disrupt classroom activities, and seek to undermine our authority. On the contrary, the objective of using methods that modify behavior is precisely to eliminate or at least greatly reduce the incidence of such kinds of unacceptable behavior. You will learn many strategies for accomplishing this during your student days and early years of teaching. One useful approach to try when you first encounter hostile behavior is to remember that hostile behavior may have its roots in problems people may have about feeling in control of their own lives. For example, students vary on how much control they feel they have in social situations. A study of junior and senior high school students has shown that those who feel they have some degree of control over what happens to them tended to exhibit prosocial behavior in the classroom; that is, they were rated by teachers as being task-oriented and considerate in contrast to distractible and hostile (Bradley & Teeter, 1977).

What is the practical value of such a finding? If disruptive students believe that luck almost totally controls how they make out in school and other social situations, then changing this belief may modify their behavior. How could a teacher change this belief? Would setting up a contract that rewarded them for their own successful performance help the students learn that they can have some control over the outcome of situations? Would involving the students in decisions about their punishments help them develop a feeling of control and decrease misbehavior? These are effective measures, although they do not always succeed in changing every student's behavior. Only by trying them can you know whether they will work in your classroom.

THE INTIMIDATING STUDENT

Ruby had a different and more serious problem than any we have yet examined. About 6 weeks into her student teaching, she began to understand that she, as a teacher, was afraid of one of her second graders:

> 2/28: I didn't realize until this morning that my feelings about one child in particular, George, are becoming terrible. George is the one who gets and keeps the class out of hand, and when he isn't there, things go so smoothly. I can do extra things with the class which are a flop when George is there. This morning I found myself hoping that George would be absent. I think that I'm afraid of him.

To begin with, Ruby's assigned class was hardly the most conducive to good teaching. Her cooperating teacher had been given all the "problem children" in the grade. Ruby silently disapproved of some of the cooperating teacher's practices, especially her frequent shouting. The cooperating teacher openly disapproved of Ruby's quiet manner, insisting she must shout at the children. The cooperating teacher was absent frequently, and there was a turnover of substitutes. These circumstances made life difficult for Ruby. Her experiences are instructive, however, because even with better conditions, student teachers, and experienced teachers too, find themselves at similar loggerheads with one learner or another.

Next we analyze the reasons for the development of fear on Ruby's part, an emotion that can immobilize a teacher and make him or her an ineffectual classroom manager. In doing so, we refer to journal entries made earlier than the one just cited. About 7 weeks before that entry, Ruby made her first reference to George in the journal, and made her first series of mistakes:

> 1/11: George is testing me to see how far he can push me. I don't quite know how to handle it. Today he and Matt were having an argument over who Mrs. W. had said could take the ball out. Matt had the ball and George walked up and hit him in his stomach. I separated them and George said, "I'm going to kick his butt after school on the way home." I said, "No, you're not." He said. "Yes, I am too." I said, "Do you want to stay in for recess?" He said, "I'm not staying in nowhere." I didn't really want to make him stay in and I didn't want him to fight with Matt, but because of other encounters that we have had I felt that I should do something. Just as this happened, Mrs. W. came in and told everyone to go outside. I didn't say anything.

Ruby interpreted George's behavior in a personal way—that he was testing her. She was being tested as a teacher but not by design; George was behaving in his characteristic manner. She got enmeshed with George as much as Matt did, responding to George's threats to Matt in an unrealistic way (a teacher cannot police children on their walk home from school). She then threatened punishment (staying in for recess) and did not carry it out. Ruby, it should be noted, gave him his choice, to cease being belligerent or stay in during recess. When she failed to carry out the punishment, he learned that she wilted under his domination. Nothing so quickly undermines the authority of a teacher than failure to carry out the consequences of unacceptable behavior:

> 1/20: Today I had my first crisis in the classroom. George started about three little battles in the classroom. After I settled the third one down (between George and Raymond), George hit Raymond with his fist on the side of his face. Raymond was crying and George was threatening to beat him up after school. While this was going on, the class was getting completely out of hand. I had no idea where Mrs. W. was, and all I could think of was to take George up to the office and come back to quiet the rest of the class. Raymond was still crying when I came back down. I quieted the class and tried to talk to Raymond. He wouldn't talk, but the side of his face was swelling pretty badly. I took him to the office.

> 1/23: I had problems with George today. He was disturbing the class, running about the room, talking and constantly out of his seat. I finally had to take his recess away. He said he wouldn't stay in. I talked to Mrs. W. about it, and she said I couldn't handle George the way I handled other kids. (This was obvious.) Authority turns him off. Mrs. W. suggested that I talk privately with him, discuss what he'd been doing, and let him choose his punishment. I couldn't let him go out after that, so I told him that I wanted to talk to him during recess. He waited without much fuss. We decided that he was talking and that he should stay in. I turned my back to talk with a reading group and he left. When he returned we talked again and decided that he had to give up half his recess tomorrow. I was afraid that it might look to the rest of the class as

if I were favoring him, but Mrs. W. said that they didn't pay that much attention and this is the best way to handle George.

1/24: George didn't come this morning and afternoon recess was only 5 minutes long, so I ended up letting him go to recess.

Ruby has now "taught" George that he can control the classroom situation. On January 23, Ruby took her cooperating teacher's advice and gave him his choice of punishment. She then failed to carry it out, both on that day and the following. So, 2 days in a row George's earlier lesson was reinforced—the new teacher (Ruby) doesn't carry out punishments.

Two weeks later (February 7), Ruby recognized again that George was the key to the problems she was having with the few children who were disruptive, but she continued to show her hesitancy about being the adult teacher, the rational authority in the classroom. The next day (February 8), she was "amazed" to find that this child behaves like a child when the authority figure behaves like an authority figure:

2/7: Today was about the same as most days except for an unusual number of problems with George, Chad, Alex, and Stewart. George seems to incite the problems and the others follow. Once this happens it is almost impossible to get things running smoothly. George was really bad today, but I can't tell how far to let him go before stopping him.

2/8: Today was a very short day, but George was disturbing the class again. I decided that I had to stop it early today. I took him by the hand and took him outside of the classroom and talked to him and he agreed to stop. I was amazed. He was completely submissive to being taken out, reasonable and honest in the discussion, and much better behaved in the classroom. The class behaved much better too.

Students like George, who have learned to behave disruptively, do not change as a result of one good experience with a teacher, or even after several good experiences. They fluctuate from day to day. Of course, so does the behavior of the teacher who is inconsistent in acting the part of the adult leader.

About 3 weeks later Ruby realized that fear was at the root of her relationship with George, as she had written in her February 28 journal entry, quoted earlier. He was absent for several days, during which time Ruby reported good and enjoyable hours in the classroom. The first day he returned, the first sentence in her journal entry was, "George came back today and everything eventually went back to the usual upset." In Ruby's March 3 journal, the last on George, you see how her cooperating teacher had put George in an exceptional position in the classroom, and how that handicapped Ruby in dealing with him effectively. With her cooperating teacher absent, Ruby asserted herself:

3/3: George was here again, but things went much better. He didn't want me to do my unit and he insisted on running all over the room and talking until the kids couldn't possibly remember anything I said because every sentence was broken by my having to correct him. Finally, I just told him to get into the coat room until we were finished.

He will have to do his unit work at recess on Monday. If the substitute hadn't been there, I wouldn't have been able to do the lesson smoothly for the rest of the class because George would not have let us. She sat near him and watched to make sure that he was doing as I said. George is afraid of only one thing, going to the office, but I'm not even allowed to send him because Mrs. W thinks that he should be allowed to do more than the other kids are allowed to do.

George needs help, much more than Ruby can provide. Only an investigation of his personal life, and of his health and school histories, could give us clearer notions about his school behavior. The student teacher has neither the time nor the competencies to accomplish that. If student teachers are to survive and develop as teachers, they must be able to cope with the Georges they encounter. That means they must overcome fear when it arises; they must be the adult to the child.

At several points when Ruby had more pleasant exchanges with George, largely through her own solicitousness, she thought she had won him over. Those were acts of trying to placate someone who was feared, a kind of behavior that is just as ineffectual in the classroom as anywhere else. George's behavior must be dealt with firmly, decisively, and rationally. Such action requires careful and systematic thought, the kind associated with systematic problem-solving methods like CONTROL-C.

Using CONTROL-C With the Intimidating Student

If Ruby had used CONTROL-C in planning her work with George, it would have very likely led to the following:

- Private talks with George to explain that although nonparticipation is acceptable, providing it does not disrupt the class, Ruby would like to help him to participate, to become stronger, to learn more, to be successful.
- Firmness about disruptive acts without exception: Firmness, not vindictiveness, firmness preferably through methods that end the disruption and at the same time bring him back into class activities (e.g., "No, George, you may not run in this room. You are disturbing us. Return to your seat. I want you to do the work we are all doing. And even if you don't work, you must sit at your desk").
- Some special tasks to use George's energy and to give him a sense of accomplishment, such as handing out some materials (but not after an act of aggression so that misbehavior gets rewarded, and not out of fear, to placate him).
- A reminder to Ruby that George is a child and a victim of some unhappy experiences. We do not need to delve into his history, although knowing it will help us understand him better.
- A reminder to Ruby that sometimes a teacher's "fear" is really a fear of letting loose anger against a student who has made classroom life hellish. Children are not hurt by the appropriate expression of anger by a teacher who is trying to help them control their self-defeating behavior. They will generally respect

expresses anger and finds it accepted can free herself from restraints to respond spontaneously to the quickly changing scene in the classroom.

- A reminder to Ruby that in many classrooms under present circumstances, there is at least one student, and sometimes many more who, for reasons not of their own making, get minimal help in school, if any. As a teacher, you do everything possible to understand and be supportive to such youngsters while still protecting the class from disruptive behavior.
- A reminder to Ruby that in 10–15 weeks or so, she should not expect to accomplish what regular teachers are unable to do with children like George in a year.
- A reminder to Ruby to reinforce George (and others like him) when he is engaged in school work or other appropriate behavior.
- A reminder to Ruby that seating arrangements have some profound effects on the activities and behavior of the children. One of us studied the impact of various seating arrangements on behavior, attention span, and teacher's attitude. We found, for example, that being assigned seats in the first rows closest to the teacher led to better student work and gave the students the most teacher attention (Schwebel & Cherlin, 1972). Comparable results would very likely be obtained in a study of seating in less traditionally arranged classrooms.

With regard to seating arrangements, there is no point in juggling them unless the teacher knows the learners and has a clear purpose. One student teacher in a middle school lost all benefit from seat reassignments by doing it on almost a daily basis and as a form of punishment. "Since you two talk all the time, I'm separating you." The student teacher was not dismayed when she found that those two talked during class no matter where they were placed: She continued to move them and others, but to no avail. Optimally, seating assignments can be made for positive reasons: Students who can help each other and work well together are placed in adjacent seats.

THE STUDENT WITH LOW SELF-ESTEEM

Many students with low self-esteem go unnoticed because they are not troublemakers. For example, only after student teachers manage to deal with the aggressive students do they become aware of the passive, withdrawn ones. A student teacher who recognized this important issue in teaching asked for advice from colleagues in his seminar. "He never raises his hand, talks almost in a whisper so that I can't hear him, and has no friends. Except in geography, he barely has passing grades. What can I do, especially to get him to learn more?" This is the advice he got:

This student has a many-faceted problem and you, as his teacher, have to understand and treat it accordingly. First apply a systematic problem-solving procedure like CONTROL-C to develop a list of options. Possibilities might include:

1. In geography: Use the student's strength to build his self-confidence through positive reinforcement. Call on him to answer questions, and praise his responses immediately after they are given. Have him make a special report to the class on some phase of geography. If he should speak too softly when delivering his report (or at any other time), you could say, "I like your comments very much and I want to be sure everyone in the class can hear them. Please speak up." Then praise him for even the smallest increase in volume.

2. In dramatics: Although he is afraid to speak up under ordinary circumstances, he may be able to do this behind a puppet stage or as an actor with a small part in a class play. Choral reading or singing can benefit this student as well as the whole class. It can be followed by having small groups and then individuals alternate in reading or singing.

3. Using his peers: Enlist an outgoing student to befriend him and include him in some playground games or other activity. Arrange to have him do peer teaching in geography or be taught by another student in other subjects.

With imagination and CONTROL-C, you can delineate dozens of other possibilities. Because there is no one correct way to help this boy, you should experiment until you find one or more that work. Remember that student teachers (or regular teachers for that matter) are not miracle workers. Work toward your goal with patience, but do not expect to transform a highly withdrawn student into a highly gregarious one, not in 3 months, not in a year.

A question that stimulated extensive discussion arose in one of our student–teacher seminars. An English teacher said that a major problem she faced was that a few of her students were learning disabled, especially dyslexic. The result for them has been poor grades and low self-esteem. "What do you think I ought to do about that? Do I work on their self-esteem? Work on their reading ability? Or what?"

Her set of questions brought forth many ideas. Here is a summary of the conclusions: Most educators would agree that a quality education fosters the broadest possible growth in all individuals. So, as you suggest, it makes sense for teachers (and student teachers) to informally assess their students' self-concept and its development over time, just as they do, although more systematically, their academic achievement.

Individuals' self-concepts play crucial roles in at least three areas that can affect classroom performance: (a) Behavior: Students who do not see themselves as able are not likely to act competently. Instead they will function in ways consistent with their self-view. (b) Expectations: Students who view themselves as poor performers expect to fail exams. Thus, they are less motivated to prepare and more likely to fail. (c) Interpretation of performance: If students have trouble mastering a technique, and their self-concepts are low, they will likely blame themselves and perhaps give up trying.

One's self-concept is important at all ages. However, because adolescents go through profound personal changes, they inevitably struggle more with theirs than do their younger counterparts. They can be helped in bolstering their self-views. A teacher's first step toward providing such help requires an informal assessment of the students' self-views. If, on the basis of the information so collected, the teacher determines that self-esteem is a problem, the next steps might include the following:

1. Try to identify the basic-skill deficiencies that may presently be contributing to individuals' low self-esteem. Find or develop training materials to help them overcome the deficits.

2. Teach the students to evaluate their performance realistically, that is, what they have and have not learned; what they are strong in (for which they deserve praise); what they are weak in (for which they need help). Teaching students to accurately self-evaluate their performance takes time.

3. Teach the students to set realistic goals. Some individuals with low self-views make excessively high demands of themselves. Setting attainable goals that they must work hard to achieve is more suitable to the building of a positive self-view.

4. Praise is a great tonic. Give it to students when they deserve it; teach them to praise each other and to compliment themselves for work which merits it. Praise is unlike money in that our supplies are unlimited. Teach the students that they can benefit others and themselves by spending it freely.

Having said all this, however, we must add a caveat. Remember that self-concept is a relatively stable factor that develops over a period of years. Progress in bringing about planned improvement may be slow; yet the actions of striving for it can transform the classroom atmosphere, benefit your students, and make your work more satisfying.

THE ABUSED AND NEGLECTED STUDENT

Abuse can be emotional, mental, physical, or sexual in character, or a combination of these. Neglect includes failure of parents to properly feed, house, clothe, emotionally support, or supervise their child. Current law in your locality probably requires teachers to report suspected case of neglect or child abuse to appropriate authorities.

Teachers are in a unique position in students' lives. They are often the only adult outside an immediate family to whom a student can turn for help. Teachers have an enormous responsibility in this area—to be alert to students in need. The physical signs of youngsters in need of help may be obvious: burns, bruises, cuts, inadequate clothing during cold winter months. The behavioral signs, such as listlessness, fearfulness, aggressiveness, and emotional instability, however, may be symptoms of problems other than abuse and neglect, so that one must be cautious about coming to premature conclusions. In any event, if you have suspicions, share them with your cooperating teacher who, in turn, would in all likelihood discuss them with the school nurse, counselor, principal, or social worker.

Teachers who become familiar with community resources and who maintain good relationships with parents can be helpful in many ways. As a student teacher, it would be wise for you to find out as much as possible about the resources available in your school's community: services of food pantries for the hungry; sources of free clothing; settlement houses that might provide after-school tutoring or supervised activities for latchkey children, or emergency help with utilities; housing shelters for a battered mother and her child, or the homeless.

Often a student is unable to concentrate in school because of overwhelming problems at home, such as the unemployment of the parent, a sibling's serious illness, or parental marital conflict. Although a student teacher cannot change a student's life, it may be possible at times to ease some of the burden. Parents generally welcome any offer to help them with their child's well-being. Some are too afraid or ashamed to ask.

SEXUAL ISSUES

Problems in class in regard to sex often shake the confidence and comfort levels even of experienced teachers. Chances are, most student teachers receive little instruction, if any, in coping with sex-related problems, such as the kinds of difficulties Sheryl and Carla faced. Sheryl wrote the following in her journal:

> 2/15: I really had a teaching problem. Frances wrote a note that said "Steve in Meg's pussy," and Steve got hold of it and brought it to me. I really wasn't sure what to do. I took Frances outside and asked her if she wrote it and she said she wrote some and Steve wrote some. Steve denied it (I only asked him if he wrote it), and then I spoke to Frances again. She admitted writing it. I asked her what she thought I should do. She said that she should apologize, which she did to Steve very nicely. She was crying and I told her I knew her mother would be upset and that I was disappointed. I told her to rip it up, which she did. I know harsher punishment would not have helped and it would have ruined anything that I had going with her.

The best that can be said about this report is that Sheryl did not evade the situation. Although she thought that she had spared Frances, she was unaware of the fact that she had greatly magnified this little note and aroused considerable guilt about sex. Yet she had not even asked Frances why she wrote it. Compare Sheryl's behavior about this sex matter with her actions the following day:

> 2/16: Many of the boys were clowning around, and I ended up putting four names on the board to stay in for afternoon recess. Steve immediately erased it and I chose to ignore his doing that. However, when it was time to go out, Mrs. R. reminded him. He put on another fit and said, crying, he was going to be bad for the rest of the time I'd be here and punishing him like this would not do any good. I ended up letting him write something 50 times and hand it in the next day.

The boys clowned. Steve erased the names Sheryl put on the board, he put on a fit and threatened to be bad for days. For all of that, Sheryl had him write "something" 50 times. Surely by any standards of what disrupts a class, Steve's far outstripped Frances'. By any standards of what kind of behavior must be discouraged, Steve's was more self-destructive and disruptive than Frances'. Why, then, did Sheryl react as she did?

Carla's experience helps us answer that question. Carla's cooperating teacher, Sylvia, informed the class that there was going to be a "good" and a "bad" list on the board. Carla, she told them, was in charge of who went on which list. Those on the bad list would not get one of the freshly baked Valentine cookies. Carla described what happened:

> 2/11: The children would run up to me and ask me to put them on the good list. I don't know if I like labeling kids good and bad, and I don't want to be seen just as the disciplinarian—somebody who can dispense rewards and punishment—and that's all.
>
> In circle, Kelly wouldn't put a book away after consistently being told to, so Sylvia put him on the bad list (I didn't want to put anyone on bad—they were either good, or weren't on at all). Then Josh pinched me hard and he went on the bad side. Later I crossed them both off, but Sylvia said they had to stay on bad. So they got no cookie—and did they ever cry! Sylvia said there was no excuse for Josh's pinching me, and I guess I agree, but Kelly with the book? Well, I guess he'd never do what we say if our threats (no cookie) don't come true.
>
> Later Josh jumped on me and started lifting up my shirt and pressing at my breasts (and I know he meant to—it wasn't that he just happened to touch there—because of the way he looked at me as he did it). I read an article on "Sex in the Classroom" and how to discuss it, but it didn't go into a situation like that. I looked at Josh meaningfully (I hope) and moved his hands. I didn't know what else to do.

We would agree with Carla that Sylvia's lists were hardly suited to aid Carla or any student teacher. We have no knowledge about the part the lists played in Josh's behavior. We do know, however, that Carla did not raise the slightest question about Josh's first attack on her.

Does it not seem surprising that seemingly without provocation he should pinch her? (She did not say where she was pinched.) Would not any student teacher be perplexed and interested in having an explanation? But the first aggression was so overshadowed by the sexual aspect of the second one that she seemed oblivious to the cause of the first. Yet, the first was much more mysterious than the second, which was "provoked" by Josh being put on the "bad list."

Quite understandably, Carla was startled and frightened by Josh's behavior. Her description suggests some of her bewilderment. We do not know how he jumped on her or how he looked at her (e.g., was it in anger or did she see sexual passion?) or what her facial expression was like when she looked "meaningfully" at him. Did she show anger or humiliation or embarrassment?

These questions are not meant to belittle Carla's responses to a difficult interaction. They are meant to indicate the special problem we adults have over sexual acts. Carla halted the behavior and thereafter made no issue of it. We are left without knowing whether the pinch was "sexual," even whether Carla's perception of the pressure on her breasts was sexual, whether these were Josh's nonsexual reactions to a frustrating mother substitute, or whether other factors were at work. We do learn from Carla's next journal entry that Josh is socially backward for his age and "acts out" rather than "talks out" his anger:

> 2/12: Josh and Tammy and Megan all wanted to be the engineer and Josh was pushing and biting the two girls because he wanted to sit in the front chair. Sylvia put two other chairs there and said now we'll have three engineers. (Would I have thought of that? I think so.) I just wish that Josh could verbalize instead of constantly hitting and pushing and kicking and then crying when he gets hit back. I keep telling him to "tell me or tell them," but he runs over and hits.

Josh acts out his emotions. He pushed and bit because he was angry. Probably his touching Carla was also motivated by anger (rather than sex impulse), and part of helping such a child is in letting him or her know that he or she may not express emotions physically that way, with teacher or students. The child must, in fact, never be rewarded for such action as Josh was by Sylvia, the cooperating teacher, who provided extra chairs so that he and the two girls could all be engineers. Coming as that action did immediately after "pushing and biting," she simply reinforced inappropriate behavior.

In connection with sexual problems, we recommend the following:

1. Avoid impulsive reactions to sexual talk. What each of us has learned about acceptable references to sex varies from individual to individual, family to family, and culture to culture. What is acceptable to you, may be frowned on in some communities, whereas what you disapprove of or are even shocked by, may be acceptable in the district to which you are assigned. Furthermore, the code of acceptable speech that you learned in elementary and high school may have changed drastically in the intervening years. Needless to say, we are not arguing for a do-as-you-may policy in regard to the use of sexual expressions. However, we are arguing against a teacher reacting impulsively with self-righteousness or outrage. To guard against that kind of response, we advise you to curb any tendency to act based on your emotional reaction alone, and instead to be thoughtful about coping with the use of sex language that disrupts the class or upsets you.

2. In this area, as in others, preparation is a key to effective classroom management. Talk to your cooperating teacher and to fellow teachers to learn what their practices, preferences, and rules are. Ask them about what problems have come up this year and in past ones. Think about how you would handle different situations that might arise.

3. When a student uses sex language that disrupts the class, treat the behavior as you would any other. You will want to stop the disturbance, which is sometimes best achieved by ignoring the provocation. You will, in any event, want to pursue two steps in dealing with a student who makes regular use of sex language that deviates from the mores of the school. The first step is to consider the reasons for the behavior. For example, does this student come from a family very different in culture and/or social class from the rest? Or, alternatively, has this student learned that sex language gives him or her attention and relationships not otherwise

attainable with his or her repertoire of social skills? The second step is to develop a plan of action. If it turns out that the student is employing home-bred vocabulary, a discussion with him or her (and with the parents) is in order, not to express disapproval of the family's language but to explain the difference between language usage at home and at school. In the more likely event that the student uses sex expressions to gain attention (sometimes by provoking the teacher), your plan might include giving him or her attention for positive behavior.

The subject of sex has become more public and prominent during the past several decades. Complex social forces led to more open discussion of the topic and to the infusion of highly sexualized content in films, television, and popular music. Naturally, school atmosphere and class discussions are bound to be affected by these societal changes, and by the fact that children are getting a good deal of exposure to sexual issues at young ages. During the 1980s, with the rise in the incidence of AIDS (Acquired Immune Deficiency Syndrome), the nature and prevention of this disease became subjects for discussion in many high schools and, in some condoms were, and continue to be, freely distributed.

As you know, there are no easy answers to the enormous social and health problems related to adolescent sexuality. Teachers can only do their best to help students, in age-appropriate ways, to understand and cope with the effects of living in a sexually charged society.

THE DISRUPTIVE STUDENT

Disruptive students often leave the student teacher frustrated. However, the experience of working with them can be instructive, and in some instances, and to some extent, the students can be helped. But we do not minimize the difficulty of working with such students or even having them in class. It is not easy to contend with students like Donna who shouts at her second grade teacher, "Don't tell me what to do, you bitch you."

Not only do such students drain the teachers' time and patience, but if appropriate steps are not taken, they can also leave too little time for teachers to attend to other students in need. A study of 1,013 fourth grade students revealed just that: When investigators (Finn, Pannozzo, & Voelkl, 1995) examined the relationship between achievement and teachers' ratings of behavior, they found that disruptive students' achievement scores were significantly lower than the compliant students' scores; they also found that the inattentive–withdrawn students scored even lower. Teachers tend to ignore the inattentive–withdrawn while giving much attention to the disruptive. However, teachers who are aware of such dangers can use logical problem-solving techniques like CONTROL-C and develop strategies to deal with this problem. For example, teachers may use such constructive responses as to ask certain students to read aloud or to put work on the board, or teachers may call on disruptive students more frequently.

In an earlier journal entry, Julie had referred to Lucas as "the kid who's had me climbing the walls." Next, we examine how she dealt with this disruptive student:

3/3: Lucas was back to some of his tricks today—banging his feet on the floor during show-and-tell. When asked to stop he replied, "I don't care—I don't want to see anyone's show-and-tell. . . . I don't have a show-and-tell anyway."

On the other days I had answered angrily and tried to outshout him. I knew that didn't work and I'd better try something else. I tried to handle his statement in the best way, a considerate way. I explained that show-and-tell was a time to listen and that the class members have something they want to share with us. It is important that we are polite and listen together. I also invited him to bring in something for show-and-tell. I reminded him that show-and-tell objects can be lots of things—an interesting rock you find on the way to school, pine cones—things that he may be able to find.

A few days later Julie had the kind of poignant experience in her relationship with Lucas that represents some of the rewards in the difficult profession of teaching. Julie shows, too, that she is a realist and does not expect that a few constructive interactions with a child can counteract all that is destructive. She also demonstrates how positive a force a student teacher can be, whether or not that experience elicits a permanent change in the child's behavior:

3/8: Today Lucas again was disruptive (singing, stomping his feet, pounding his hands) during show-and-tell. When I asked him to stop, he continued saying, "I don't want to listen." I got to the point where I just tried ignoring his behavior, knowing that attention was only reinforcing his behavior. But he persisted.

At library time I stayed in the classroom with Lucas (he had not returned his library book and said he didn't want to go to the library anyway). I asked him why he thought I had kept him from the library today, and he knew exactly why. We began just to talk, and he was very open. I didn't want to lecture him. I wanted to try and get through to why he is so unhappy. At one point I just wanted to cry for him. He asked me why he had no friends, and I explained that whenever anyone tries to be his friend he hits, bites, or kicks them and people don't like that. I told him that he had to be nicer to others and they'd be nicer to him. He then asked, "How can I like other people when I don't even like myself?"

What a horrible thing for a 6-year-old to be going through. No amount of discipline is going to solve Lucas's problem. He seems crushed, feels he can't do anything right. He has no self-esteem at all. I could only encourage him and point out all that he has to offer all of us. At the end of our talk he seemed more convinced of his worth, but our one little bull session alone can't change him. As we walked down the hall to the library from the class, he reached over and took my hand to walk with him.

At that point I felt something very special. He had confided in me and that made me happy. And he showed me how much he needed encouragement. . . . I don't want Lucas to be a puppet—doing everything I ask him to do without any comment. I just want him to be a happy little boy for once in his life (I have never seen Lucas laugh).

3/9: Today I made a special point to talk to Lucas individually. I feel that he needs the extra attention desperately. He had a show-and-tell today. As much as I have mixed feelings about this activity, I was glad to see him get involved. His show-and-tell was a poem he had copied for his mom. . . . He did a neat job, and I made sure that I praised his good work.

Lucas, as Julie now understood, had not sprouted angel's wings! He was a troubled boy, and she knew she would be pressed to contend with him in ways that would protect the class from disruption and him from behaviors that alienated him from the class. Now at least she understood him better and also was not setting impossible goals for him or herself. Julie was shaken when Lucas asked how he could like other people when he didn't like himself. Had she realized that he was probably parroting a parent or teacher when he spoke those words, she might not have reacted so strongly.

Like Julie, Jane, too, comes to realize that she has been expecting too much too soon. In her journal she explains that, after much thought and soul-searching, she came to realize that, to date, she has done little "actual teaching" in her cooperating school. She continues:

2/25: All I have done is just discipline these kids. But every time I think I am getting somewhere and have a few rules set up, they fall apart when Miss F. tries them. I like her and I think she has some fantastic ideas about teaching, but she has not helped these kids form any self-control at all. I don't know how to do it either and sometimes I feel down about it, but now I'm getting the feeling that I need time. This year, next year, I don't know when, but I'll help the kids in my class.

Dorothy had a different problem. After one week of student teaching, she had that desperate feeling that is so common to the student teacher: They do not take me seriously. It's the sensation that leads the young teacher to yearn for Friday afternoon and to dread Monday morning. For the stout-hearted student teacher that feeling is also a challenge. Dorothy was stout-hearted. At a critical time she did not collapse, even under the turmoil she experienced:

1/14: The substitute was unable to come, so I had to take complete control of our class. I had discovered that the children did not take what I said to them seriously, because all I had been doing was threatening and not carrying things out. I kept telling April, Horace, and Thomas to stop running around the room and making jokes during my explanation of their arithmetic assignment. Was I going to be beaten by this? I decided I would not.

As soon as I got the rest of the class settled down and doing their math (accomplished this by telling them at 1:15 I would collect their papers), I took April, Horace, and Thomas out in the hall. I discussed with them how they were disturbing the class, plus I gave them an opportunity to explain their behavior. Well, all they could do was giggle and make smart remarks. Therefore, I proceeded to take them to the principal's office.

When we got there I became sick all over—the only thing I could picture was him calling their parents and the beatings they would get at home. All of a sudden I felt sorry for them and wanted to cry and tell the principal to forget it. But it was too late, and thank God he only made them stand in the corner outside his office. I'm really afraid that if he had mentioned calling their parents, I would have asked him not to.

Someday I'll have to face such a situation—and how am I going to handle it? I really don't think I can answer until I'm in the actual situation, but I must get my logic together so I can support however I react.

1/15: Continued having problems with Horace, Thomas, and Martin. Therefore I kept them in the room while the rest of the class went to a film. I wanted the punishment to be constructive, so I had them help straighten up the room, then made them sit in their seats for approximately 5 minutes. Then we four went to the film.

Firmness, plus understanding, combined with perseverance, are necessary in coping with disruptive students.

THE STUDENT WHO STEALS

Discovering that students are stealing is upsetting. One student teacher, Celia, told about an incident that we mention only to alert others to the need for care about safeguarding valuables and avoiding temptation for children and adolescents:

6/2: I got to school late and parked my car in the last faculty spot, adjacent to the student lot. I had more than I could carry in the car and left my tape recorder and papers on the front seat. I came out between first and second periods, but the tape recorder was gone.

Celia was student teaching in a suburban high school. Sandra, whose journal appears here, was assigned to an elementary school:

3/23: An unfortunate incident: While we were out on a nature walk, someone took money from my pocketbook in the coat area of our room. There is one fifth-grade boy in another class who has a record of doing this. I reported it to the school the next day because it wasn't discovered until I got home.

Thefts of this kind occur for a variety of reasons. Some are obvious ones, like wanting money for its own use. Others are indirect ones, like getting back at an authority for what has been perceived to be an injustice, an abuse, a grievance of some kind, committed by the victim or by another school person or by a parent.

A student teacher should take preventive and self-protective measures. If you are victimized and the guilty party has been identified, it is wise to avoid indignation. Instead, react like the rational authority who disapproves of the behavior: Give appropriate punishment, and try to get the individual to face up to the reasons for the offense.

One of us had an experience that was different from Sandra's in that another pupil's property was taken. In general, the reasons for such thefts are somewhat different from those perpetrated against the teacher. Although the child or adolescent can be motivated by the overpowering desire to have the money or the property taken, it can also be instigated by envy of another student's success, beauty, popularity, relative wealth, athletic skills, and so on.

In the experience referred to, one of us was the teacher of a seventh-grade class in which Ralph was seen going through the bookbag of another boy, Lewis. The teacher was not surprised by this behavior because Ralph, who was husky for his age, acted the part of bully with weaker boys after school and also surreptitiously tried to provoke fellow students in class. Following is an approximate replay of the interaction between the teacher and Ralph at the end of the class period after the other students had been dismissed for lunch.

Teacher: Ralph, is there something you want to tell me?

Ralph: What about? I don't know what you're talking about.

Teacher: About what you did in class this period.

Ralph: I don't know what you're talking about. I worked on the reports.

Teacher [looking intently but not angrily]:   You don't know what I'm talking about?

Ralph [shifting uncomfortably in his seat]:   Well . . . no . . . I don't.

Teacher: Let's just sit here until you remember what you did this period, apart from some work. Something you did that you should never do.

Ralph [after a moment's pause]:   What's the big deal? I didn't take anything.

Teacher: You didn't take anything?

Ralph: No.

Teacher: Well, just to be sure, let's get Lewis in on this. We'll have him examine his bag right here in front of us.

Ralph: No! Don't call him. I'll give it back.

Teacher: Mmmmm . . .

Ralph: I just took a Scout badge. I'll give it back [he gets up to leave].

Teacher: Hold on, Ralph. What are you going to say to Lewis?

Ralph [looking puzzled and angry]:   I don't know.

Teacher: If you go to Lewis this way you'll just cause even more trouble for yourself. I'll give you a few more minutes of my time to help you prepare.

Ralph [angrily]:   What do you want me to say—I stole your Scout badge? Here it is?

Teacher: I offered to help and you got angry. Is that what you do when people try to help you?

Ralph: Nobody helps me. I don't need it.

Teacher: Don't need it?

Ralph [after a long pause]:   I'll say I'm sorry. I'll say I won't do it again.

Teacher: Yes, Ralph, and that's a good thing to say.

Ralph [at peace for the first time]:   Can I go now?

Teacher: When will you see Lewis?

Ralph: In the cafeteria.

Teacher: All right. You may go now. But I want to see you again after you've spoken with Lewis.

The teacher's aim here is clear: to handle the situation in the most constructive way possible. This means Lewis' property will be returned, and Ralph will also learn from the encounter. A change in his behavior is the hoped-for goal. The teacher did not make him defensive, did not get aroused by his initial belligerence, and did not get angry when he denied that he had engaged in any untoward behavior. The teacher, through an understanding approach that involved following his feelings very closely, sought only to have Ralph remedy his behavior. The teacher knew that a heavy punitive approach would do much less for Ralph than one that got him to think and to change his behavior.

EXPECTING THE UNEXPECTED

Expect the unexpected because it will happen. By expecting it you will not be surprised and will be better able to cope. Some of the behaviors and events that we consider to be "the unexpected" are fights, tobacco, drug, and alcohol use, weapon discovery, health emergencies such as epileptic seizures, the appearance of strangers in class, and problems at parent conferences between divorced spouses.

We all know that we are supposed to "keep our cool" when faced with such events, and the question we ask is how to do that. The best way is through preparation and rehearsal. Preparation means:

1. Knowing your students.
2. Knowing the resources in the school, such as someone you could count on in an emergency, like a teacher, nearby colleague, principal, vice-principal, counselor, custodian, your most reliable student.
3. Mentally going through the process of cooling down the atmosphere and feeling good that you were able to take control of the situation.
4. Imagining each of the "unexpecteds" previously given, following through until you have dealt with each of them to your satisfaction.
5. Rehearsing again and again the steps you took in 3 and 4.

Here is advice from experienced educators on handling common "unexpecteds" (Westling & Koorland, 1988).

Fights: Firmly order the students to stop and separate them. If they do not respond to your order, send for help and repeat the order. When they stop fighting, get all students back to work. At this point you want them involved, no matter in what. Later, in an atmosphere of calm, discuss the fight with each of the two students separately and apply class and/or school rules and punishment. Finally, talk with them about how such fights could be avoided in the future.

Stealing: If you know who was the thief, find a time to discuss the action privately. If the theft is admitted and the item returned, the punishment should depend on whether this was the first offense. If the student does not confess, although you have no doubt he or she is guilty, explain that you are disturbed both by the act and the denial. If the behavior is part of a persistent pattern, inform the guidance counselor or school psychologist. No matter how frustrated you may be, if you have no clues, do not punish the entire class.

Foul language: Inquire whether there is a school or class rule about this. In your own class in the future, if there are no school rules, you may wish to make your own and announce and firmly enforce them.

Sexual activity: This may be heterosexual, homosexual, or autoerotic. It is wise simply to halt the activity as unobtrusively as possible. You explain, if need be, that this is not the time or place for it. It is wise not to moralize and certainly not to draw more attention to it.

Health problems and physical accidents: Deal with the immediate situation, for example, a seizure, a faint, a vomiting student, and then call for the school nurse or another person assigned to handle such problems. Don't move the student; don't administer drugs of any kind. Prepare a written report of the incident, perhaps on a standard school form. Someone, perhaps you, will be expected to inform the parent.

With mental rehearsals and experience you will learn to take the unexpected in stride. That does not mean you will ever find it a favorite part of being a teacher.

GROWTH IN COPING

Few of the student teachers' journals we collected, or the interviews we conducted, had 100% happy endings as in Hollywood films of the 1950s. What they reported was the mixture of successes and failures of real life. Many student teachers showed enormous growth during their few months of student teaching. Among their other accomplishments, the successful student teachers had become more effective in maintaining a disciplined class.

They learned that they themselves were ready to make the transition from student to teacher, and that teachers cannot help students by pretending to be their peers or by avoiding the use of the authority assigned to them. They discovered that being a classroom leader is not the same as being a martinet. They realized that freedom in an orderly system that has its own rules is different from the anarchy of a laissez-faire (do-as-you-choose) classroom. And they also came to understand that in a mere few months, some filled with despair, they had learned very much, but that it was only what it was intended to be, that is, only a beginning, with years of opportunity for growth ahead.

A study of the journals shows that student teachers began at different levels with regard to their ability to manage a class and ended at different levels too. And that is just what you would expect. But among those who encountered and successfully overcame the toughest discipline problems, there was one common element: They all employed a systematic problem-solving thought process in working things through. In other words, although most of them did not have access to a prepackaged problem-solving plan like CONTROL-C, they did, on their own, develop and follow procedures much like CONTROL-C.

This meant that these successful student teachers took whatever information they could piece together about the problem they faced in order to develop one or more solution strategies. Because they had journals, they could look back and see what thoughts they had had from the beginning. Without their journals, they could not have detected the changes that took place in their thinking. And they would have had difficulty remembering clearly what their earlier reactions were.

The most successful student teachers worked persistently at specifying the problems they were facing and struggled to understand them. To accomplish this, most talked their thoughts and ideas over with their fellow professionals (in and out of seminar) and with friends.

By the end of their assignments, successful student teachers had begun to come to terms with the real life of the teacher. Some students, they realized, came to school unhappy, angry, and belligerent. They had learned to contend with those emotions and especially the behavior that they stimulated.

Malvina was well into the term as a student teacher in the sixth grade of a New York City school, still working only with individuals and small groups. She saw first hand how classroom management problems are compounded when a student suffers from chronically uncontrollable angry outbursts. And by the end of her assignment, she had learned how to effectively cope with this:

> 3/6: During the math lesson (which followed the morning reading period), Richard started banging and whistling. Mr. B. spoke to him privately by going up to his desk. The disturbances continued, but Mr. B. ignored him. The noise was beginning to have its effects on the rest of the class. I hesitated, but finally decided it wasn't worth it to the rest of the class to let the commotion go on. I asked him to stop; he now put away the mirror that Mr. B. told him to stop playing with. The disturbances continued. I asked him if he wanted to come to the back of the room so I could babysit for him. He was unwilling to come and I wasn't going to physically force him. The noise still continued. I took my chair and my work and sat next to him. I kept him calm enough so he did not upset the whole class (and I felt that was crucial).

Student teachers like Malvina who have gone to disciplined schools and then to college are upset at first when a boy like Richard (age 13 and above average in height and weight) bangs on his desk and whistles with no evident provocation and, furthermore, continues after his teacher tells him to stop. Two months later, Malvina, who had been stunned by his behavior earlier in the term, handled it in stride. That means she kept Richard from further disruptive outbursts. By the end of that same week, she had an experience with him that gave her hope, very tentative, but hope nevertheless:

5/10: I had my first good experience with Richard today. The kids were allowed to make Mother's Day cards. Richard wanted some help in writing something. I had him respond to "What does your mother do for you?" He mentioned close to ten things. I listed them in a nice poetic arrangement. He just sort of looked at me in the end and said distinctly and with feeling, "Thank you, Miss R." Mr. B. saw and heard him do it and nodded to me. He apparently felt as I did. I had really "reached" Richard for a moment—and that's a hard thing to do.

Malvina had indeed reached Richard. Her success, momentary though it might have been, shows how much in the way of understanding, attention, and support some students in our schools need. This can be done only on an individual basis, and to do that teachers typically require more assistance and smaller classes than they get. However, as in Richard's case, attention such as Malvina gave can help, even if it is not enough to reverse the damage and the present distress. In any event, Malvina's hopes were set back a few days later:

5/14: During a morning lesson time, Mr. B. indicated he had to step out for a moment. I continued with the lesson. All of a sudden a chair is turned over and Richard starts shouting. I had seen Richard go off like this once or twice before. He climbed to a chair, to a desk and kept challenging and baiting Harold to fight him. Harold, normally very patient with Richard, wouldn't put up with it any longer and started to fight. The rest of the class grew rather quiet and inactive. I moved to the back of the room and attempted to separate the boys by placing myself between them. Harold came (with my urging and pulling, if I remember correctly) to the front of the room. Richard kept baiting him and he began to fight again. I called to the boys in the class and asked for some help. I had them hold Harold back. I also had worked hard to calm Richard, telling him it couldn't be settled by fighting in school and that I didn't want to be hurt. I took Richard out of the room.

By this point in the term Malvina has become almost expert at handling these crises, even to the extent of getting the help of the other students. Following the principle that there can be no learning in a class devastated by conflict, she took action to quell the fight and to win a degree of tranquility. Malvina began to look for a pattern to understand Richard's behavior and she found one:

5/21: I noticed something rather interesting about Richard. At the end of the trip today he began to "go off." I have the feeling that when things begin to go too well, Richard finds something to "go off" for. During our trip today Mr. B. and I were able to give him more attention—instead of making him happier, he acts up. And it's been true when things get good in the classroom too. This also fits with his answer to the psychologist's form when he said he usually expects bad or unhappy things to happen. How do you deal with a problem like this?

Some people are so accustomed to "things going wrong" that not only do they expect it, but also they make it happen. They help bring it about so that the world behaves in the only way they know. They are not happy in that state, but they are at least accustomed to it. A teacher's task working with Richard (and those like him) is to try to help him learn and grow, to become accustomed to things going well.

Malvina tried to do that, but she had no illusion about the obstacles both within Richard himself and in the circumstances in the school.

If we are to be effective classroom managers in coping with tough problems, we benefit by taking both a broad and a narrow view of the situations we face. We ask ourselves what, if anything, we might be doing to create or maintain discipline problems and, further, what we might be able to do to curb them. At the same time we are aware that some disruptive behavior has been stirred up elsewhere, perhaps by conditions at home or by those in school but not in our classroom. In this case, too, a logical problem-solving technique like CONTROL-C will help us develop techniques useful in managing the classroom and coping with tough problems.

CRITICAL ISSUES

- What is your reaction, emotionally and behaviorally, when a student disrupts the class?
- What approaches will you feel comfortable using to handle disruptive students? Intimidating students?
- What steps can you take to prevent outbreaks in class?
- What help do you feel you need to learn to manage the tough problems?
- What results did you have in applying a problem-solving method (like CONTROL-C) to tough classroom problems?

PART IV

Today and Tomorrow

11

The Student Teacher As a Person

In actuality, student teachers as persons are hardly separable from student teachers as pre-professionals. Only for the sake of emphasis do we have a chapter of this kind.

In this chapter the focus is on the persons behind the student teachers and the human emotions they experience. Former student teachers share their feelings with you as those are expressed in their journal entries and interviews.

We present nine kinds of experiences common to student teachers. All of them have the potential for promoting personal growth.

COPING WITH CONTROLLED EXHAUSTION

Many student teachers find their experience exhausting. Knowing that their future career depends on success during this period, they invest their whole selves into it. Contending with the behavior of unruly and disruptive students takes a further and heavy toll of energy and peace of mind. Beyond that, the tension from being under observation is, by itself, fatiguing. This last factor is sometimes compounded by overt and covert differences about important matters, most significant of which is whether the student teacher will be permitted to teach in a way that fits his or her personal style.

Besides all this, sometimes the student teacher has further academic requirements to meet during this time. Then there is one's personal life. "How can I leave the worries and pressures of my class behind," the student teacher wonders, "so that I can enjoy tonight's get-together with my friends?" Here is Joyce, halfway through her student teaching:

2/11: Boy, it's Friday. TGIF. Change of pace for a weekend. Teaching can really get you down. I haven't developed the ability to leave school at school. Maybe it's because I'm always so busy planning for tomorrow.

In my opinion, teaching this quarter has made me aware of the stamina I'm going to need if I get a regular position. Like, I'm almost totally exhausted after 5 or 6 weeks. What will I be like after 5 or 6 months! Beats me.

At points, the time pressures can become so great that even medical appointments are put in second place. Ruby tells about that:

2/18: I had a lot of trouble controlling the class, perhaps because it was Friday or perhaps it was just because I hadn't been here on Thursday. . . . I went back to do my bulletin board and it took me from 3:00 to 7:15, which meant that I had to cancel my doctor's appointment. I'll have to get my iron shot Saturday.

Some fatigue is due to inexperience in performing a task that is in itself tiring. Gary, a high school English student teacher, explained:

3/11: This week, at last, I got the chance to read the students' papers. I wrote comments and put grades on them (lightly in pencil). Great, but I feel I've been through the meat-grinder. Four classes turned their papers in on the same day (it's the end of the marking period). How much of this can you stand? Or do you get used to it?

But, as demanding as student teaching is, most individuals muster the energy and the hours necessary to emerge from it stronger as teachers and people than at the beginning. Awareness of the limited time frame is one positive factor. Even more important is the conviction that this road leads to a lifetime profession.

If exhaustion is sapping your strength, take steps to adjust. Set aside time each day for relaxation, pleasure, reading, a jog around the block, a favorite television show, or playing the piano. Frequently, the emotional demands of student teaching, not just the long hours, bring about that exhausted feeling. Putting your life into balance, with time set aside for pleasurable activities, will help you manage your emotions and combat that feeling of exhaustion, both now and in the future. Some of the suggestions in the section on coping with stress later in this chapter will also help you contend with exhaustion.

REACTING TO BEING CRITICIZED

Criticism is an essential ingredient in the development of professionals. Artists, actors, and athletes depend on it to enhance their growth in their respective fields. We as teachers need it too.

Teachers regularly use imaginative ways to translate their classrooms into effective learning environments; that is, classrooms that are physically and psychologically conducive to learning. When their innovations are effective, they excite and generate great interest. However, one cannot expect that every new idea will work as planned. Some do not. Criticism and self-criticism, as long as they are constructive, will help the teacher learn from ideas that did not work as expected and to develop professionally.

As for student teachers, criticism may be forthcoming for a number of reasons and most of all because a method used was simply not effective. Sometimes a method is not used effectively because it has been learned from a professor's lecture and then applied to an inappropriate situation. In other instances, the method may fail because it is too different from what the students are accustomed to. Sometimes, as a result of the "strangeness" of a method, criticism may come from quite an unexpected source, as Laura discovered:

> 1/29: Today was a good day with one exception. One of the girls told me that a boy said I was a stupid teacher. That really hurt. I couldn't figure out why he would have said it. I hadn't reprimanded him or anything like that. The only thing I could think of was that I had done some things differently from Mrs. W., so that maybe that's why he thought I was stupid. It was a blow to my ego, but I suppose it won't be the only time it will happen.

Hearing about criticism from one's students is infrequent. Most criticism will come from cooperating teachers, as the very purpose of student teaching is to have practical experience accompanied by vigorous and constructive critiques. For some student teachers, however, the criticisms are difficult to cope with, even when the student recognizes them to be valid. With time, a growing comfort in the classroom, and confidence in oneself, criticism becomes increasingly easier to accept and to use.

Occasionally, however, a difference in a temperament or teaching style leads to ongoing, difficult-to-deal-with criticism such as Lynn was subjected to:

> 3/5: Today was another bad day. Mrs. S. thought I took too long doing the math paper with the children. She felt the children would grow to dislike math if the papers were drawn out too long. I must be in a sensitive mood because I really feel low. I mean, her criticisms really got to me. I'm beginning to doubt whether I'll ever make a teacher and in fact if I want to be one. If I had to teach this way in a regular teaching position I don't think I could last.

Mrs. S. criticized Lynn for the same faults day after day. Why? Mrs. S.'s way of teaching worked. By that we mean that what she did (i.e., employed a crisp, thoroughly controlled form of drill), she did effectively. She believed that it was in the students' interest for Lynn to use this same mode of instruction. However, Lynn resisted, preferring an approach she had used during an earlier school field experience.

Lynn's journal alerted the college supervisor to this problem, and a conference with Mrs. S. and Lynn softened the cooperating teacher's stance and Lynn's strong reaction to criticism. Lynn then tried Mrs. S.'s method and found that she could work with it, a discovery that gave her more confidence in the classroom, and also increased her repertoire of teaching skills.

The skills you develop during student teaching are often very different from those you acquired in your education courses. In those courses you were responsible for more abstract learning, writing papers that demonstrated your understanding of concepts and a broad base of knowledge. But when you teach, you need other skills: personal presence, the ability to hold the youngsters' attention, flexibility in planning, and "eyes in the back of your head."

Your cooperating teacher's role is to help you learn these new skills. Still, these are new skills and you may have difficulty rapidly incorporating them into your repertoire of behaviors. You may feel angered, frustrated, and uncomfortable when your cooperating teacher criticizes you. If his or her criticism gets you down, use CONTROL-C and consider discussing the problem with your supervisor.

Maureena's comments during her interview show that she finally recognized the benefit of her cooperating teacher's criticism: "All term long Jan criticized my teaching. Day after day. I didn't keep the kids' interest (hey, they are high schoolers and almost adults), I didn't stick to my schedule every period (hey, I finished all the units on time), etc. But listening to her and working hard paid off. When I got my written evaluation and letter of reference, I was mucho pleased. They were very positive."

DISCOVERING THAT TEACHERS ARE PEOPLE

Perhaps you can recall an experience years ago when, by chance, you encountered a teacher of yours in a supermarket or at a mall. You may have been surprised to see her engaged in so prosaic an activity as shopping. One of the rarely discussed benefits of the student–teaching experience is the opportunity it provides to shatter myths. Teachers are people. They are very human.

The humanness of teachers leads them at times to be less than saintly in their personal behavior. You will find, when you spend a free period in the faculty lounge, that teachers do not often discuss Schopenhauer's philosophy or Greek tragedies or even the newest educational practices. They often discuss their classes and students, but as often they will be found discussing recipes, their children, football games, vacations, their families, dates, and yes, school gossip.

Some student teachers come to their first teaching experience with "stars in their eyes," expecting their teacher peers to be like the idealized version of one or two exceptional ones in their own past. What disenchantment to witness teachers expose their feet of clay, as Amy reported.

3/1: The time I spent in the teacher's lounge today disillusioned me. All I heard was malicious gossip. I wonder what they said about me when I walked out!

One day during one of my free periods, I was on the phone for about 5 minutes with my roommate. I had been in the midst of some personal problems, and was in a foul mood; however, I managed to keep my voice slightly above a whisper when she asked me how school was going. . . . I was later informed that one of the teachers who had a reputation for eavesdropping at every chance had heard my conversation and repeated it. This is one example of how the teachers in this school constantly work against one another. It is true that what I said was not complimentary; however, the important thing, as far as I am concerned, was that my attitude did not conflict with my teaching, which was my sole reason for being in the school.

Perhaps the behavior of the informer in Amy's case could be attributed to an excessive and mindless loyalty to the school, or, to be charitable, even to a more admirable motive: concern about Amy's dissatisfaction and a desire to have her obtain more assistance. Regardless of the eavesdropper's motive, the lesson is the same. Use the same good sense in sharing thoughts about your school experience in the teacher's room as you would in the staff room in any other organization. Specifically, as Amy painfully learned, it is hardly the place to talk in uncomplimentary terms about one's employer.

An example of the demystification of the teaching profession was reported by Ira. He attended a faculty meeting and soon discovered that the process of school governance, far from being romantic, is often a bore and a drudge even as it is essential:

3/22: What a day of enlightenment; I attended a "Teachers' Meeting" today after school. It is absolutely amazing how people can and do blow such little things completely out of proportion. I never before heard such argumentation and heated discussions over such petty items. To hear some of the conversation you would never guess that these were all educated people talking.

Over time, Ira will come to appreciate the importance of staff meetings that give teachers the opportunity to contribute to policy-making in their school building. As more school systems move toward decentralization, such meetings will assume increased importance. Even if the principal or chair of the meeting is not effective as a group leader and much time is wasted, the bottom line is this: you can only put in your view and work for change in faculty meetings if you are present and participate.

Teachers can of course be excellent as instructors without actively participating in teachers meetings or, for that matter, socially in the teachers' room. You make your own choices. Whether you choose to isolate yourself or not, you ought to do it with your eyes open, recognizing, on one hand, that teachers are indeed human and behave like human beings. On the other hand, you can learn a great deal from out-of-classroom interactions with teachers. You will also see that the welfare of your professional group depends on its organizational strength.

OVERCOMING SELF-DOUBT

One of the toughest obstacles to overcome in teaching, as in almost every human endeavor, is self-doubt. It does not necessarily announce itself or make itself known in obvious ways. It comes on wearing different cloaks. For Elaine, who had been having a relatively good time of it as a student teacher, it first took the form of insecurity about the future:

> 3/25: Besides not feeling well, I really didn't want to go to school today. I am worried about my plans for next year, about finishing courses this year, and I am preoccupied with other things. Since I am teaching, I feel kind of left out of college life. I feel like I've already graduated and am in a world of my own. I guess I'm getting kind of scared about the insecurities of the future and it is affecting my interest in teaching.

Elaine had been excessively demanding of herself. Does that kind of drive make one an exceptional teacher? The answer is an unequivocal no. People in the condition of constantly demanding more of themselves rarely find any lasting satisfaction in their accomplishments. They whip themselves so unmercifully that, even apart from any concern we might have about their personal contentment, they are so stressed that they are subject to cracking under the strain of any new tension and having, as a result, nothing to offer for a period of time.

Elaine was so stressed that her confidence and self-esteem showed signs of erosion in the presence of a substitute teacher. Note that these losses were not caused by any identifiable behavior on the part of the substitute, but by Elaine's conclusion that under a set of new circumstances (the hospitalization of her cooperating teacher and the arrival, on March 31, of a substitute) she had to prove herself all over again:

> 3/30: Today did not go well at all—I didn't get "good vibes" from the kids nor did I feel much was accomplished. I am so frustrated by the fact the kids are dependent on adult direction; also, the room, the way it looks is not making me too happy. I wonder if I am being "lazy" and not doing enough. Today I found out Mrs. R. had gone into the hospital and I had the full responsibility for the kids—it was all on me. I am glad today is over.

> 3/31: Today was no better. I feel as if the substitute was looking at me very curiously and saying to herself: She doesn't know what she is doing—I would do it this way. I "won" Mrs. R.'s respect, and now it's as if I have to prove myself all over again. I think I'm afraid to assert myself today with her. I don't know my limit or how far I should go. I'm beginning to wish everything was over.

> 4/1: I have the same doubts today as I did Tuesday and Wednesday. I had the confidence that what I was doing was right, but now I'm beginning to wonder. Having to win approval of the substitute is really putting pressure on me. I seem so uncreative and unimaginative compared to her. I don't know. I feel as if I'm doing a terrible job with the class. I don't think I'm enjoying my experience as much as before. I sense I can do it, but I feel her critical eyes all over me all the time. I'm glad the day is over!

On March 30, Elaine learns that her cooperating teacher has gone to the hospital. She is alone with the children, and there is no substitute teacher. She feels "lazy" as if, when there is no one present whose approval she has to win, she does not have to expend energy. She is also concerned with the "looks" of things. Ironically she, who seems so dependent on how other adults react to her, is frustrated that the kids are dependent on "adult direction."

By March 31, her self-doubts have reached the point at which she is projecting them on the substitute, that is, she acts as if she knows, without being told, that the substitute has a poor opinion of her. (Chances are the substitute had never been in a class with a student teacher and she herself had to adapt to a new situation.) Elaine tells us that she had to win the respect of the cooperating teacher and feels she has to start all over and do it again with the substitute.

On April 1, her confidence ebbs as she compares herself with the substitute. Instead of benefiting by this opportunity to observe still another person's work as a teacher, Elaine used her observations to put herself down—nothing short of that. Instead of seeing teachers as colleagues from whom she can learn, she sees them as threatening "big people," as if she has to perform to win mommy and daddy's love. She feels "critical eyes all over me all the time." With her supervisor, she even raised the possibility of quitting.

Fortunately for Elaine and for everyone concerned, she had a capable and sensitive supervisor. On the margin of the March 31 journal entry, the supervisor wrote, "Elaine, we need to talk!" At the end of the April 2 journal entry she noted:

> Elaine, bring this week's journals and let's get together. I've observed you and I know several things about you: (1) You have fine qualities; (2) You are doing many good things; (3) You are sensitive; (4) You are willing to try. The question is, why don't you know this? In my own opinion, you have the potential of becoming an exceptionally good teacher, not just average, and I guess I'm wondering how we are seeing this at such opposite extremes.

Having a mini-crisis of self-doubt, as Elaine's was, is part of life. It should not be the cause for withdrawing from teaching unless, at the end of the student teaching and after very careful analysis, a person decides the field is not for her or him. Instead, the individual should do what Elaine did, with help from her supervisor. First, she examined her journals. Through that process, she discovered that she was faced not with the problem of becoming a teacher, but with the problem of becoming an adult. She saw that she was dependent on the approval of her cooperating teacher, which we hasten to add is different from wanting healthy approval for her work (in the form of positive criticisms and a good grade).

Through conversations with her supervisor and others, Elaine saw that she constantly struggled with an urgent sense of anxiety that if she—her classroom or her teaching—did not look right to people, they would consider her a complete failure. Having seen this, Elaine learned to catch herself when she was having irrational thoughts that made her tense. When she felt others were criticizing her teaching—doubting her ability—she reminded herself of what was fact: She had been assured already that her work was much more than passable.

After this crisis, Elaine completed her student teaching with relative ease and, after having a successful job interview, took a full-time teaching position.

Other student teachers who had extremely difficult times withdrew from teaching. Skolnick (1986) explained in an amusing article, "Why I'm Sorry I Don't Teach English," how nervous and insecure she was when she started teaching English to ninth-grade nonreaders. She explained that during her month of teaching she was a failure: She was easily flustered and had trouble disciplining the students effectively and holding their attention. Although she said she is sorry she is not teaching, by her own report she is better off working for a publisher, and so are those who would have been her students.

Self-doubt is like any of the other problems student teachers encounter, and can be effectively dealt with in the same manner. If self-doubt begins to concern you, address it squarely. Use CONTROL-C or another logical problem-solving plan to delineate the issues, to outline alternatives, and to develop a solution.

One of the best ways of countering self-doubt is by being open to good feelings. If you are open to them, you probably will experience some very positive feelings that will permeate your life. Brenda and Danette wrote about theirs. Danette's joy is apparent in the following journal entry:

> 1/28: Today went very well. The activities planned were great, and [the students and I] thoroughly enjoyed ourselves. My only disappointment is that the days go by so fast. I only wish there were more of them.

Here are excerpts from two of Brenda's journals that show her professional development and its effect on her personal life:

> 1/28: I feel more confident than yesterday: The children responded more to me when I took over the morning routine, more than yesterday. For the first time I worked individually with a child while everyone else played. Also I observed Kelly today. I'd like to help him deal with his bad temper. I'm starting to think about the meaning of being a teacher, and how I must think of myself as a teacher. It's really a nice feeling being loved, having the children hang on to you and hug you, but I must begin to think of what they are learning. Aren't they learning dependence by hanging on to me? What am I trying to teach them?
>
> I feel that I must gain more confidence in myself (and I feel confident I will) in order to be more effective not only as a teacher, but as a person.
>
> 2/13: I found that some confidence I am gaining here is spreading into a lot of my relationships outside of the classroom. I had been feeling stagnant, like I wasn't changing anymore, but now I feel more change and more confidence in dealing with both my Sunday school class and with certain close friends of mine, particularly ones I found it hard to talk to. I feel more able to talk now. I feel less afraid.

Student teaching is often a professional stepping stone and a transition point as one moves forward into adulthood. No longer solely a student, you are on the front line, sharing responsibility for directing the education of others. This responsibility requires new skills and new ways of thinking about yourself so that you come to fully enjoy your professional work.

COPING WITH STRESS

We have become keenly aware in recent years that life is filled with stress. Life events like a death in a family, a divorce, a sickness, or unemployment create stress, but so, too, do some positive events like a marriage, a promotion, or a vacation trip. Furthermore, life's daily hassles such as commuting (to work, school, or college/university) or shopping can be stressful. Psychologists have come to understand that individuals cannot live a stress-free life. We can, however, learn to cope with stress in effective and constructive ways, rather than living with tension and headaches or, worse yet, resorting to alcohol or drugs as an escape.

Before we review good coping techniques, let us look at some findings about stress in student teaching. Forty-four secondary-school student teachers, some graduate, some undergraduate, in their last week of student teaching, completed a questionnaire designed to gather information that might enable faculty to reduce the stress of student teachers (Davis, 1990). The respondents were asked questions about when they felt most stress during student teaching, how intense it was, what factors contributed to the stress, which of the factors they considered the major cause of their stress, and what preventive measures might be taken.

Forty-three of the 44 said they experienced stress during student teaching. They used words like: "pressured," "anxious," "overwhelmed," "tense," and "overburdened" to describe how they felt. Given a choice as to when they felt most stressed (beginning, middle, end, throughout), "beginning" was chosen most, but "throughout" was chosen almost as often.

The respondents listed these reasons for their stress at the beginning: new experience; new role; leaving college; entering the work world; unfamiliar setting; unfamiliar people (teachers, students); ambiguity about the role; ambiguity about evaluation; and so forth. The reasons why the student teachers felt stress throughout their student teaching assignment included time pressure (not enough time to plan lessons, construct tests, grade papers, etc.), classroom situation (problems in maintaining control, dealing with unmotivated students, etc.), and cooperating teacher (the expectations and demands of that teacher, sometimes combined with a lack of direction or a personality clash).

Davis' study reported some silver linings. First, although the student teachers felt stressed completing their day to day school activities, most said that their feelings of stress would come and then be gone for a time. Another silver lining in connection with the intensity of the stress: On a scale that ranged from *slight* to *intolerable*, on the average the student teachers chose *moderate*. Occasional, moderate stress can be managed, especially if you learn how to reduce its intensity and prevent the occurrence of some of it.

Three useful ways to deal with stress (Lazarus & Folkman, 1984) are:

1. Prevent it to the extent possible. Do so by being prepared for each class, by learning all you can about classroom management, by having a thorough understanding of what the cooperating teacher expects of you, by arriving in school on time, by not carrying another job during the student teaching term, and so forth.

2. Modify the stressors to the extent possible. Do so by arranging a conference with your cooperating teacher if uncertainty about his or her demands are stressful; by modifying your classroom behavior so that you can keep a better eye on the students; by applying your discipline plan as soon as student chatter is occurring and irritating you; and so forth.

3. Modify your reactions to the extent possible. Do so by keeping things in perspective. Remind yourself that although student teaching is important, it is not the end all and be all of your life. Remember that there is life after student teaching. Here is how you can do that. Let us say that a few students are particularly troublesome one day, or more troublesome than usual, or that the cooperating teacher seems to ignore you or is more irritable one day. It is good to be able to appreciate that their own life's circumstances probably account for their behavior and not allow it to depress you. Another way to modify your reactions is by maintaining a balanced life. Do that by seeing that you incorporate relaxation and pleasure into your life during this period.

COPING WITH ETHICAL ISSUES

Ethical issues belong in a chapter on the student teacher as a person because they touch on our individual values. Ethical issues arise over a wide spectrum of behavior on the part of both teachers and students. We discuss only a few ethical issues to illustrate the questions they raise and some coping (as well as preventive) measures you can take with regard to these issues. Finally, we introduce you to an educator's code of ethics.

As a student teacher you may not have to make difficult decisions that involve complex ethical issues. You may, however, witness your cooperating teacher involved in that kind of decision making, perhaps in connection with cheating on exams or homework, or in deciding how to punish a student. And you may even, like Karen, have strong differences over school policy:

1/6: I have a difficult question, I think an ethical one, and it's about a situation that really annoys me. Sally had her head down on her desk during today's history lesson. After I assigned the class seat work and everyone had begun working I approached her and asked what was wrong. She hesitated a bit and finally said something like, "It's that time of the month."

She really looked terribly uncomfortable, so I suggested she go to the nurse and get an aspirin. She returned in 10 minutes to tell me that the nurse couldn't do anything for her, that school nurses were not permitted to dispense unauthorized medication. I had aspirin in my purse and was about to give her one when my cooperating teacher stopped me (she had been out of the room earlier when I had sent Sally to the nurse), saying it was against the rules. I really felt it was an awkward situation. Why should Sally have to suffer? Why shouldn't I have given her the aspirin?

We can empathize with Karen's frustration. At the same time we can appreciate the importance of regulations. Many rules that have been established by the school and school board are for the protection both of students and teachers. (The occasional student could be allergic to aspirin or develop a serious disorder from ingesting it.) Because the dispensing of medication of any kind brings to bear all sorts of legal questions, it is best to advise students like Sally to bring their own medication to school on those days they feel they might need some.

Karen's annoyance is understandable. She knew that the aspirin in all probability would have relieved Sally's discomfort, and she found it hard to accept a regulation that disallowed it. She is not alone in having that feeling. There is another side: If you were to provide assistance in the form of medication for this type of pain, at what point would you stop? Earache? Toothache? Digestive problem? Broken toe?

To learn the particulars of the relevant laws in your state, discuss the issue of medication with your school nurse. The deeper issue is the ethical one, namely, the right thing to do in a situation like that with Sally, and like that raised by Larry in the following:

3/26: By chance I overheard several students in the hall talking about book reports which were due today. One said, "I was too busy so I handed in an old book report of my brother's." These are the questions that ran through my mind: What should I do? Tell my cooperating teacher, talk to the student directly, or ignore the whole thing?

This kind of problem has been common in the past and will continue to be so as high-tech advances make it easier for students to transfer material from a source into their own paper with a push of a button. No matter how tempting it may be to "ignore the whole thing," that would be unwise. It would certainly not be helpful to the student. To act professionally and ethically, you want to cope with the problem in a constructive, nonpunitive way. Your aim would be to teach, not to make the student suffer.

As a student teacher, share the information with your cooperating teacher. He or she will have to decide how to deal with the problem. For your sake in the future—every teacher is confronted with some form of cheating, usually with many more varieties than we like—and because your cooperating teacher might ask for your thoughts, you should consider the following approach: First, quickly dispel whatever anger you may have toward the student, because its presence can be counterproductive to your own clear thinking. Second, ask the student why he cheated and what he thinks the consequences were (e.g., that he was really cheating himself). Third, ask the student how he proposes to resolve the problem he created. Finally, tell the student what your intentions are. Your intentions would probably depend on the student's responses to your questions and could range from no penalty (if he was genuinely sorry and promptly submitted his own book report) to failure.

This approach is first and foremost an educational one. Its purposes are to have a student learn from the experience and to prevent recurrences. That orientation, a preventive one, has been recommended by researchers (Bushway & Nash, 1977) who reviewed past studies on cheating. Their review revealed the following:

1. Cheaters and noncheaters differ in some personal and behavioral characteristics, including cheaters (a) being lower in school achievement, (b) being closer to others in their class, and (c) being more tense and anxious;
2. Situational factors are important, including (a) the moral climate of the school, (b) the likelihood that students could be successful at attempts to cheat, and (c) the teaching style of the teacher (e.g., assignments and tests that are too difficult, or use of the curve in grading);
3. There are many different reasons for cheating, including pressure to get high grades for college admission or to allow participation in interscholastic sports.

These researchers found cheating in the classroom was widespread. They urged researchers to turn their attention to strategies that prevent or reduce cheating. That is also good advice to a beginning teacher, who is helped by knowing what types of behavior students classify as cheating, how serious students consider each particular type of cheating, how often they practice those types, and how students' responses about cheating compare with responses of administrators and teachers. Research provides some answers to these questions. McLaughlin and Ross (1989) administered questionnaires about cheating to 130 middle-class high school students in Memphis, Tennessee, and to 10 administrators and teachers.

The vast majority (90% or more) of the students classified both copying during an exam and looking at notes during an exam as cheating. Faculty/administrators and students showed considerable agreement about what constituted cheating, although faculty classified more behaviors as cheating and regarded more of them to be serious. For example, all faculty, but only 69% of the students, classified allowing someone to copy homework as cheating. Also, faculty considered allowing another student to copy on a test to be more serious a violation than students did.

Although students knew what behaviors were unacceptable, they cheated frequently. Some admitted to copying homework, even taking turns in doing that.

During your student teaching you will be guided by school rules and by your cooperating teacher. You will have the opportunity to think about your own values. When you have your own class, you may decide to take action to discourage cheating early in the school year, when there is less pressure to cheat. You also will want to carefully monitor tests and conduct open discussions on the subject of moral behavior in school and outside.

In connection with thinking about ethical issues and discussing them with colleagues, you may find helpful the National Education Association's "Code of Ethics of the Education Profession." Approved in 1975, the Code appears in the annual NEA Handbook (see Table 11.1).

TABLE 11.1
Code of Ethics of the Education Profession

Preamble

The educator, believing in the worth and dignity of each human being, recognizes the supreme importance of the pursuit of truth, devotion to excellence, and the nurture of democratic principles. Essential to these goals is the protection of freedom to learn and to teach and the guarantee of equal educational opportunity for all. The educator accepts the responsibility to adhere to the highest ethical standards.

The educator recognizes the magnitude of the responsibility inherent in the teaching process. The desire for the respect and confidence of one's colleagues, of students, of parents, and of the members of the community provides the incentive to attain and maintain the highest possible degree of ethical conduct. The Code of Ethics of the Education Profession indicates the aspiration of all educators and provides standards by which to judge conduct.

The remedies specified by the NEA and/or its affiliates for the violation of any provision of this Code shall be exclusive and no such provision shall be enforceable in any form other than one specifically designated by the NEA or its affiliates.

Principle I

Commitment to the Student

The educator strives to help each student realize his or her potential as a worthy and effective member of society. The educator therefore works to stimulate the spirit of inquiry, the acquisition of knowledge and understanding, and the thoughtful formulation of worthy goals.

In fulfillment of the obligation to the student, the educator—

1. Shall not unreasonably restrain the student from independent action in the pursuit of learning.

2. Shall not unreasonably deny the student access to varying points of view.

3. Shall not deliberately suppress or distort subject matter relevant to the student's progress.

4. Shall make reasonable effort to protect the student from conditions harmful to learning or to health and safety.

5. Shall not intentionally expose the student to embarrassment or disparagement.

6. Shall not on the basis of race, color, creed, sex, national origin, marital status, political or religious beliefs, family, social, or cultural background, or sexual orientation, unfairly—

a. Exclude any student from participation in any program.

b. Deny benefits to any student.

c. Grant any advantage to any student.

7. Shall not use professional relationships with students for private advantage.

8. Shall not disclose information about students obtained in the course of professional service, unless disclosure serves a compelling professional purpose or is required by law.

Principle II

Commitment to the Profession

The education profession is vested by the public with a trust and responsibility requiring the highest ideals of professional service.

In the belief that the quality of the services of the education profession directly influences the nation and its citizens, the educator shall exert "every effort to raise professional standards, to promote a climate that encourages the exercise of professional judgement, to achieve conditions which attract persons worthy of the trust to careers in education, and to assist in preventing the practice of the profession by unqualified persons.

In fulfillment of the obligation to the profession, the educator—

1. Shall not in an application for a professional position deliberately make a false statement or fail to disclose a material fact related to competency and qualifications.

2. Shall not misrepresent his/her professional qualifications.

3. Shall not assist any entry into the profession of a person known to be unqualified in respect to character, education, or other relevant attribute.

4. Shall not knowingly make a false statement concerning the qualifications of a candidate for a professional position.

5. Shall not assist a noneducator in the unauthorized practice of teaching.

6. Shall not disclose information about colleagues obtained in the course of professional service unless disclosure serves a compelling professional purpose or is required by law.

7. Shall not knowingly make false or malicious statements about a colleague.

8. Shall not accept any gratuity, gift, or favor that might impair or appear to influence professional decisions or action.

—Adopted by the 1975 Representative Assembly

BECOMING SOCIALIZED

After years as a student, how, during the student–teaching experience, do you make that step to the other side of the desk? An interesting study by Friebus (1977) sought to identify those individuals through whom the culture of the school and the role of the professional teacher are communicated to the student teacher.

Friebus interviewed 19 student teachers six times each. To ensure representativeness, he selected student teachers who had assignments that varied on several relevant dimensions (grade level, school neighborhood, supervisory arrangements, etc.). In analyzing the data he looked particularly for information in areas that had proved useful in studies of other professional groups, three of which are defined next, along with his findings.

Coaching

Friebus found a surprisingly large number of individuals who served as coach. He defined a coach as somebody who "guides and advises the trainee, provides . . . encounters with new activities, and challenges to old identities" (p. 264). The coaches included, in order of importance, the cooperating teacher, college supervisor, other teachers in the school, self (the student teacher), professors, students, principals, friends, relatives, and student–teacher peers. These people did the coaching by providing ideas, information about teaching, encouragement, performance evaluation, and certain expectations.

That the cooperating teacher should top the list, followed by the supervisor and other teachers at the site, is not unexpected. The high score for "self" is surprising, however, and it suggests that student teachers are using their own observational skills and sensitivity to learn "how things work" and to generate advice for themselves. How does this work? Friebus provided this interchange between an interviewer (I) and a student teacher respondent (R):

I: Did the mid-term review give you a sense of progress?

R: Didn't need it. My progress came from within myself, was evaluating myself.

I: Who is your main indicator of progress?

R: Me, you can tell me I'm excellent but if I don't have the feeling within myself it doesn't mean anything.

I: If you had problems or a question about what you were doing, who was your main source of information?

R: First and foremost it was me.

Peer Involvement

Friebus found that contacts student teachers have with their fellow student teachers serve two important functions. First, individuals can compare notes and see how their situation stands in relation to others. Through this process they assess whether they are teaching a fair share of lessons, whether they are overworked or under-worked, and so forth. A second function served by peer involvement is support and comfort; that is, having much in common, peers are ideal people with whom to share the varied feelings and inevitable dilemmas student teachers encounter. Out of the sharing can come some profitable exchanges and useful ideas.

Legitimacy

The behavior of others toward her or him confirms the student teacher's growing feeling of being a professional. The behaviors include obedience by students in response to the student teacher's directions, an invitation from a teacher to join him or her for lunch, a comment by a parent acknowledging the difference the student teacher had made for the child, and so on.

Friebus found that the students and cooperating teacher were by far the greatest reported sources of instances of legitimation. That the students top the list is a fascinating example of human interaction. Student teachers, who devote so much of their energy to helping their learners develop academically are, in turn, helped by the learners to develop professionally and to feel like an adult leader in the classroom.

Very likely, you, too, will be socialized through your interactions with your coaches, peers and students. And among your coaches, one of the leading ones will be you.

APPRECIATING THE COLLEGE/UNIVERSITY SUPERVISOR'S SUPPORT

Repeatedly, the experiences of our student teachers point to the crucial role of the college supervisor and the cooperating teacher. Children can be expected to behave like children, and teenagers like teenagers, and when twenty or thirty of them are together, there are bound to be problems, even just the problems of people living and working together. For the student teacher, the major purpose of the apprentice-ship experience is to learn to take these problems in stride, in order to deal effectively with them.

If you have your cooperating teacher and college/university supervisor on your side and have their advice and especially their support, your chances of having a valuable, even if difficult, teaching experience is increased many times over. However, in those instances when the cooperating teacher is hostile toward the student teacher and competitive with her or him, and especially when these attitudes are covert and masked by occasional acts of false solicitousness, then the student teacher can have her or his confidence and self-esteem shaken to the core. Kate had such a cooperating teacher:

1/27: I went home Friday feeling quite discouraged. After 3 days of student teaching I still felt like a stranger with my cooperating teacher and even with the kids. After listening to everyone's glowing accounts of their experience in Thursday's curriculum class and reflecting on my own experience, I was really depressed. I thought about it all weekend and tried to explain my feelings to my friends. But I couldn't seem to verbalize exactly what the problem was. I had been so realistic over vacation, but I guess I was picturing things like they were at the end of my field experience, a wonderful relationship with the teacher. Probably I was expecting too much too soon. Also I was used to kids who craved extra attention. Now faced with kids coming from a totally different background who are much cooler in their reaction to strangers, and a cooperating teacher who seems aloof, I have to modify my expectations. All these things were running through my head.

After 2 months of frustration—of no support from her cooperating teacher, despite ever increasing effort on her part—her confidence was undermined to the point that Kate wrote:

3/29: I am beginning to experience this feeling of anxiety creeping over me. As I make the valiant effort to finish my proposal for my course in School and Community, my mind keeps wandering. I feel very confused. I keep thinking I should throw my proposal down and concentrate on tomorrow morning, but then I realize that the kind of situations I need to prepare myself for just can't be planned. My lessons are ready to go, the materials are set, but. . . .

I don't think I would be so scared except that I feel the issue of taking total control, rather than seeming like a logical, natural step, is beginning to feel like an insurmountable hurdle. Maybe the problem is that I am still unclear.

Maybe I am looking for a simple solution when there is none. I'm afraid to show doubt in myself because then everyone else will doubt me. But at the same time the doubt is beginning to overpower me. Where is all my self-confidence? I know, it's sitting on 3½ years' worth of papers, test grades . . . and somehow I haven't managed to translate it into the real world.

How can a person try so hard and not even come close to achieving a desired goal? Maybe it's the wrong goal? Maybe the answer is that I care too much and I'm getting sick of "maybe's."

The story has a happy ending. Her supervisor helped Kate to recognize what Kate had surmised—that her cooperating teacher had been a destructive force, a person rare among cooperating teachers, who seemed intent on giving Kate nothing but negative feedback or, at best, no comments whatsoever. Kate completed her 10-week period and went on to another student–teaching experience in a middle school, during which she herself became finally convinced that she had the makings of a superb teacher. The second school offered her a position, which she accepted.

Ideally, the student teacher and cooperating teacher form a working team, directing their efforts toward common goals. When this does not happen, when the student teacher does not get the support he or she needs, the best resource available is the supervisor. Although supervisors typically will be ready to listen at any time, and particularly as soon as the lack of support begins to become a problem, it is likely that they can be most helpful after the student teacher has begun to apply the first steps of a problem-solving approach, like CONTROL-C.

GROWING IN THE "SCHOOL OF HARD KNOCKS"

Dorothy had a gift for teaching. This was apparent to her supervisor early in the term, although her cooperating teacher never recognized it. Despite the obstacles she encountered, through dogged persistence, through imaginative plans, and through the honest expression of her feelings, as in the following passage, Dorothy had a great measure of success with her class:

> 1/20: This morning the class was misbehaving and I lost control of myself. Tears started rolling out, and I said to the class, "I don't understand you kids. I go home every night and work on new and interesting things for you to do and I receive no response or respect from you. All you can do is disturb the class. Do you realize I do these things only because I care about you and what will happen to you in the future if you don't learn?" No discipline problems the rest of the day. But I do realize I need to control my emotions, and it is something I will have to work at.

Again and again, Dorothy found renewed strength and inspiration from the students themselves. The next journal entry conveys the kind of devotion to students that becomes apparent to them and elicits their warm and positive response:

> 3/3: It's the usual Friday. The children are tired and restless. Very excited about the weekend, questioning me about leaving. Timmy kept saying in reading group that they were going to spring a surprise on me, and Larry would say, "Be quiet, Timmy." The school counselor came in and talked to me today, and I told her that it had been a hard quarter plus a period of shattered dreams and idealism; that I found out that many things the university teaches you cannot be used; also, that I feel the structure of schools increases discipline problems and that every time I punished a child I thought: We are punishing him for many things he cannot help, things forced upon him by the school and home environment. It ran through my mind, and every night I go to sleep thinking of this. But as my father and I discussed, I have to teach the child the appropriate behavior set up for him by this society or he will have many difficulties adjusting later.
>
> . . . Isn't it sad that this is what is happening every day in many schools?

Institutions that educate teachers help them develop conceptions of what schools should be like. Sometimes student teachers and beginning teachers who have fine aspirations have not had the experience in the "school of hard knocks" to appreciate the power of the principle of inertia. The status quo is not easily changed, and those who learn that fact of life and understand the reasons for it are more likely to work for modest, realistic goals. Dorothy learned that fact of life and, although saddened, was strengthened by it. Nonetheless, even under these less-than-ideal circumstances, over the course of 3 months, her devotion to her students paid off by making a difference in many of their lives.

Dorothy was fortunate in being able to mobilize herself so that she did not suffer from continuing doubts, no matter how discouraging a day or week she encountered. She felt early that in her situation the cooperating teacher was more enemy than ally, and that the only kind of criticism that she could depend on getting was the kind that put her down. But she would not allow that relationship to be defeating.

Dorothy was reinforced by the support she received from both the supervisor and her colleagues in the student–teaching seminar. For one thing, her classmates agreed that her cooperating teacher was being grossly unfair and unhelpful. For another, when she heard how her fellow student teachers received extra support from their cooperating teachers, she was reassured that most teachers actually are helpful to newcomers and that her unfortunate experience should not dispel her expectation that she would in the future find herself working with kindly people.

Near the end of her student teaching, Dorothy used her journal to define for herself the role that her cooperating teacher had played and to put her experience in perspective. This prepared her to appreciate her last 2 days and to take full and clear note of the children and of their feelings toward her. Like every other teacher—of kindergarten, sixth grade, eleventh grade, or university—who gives the students the feeling that he or she genuinely cares and works unstintingly, Dorothy got the evidence that they cared and that she had been important to them:

3/9: I must admit I had fun with the class today, because for the first time I stopped worrying about pleasing Ms. K. We had our usual reading in the morning, but in the afternoon we did choral reading and had the boat race with the children screaming. I read stories to them, then we had gym together. It was great. The class even talked about how much they enjoyed it!

3/10: What a day! the children brought me earrings, pins, a rabbit, and a lamp plus a letter that meant a lot to me . . .

Sometimes I feel Ms. K. was truly trying to stifle my progress! She definitely had me feeling like a failure on and off through the entire quarter, but thanks to a great deal of thought I gave it Wednesday and Thursday, and encouragement from my supervisor, I have come to realize I am capable of being a very human teacher. Reconsideration of myself plus positive responses from the children and my supervisor helped.

Ms. K. laughed when she saw several of the children crying over me leaving. I feel sad that these children had to suffer this hurt, but I feel good about it too because I realize I have radiated some warmth toward these children which I feel is very necessary in a healthy human development. Geraldine said to me, "I want to tell you before you leave that you are the best teacher I have ever had." Another little girl said she was going to kidnap me. Then Lisa said I was better than the teacher she had before she came to this school. I realize now that instead of listening to Ms. K. so much I should have listened to the children's responses to me all quarter, because I did know they enjoyed me, but instead I worried about Ms. K. and my evaluation.

I'll miss the children, but I feel like a thousand pounds have been taken off my shoulders.

Such are the dramas in the life of the student teacher. They are moving, and they are yours to appreciate. Those who choose teaching, knowing it is an occupation of decision making and intense human interactions, are likely to have relatively good endings to their own dramas.

CRITICAL ISSUES

- What methods do I use to
    (a) Manage to benefit from criticism?
    (b) Handle self-criticism?
    (c) Cope with stress?
- In what ways is *constructive self-criticism* part of my thinking?
- In what respects am I already feeling like a teacher?

12

From Student Teacher to Teacher

About a century ago, Sigmund Freud said that the mark of adulthood was the achievement of satisfaction through work, sex, and family. Although some of Freud's ideas have fallen from the preeminent position they held in years past, most people would agree with his statement about adulthood. With regard to work, no one would deny that, for many people, having a career is one of the highest priorities in life. That, after all, is the ultimate goal toward which you and your classmates have been striving.

True, there may be days during the student–teaching period when you would like to toss the ringing alarm clock out of the window and go back to sleep. Most days, though, you will find student teaching a challenge, as well as the route to a secure career and way of life. Moreover, you will enjoy the satisfactions, so important in life, of being identified with an organization (e.g., a school), of being

234

part of a group of co-workers (e.g., faculty and staff), of utilizing a body of knowledge about students (e.g., stages of cognitive development), and of having a discipline (e.g., elementary education, language, or science) and developed skills (e.g., to teach students to read, to converse in French, to solve physics problems).

Looking forward to next year, your wish is probably like that of others in your position: to feel successful in the classroom. As a recent study shows, this feeling is important in separating those who stay on and make teaching their career and those who leave after a year or a few years.

The investigator, an experienced teacher (Yee, 1990), queried current and former teachers to find out what led most to remain in the field and some to leave it. She found that remaining in teaching and deriving satisfaction from it is associated with:

- Workplace conditions such as positive support from administrators and peers, positive community and parent attitudes toward the school, and adequate budgetary support for the school.
- Extrinsic benefits such as favorable pay and job security, promotion opportunities, and schedule and vacations.
- Intrinsic benefits such as seeing oneself successful as a teacher, viewing students as the chief source of intrinsic reward, and feeling a sense of professional growth.

All three categories are important. The first one (workplace conditions) helps make the third (intrinsic benefits) attainable, and the second one (extrinsic benefits) can surely make life more pleasant. Still, there is no formula that can predict who will remain in teaching and who will not.

Some teachers, Yee found, stay for the extrinsic benefits (e.g., summer vacation) even when they are not getting satisfaction from the intrinsic ones, the work itself. That condition is not unique to education; you may have already encountered lawyers, nurses, accountants, and others who are unhappy with their work but stay for the extrinsic benefits. That we share this condition with other professions does not make it any more satisfactory, either for the unhappy teacher or the unfortunate students.

Yee also examined the effects on teachers of frustration with their lack of classroom success. She concluded that some who fail but do not physically leave the profession "withdraw emotionally and psychologically, effectively retiring on the job" (p. 120).

We believe that the careers of many teachers who became dissatisfied or frustrated did not have to turn out in that unhappy way. Perhaps they might have had more favorable career outcomes if their circumstances had been different during the early, crucial stages of their teaching. This chapter is designed to help you move forward as successfully as possible into the next step in your career—to assist you in effectively making the transition from student teacher to teacher.

ESCAPE FROM FREEDOM

A quality job search, writes an expert in the area, involves much time and the willingness to expose yourself to the risk of being rejected (Kimeldorf, 1993). Every step of the search is time consuming, from networking and contacting potential employers to scheduling and preparing yourself for interviews. Furthermore, as you know, even the most talented of applicants will receive some letters of rejection. In the face of such letters, the effective job search requires you to persist. Most of those who do so will find a position.

It is useful to consider the psychological as well as practical factors involved in the job search process. When Erich Fromm used the title *Escape from Freedom* (1976) for one of his books, he captured the essence of a problem that plagues many of us. We want the satisfactions of adulthood, yet at the same time we have much anxiety about them. (The anxiety is sometimes at such a low level of consciousness that we have only a vague sense of it.) What we are experiencing is a throwback to an earlier time in our lives when we wanted at one and the same time to imitate the behavior of an older brother or sister or a neighbor's child, but did not want to give up being mom's or dad's little boy or girl. We wanted to stay overnight at a friend's house (or later go on a first date), but how much "safer" it was to stay at home!

Elements of the insecure or frightened child lead us to "do and not do" at the same time, to go after a job opening and yet to drag our feet, to take the initiative in arranging for an interview and yet to manage to leave doubts in the interviewer's mind about our single-minded interest in being a teacher in that school. If we are not careful, these elements can lead to self-sabotage, making us a day late in submitting an application or a half-hour late for our appointment about a position. They induce us to "forget" to contact the faculty member we met in the teachers' room in our student–teaching school, the one who knew of an upcoming position in a nearby school district.

STARTING THE JOB HUNT

Such costly anxieties and ambivalent feelings do not make you abnormal, nor do they ordinarily require professional treatment. However, by being vigilant during your job search, you can guard against any self-destructive behavior they may cause.

Ask yourself, have I established a plan or am I going about the search process without direction? Am I following my plan faithfully or so haphazardly as to raise suspicions about conflicting motives (e.g., to want to find a job and to not want to find a job)? Is the plan operating effectively? Am I getting responses to applications? Requests for my college placement credentials? Appointments for interviews? If the answer is negative to any of the questions, consider using CONTROL-C and the corrective measures that follow from its use. There is no profit in pursuing a plan that is not producing opportunities.

If you are getting repeated turndowns, one possibility is that the competition is very great. Another is that your letter and resume do not do you justice, or your letters of reference are not helpful, or that in your interview you convey a defeated attitude. A discussion with your college placement officer is in order at such times.

If your field of teaching is especially oversupplied, another plan can involve trying for a different teaching level, such as seventh-grade instead of twelfth, or nursery school instead of kindergarten; or a different setting, such as a training program in industry or an adult program for senior citizens. Or you may want to consider job possibilities in other geographic areas.

Studies about how people land a job consistently show that friends and acquaintances are among the top sources of leads. It pays to talk up your job hunt, to let it be widely known, to encourage others to give you tips about openings, and to follow them vigorously. A personal contact usually means that you are more than just another candidate to those who make the appointment. It means that in circumstances when you are among a group of equally qualified finalists, you have an edge.

Of course you will have an edge if you student teach in a district that hires most new teachers from their pool of student teachers (Kolze, 1988). One school superintendent described the ambitious program used by his district to recruit student teachers and to give them rich experiences. He and his staff do this not only to prepare many excellent teachers, but also to choose people whose demonstrated performance shows them to be first-rate prospects. The quality of this program is further shown by two end-of-student-teaching activities:

1. The assistant superintendent for personnel conducts a seminar on "How to Get a Job." This includes tips on the job hunt, writing resumes and cover letters, preparing for interviews, and checking on qualifications for state certification.

2. The assistant superintendent holds individual sessions with student teachers to discuss ways to make them more marketable.

Most colleges and universities have active placement bureaus that serve students at little or no charge. Although you may feel too overwhelmed in the midst of a busy senior year to register with that bureau, the effort will be well worth your time. This office will send records out for you, no matter how many positions you apply for. As a result, you will not have the burden of asking professors or others to write letters of recommendation repeatedly.

Further, you will be building a file at the placement office good for lifetime use. You will need only to keep it up to date, to have it available and fresh should you apply for another position 1, 3, or 10 years from now. That is all the more reason to give your best thinking to the material you ask the placement office to include in your file.

As you draft whatever written material they suggest, bear in mind that your chances of success can be greatly increased if you are able to take the perspective of your potential employers, the recipients of your placement credentials. If you were an employer, what kind of statement would most impress you?

Determined job hunters will systematically review newspaper and other resources with advertisements. They will have ready to mail a resume and a prepared letter of interest, both concise and to the point but striking and well-written so that they will stand out from those of other candidates. They will also acquaint themselves with the resources available to help in their search. Among those resources is the nearest branch of the state employment service that offers placement services for professional people. Consider registering there, especially if you seek a professional position other than teaching, or at least other than teaching in a public school.

YOUR RESUME

To present yourself to prospective employers, you will need a personal resume. Learning to compose a strong and appropriate resume at this point will help not only in getting your first job, but later ones as well. A resume should be written so that the potential employer scanning it knows almost instantly the highlights of your background. Because your resume plays such a crucial role in your job search, we suggest you consult a recent book on resume writing or the section on that topic in a book like *Educator's Job Search* (Kimeldorf, 1993).

Writing a strong resume is a time consuming task, much like writing a term paper that would earn an A in the toughest English class. You will probably have a stronger final product if you write a draft and put it aside for a day or two before reviewing and revising it again. After preparing the next draft, ask others for comments and criticisms.

In Table 12.1 we present the kinds of information that should be included and a recommended format with explanatory footnotes. Modify both of these (content and form) to your personal taste and especially to highlight your particular strengths.

If your experience cannot be subsumed under the given headings, add others. For example, if any of your writings have been published, by all means include them under a "Publications" heading. Similarly, if you have been a volunteer (e.g., in a "Y" or 4-H Club) or have engaged in public service (e.g., a voter registration drive), include such items under an appropriate heading. The resume is, after all, a vehicle to present yourself well and give recipients a clear notion of what you are capable of doing.

Although everything relevant should be included in your resume, the document should be brief and to the point. As Chris Smith did in Table 12.2, use concise phrases to make your resume easier to read. Finally, to state the obvious, make sure your resume is visually appealing, printed on durable, professional paper, and organized in a way that does not look busy or crowded.

YOUR PORTFOLIO

Besides your resume, you may want to develop a teaching portfolio. The portfolio is a set of materials selected by you to represent your teaching practice and to give evidence of its effectiveness.

The portfolio will always include your resume. It could also include any of the following:

TABLE 12.1

RESUME

NAME
Address
Telephone: home and/or work (if available)
Fax number and/or e-mail address (if available)

POSITION DESIRED

EDUCATIONAL HISTORY

HIGH SCHOOL
School Name, Year Diploma Awarded
Address
Program[1]
Extra-Curricular Activities[2]
Recognitions, Awards, Honors[3]

COLLEGE/UNIVERSITY
Degree
Academic Program[4]
Name of College/University, Year Degree Conferred
Extra-Curricular Activities[2]
Recognitions, Awards, Honors[3]

CERTIFICATION

WORK EXPERIENCE[5]
Employer
Employer Address
Dates of Experience; Position or Job Title
Brief Description of Duties and Responsibilities

MEMBERSHIP IN PROFESSIONAL ORGANIZATIONS

RECREATIONAL ACTIVITIES[6]
REFERENCES[7]

[1]Indicate your specific course of studies (e.g., agriculture, business, college preparatory, music or art, or vocational).

[2]Cite activity and number of years involved, highlighting those that could make you a more attractive candidate.

[3]Honor societies, class offices, or awards for scholarship, leadership, athletics, or other activities.

[4]List major and minor fields, other areas of concentration, and relevant electives (e.g., major in early-childhood education, minor in children's literature, concentration in math education, and four semesters of music education).

[5]Start with the most recent employment and continue to the earliest. Include all types, because diverse experience, even unskilled, is valuable to one's personal and career development and is appreciated as such by employers. Also include unpaid community work, such as hospital volunteer.

[6]Include these only if relevant to the position you are seeking (e.g., if you apply for a position in English and you write poetry or, if you apply for one in science and astronomy is your hobby).

[7]Although the current practice is to state "References available on request," we recommend that you identify your references, giving names and addresses. This will be to your advantage because it will make it easier for potential employers to obtain further information about you.

Give four or five names, preferably persons like your cooperating teacher and supervisor, who can speak authoritatively about your promise as a teacher. Among them, also choose references who can report on the quality of your work on related jobs (e.g., camp counselor, assistant scoutmaster).

If you already requested references from these persons for your college placement office file, you do not need their permission. We suggest that you alert them to your search and give them a copy of your resume.

Following the list of names on your resume, you will want to note: "I am registered with the [Blank] College/University Placement Bureau. At your request I will have a set of credentials including (confidential) letters of recommendation forwarded directly to you. "

Note that the word confidential is enclosed in parentheses. Whether you include the word depends on your decision about waiving your right to see copies of the letters in your placement file. If you waive that right, indicate that the letters are confidential. There are obvious advantages and disadvantages to waiving that right.

TABLE 12.2

Using the Recommended Resume Format

RESUME

CHRIS SMITH
123 Main Street
Anytown, Any State 00000
(000) 767-1212 (home)
(000) 337-4830 (work)
(000) 896-7134 (fax)

POSITION DESIRED
English teacher, high school

EDUCATIONAL HISTORY

HIGH SCHOOL
Washington High School, 1992
City, Any State 00000
College preparatory program
Drama Club, 1985–1989; Basketball Team 1986–1989
English Award, Outstanding Senior

COLLEGE/UNIVERSITY
State University, 1996
City, Any State 00000
Bachelor of Arts
English major; History minor; concentration in American Studies;
three semester courses in athletic instruction and administration
Extra-Curricular Activities: Reporter and Feature Writer
University Student Newspaper; Basketball Team; Nature Club
Honors: Member, Silver Bell Honor Society

CERTIFICATION
Will complete requirements to teach English in secondary school by end of academic year

EXPERIENCE
Student Teacher: English in 9th and 10th grades,
January–May, 1996, Jeff High School; Anytown, Any State 00000
Camp Counselor: 10–12-year-old, Summers, 1994–1995,
Community Day Camp, Anytown, Any State 00000

MEMBERSHIP IN PROFESSIONAL ORGANIZATIONS
Student Member, Any State Education Association

RECREATIONAL ACTIVITIES
Hiking, basketball, reading mysteries, and writing poetry

REFERENCES
Kelly Baskin, EdD, Associate Professor of Education
State University
City, Any State 00000
Leslie Simon, PhD, Professor of English
State University
City, Any State 00000
Jan Robbins, MA
Chair of English Department
Washington High School
City, Any State 00000
Toby Bristol
Director, Community Day Camp
Anytown, Any State 00000

I am registered with the College/University Placement Bureau. At your request I will have a set of credentials, including confidential letters of recommendation, forwarded directly to you.

- A table of contents.
- A description of teaching experience as well as non-teaching but related experience, such as camp counselor, day-care center assistant, or sports team coach.
- Samples of course material that you developed for use in your student teaching.
- Records of the evaluations of your student teaching and prior school practicums.
- A brief videotape showing you teaching the whole class.
- A brief essay on your goals and ideals as a teacher.
- Any letters received from your students or their parents.
- Any other item that helps the recipient know you and appreciate your qualifications for a teaching appointment.

The materials in your portfolio should be organized in a logical sequence, with the resume placed first. Make the portfolio neat and eye-pleasing.

The effort in preparing it is very much worthwhile because the portfolio puts you at an advantage. It contains a much more complete picture of you as a teacher than you could convey orally during the interview.

Beginning the Search

Keep in mind that personnel in two school districts know you better than any others. The first is the one that you attended. They knew you even before you started your job hunt. True, they have not observed you teach. On the other hand, they have knowledge about your character and personality, and about the kind of student you were. Together, these add up to a lot of important information about a potential teacher. It is very much to your advantage if your former teachers pass the word on to hiring principals they know that you are a dependable and conscientious person, or that students will appreciate you as a teacher.

The other district is the one in which you do your student teaching. They have seen you as a teacher. They do not have to depend on letters of recommendation or your grade in student teaching to make a judgment about your teaching ability; they have much more reliable evidence—what their own eyes and ears have given them. The school district may not want to lose you. Let them know as early as possible if you plan to apply for openings they will have.

Most likely, you will want to cast your net beyond those two school districts in your job search. Identify the school districts in the geographic area(s) in which you want to live, and follow leads generated through your networking. When ready, you can contact these districts to obtain application materials and to learn about the hiring process.

Obtain application materials far enough in advance so you can prepare your materials and have ample time to review and edit them. There are at least two issues that are obvious in this regard but that bear repeating. In these materials, which include the application, your resume, and a cover letter, you want to present yourself in a favorable manner that will make your application stand out and, concomitantly, you want to avoid flaws that will make it easy for the selection committee to reject your application. Such flaws include misspelled words, applications that do not conform with the instructions, resumes that are not professional in appearance, and so forth.

One day you will receive a phone call or letter informing you that you are a candidate for a position and inviting you to come for an interview. It is a thrilling moment: The hiring official was already impressed enough to make you a candidate.

THE INTERVIEW

Preparation for the Interview

The personal interview is your opportunity to exceed whatever assessment has already been made of you—that is, to show that you are at least as good as your resume and your placement credentials indicate, and as good as your college supervisor and cooperating teacher have rated you. In short, the interview provides you with an opportunity to show that you are an excellent choice for the vacant position.

We have frequently been asked about preparation in anticipation of the interview. Our answer is deceptively simple: Prepare yourself to be yourself. A relaxed and spontaneous person is typically self-confident, prepossessing, and interesting. And a person's chances are enhanced if these qualities are apparent to the interviewer.

There is still another important area of preparation. Interviewers want to learn several things about you. Why do you want to be a teacher? Why did you choose the level (or the field) that you are in? What makes you think you can be a good teacher? What are your strengths and weaknesses? What do you expect will be your greatest problem the first year on the job? What kind of school would you like to teach in, with what kinds of children? Are there questions about the position or about the school that you would like to ask?

Questions like these are both fair and appropriate. Expect questions like these, and spend time developing and organizing your thoughts about how you might answer them. After doing this, you might want to tape record your answers or at least speak them out loud. Ask yourself, did my responses sound professional? Did I convey my needs and goals while also keeping in mind the needs and goals of the potential employer?

Another way to prepare for a job interview is by using role play. With your student–teacher colleagues, or with friends or relatives, you can simulate the real-life experience. Ask your role-playing partner to be, in turn, a male interviewer, a female one, tough, gentle, talkative, passive, directive in questioning style (e.g., "How many credits in sociology did you take?") versus open-ended (e.g., "Tell me about yourself").

Practice answering a range of questions asked over a 30-minute period. Begin with open, get-to-know-you questions ("Tell me about your training at college/university"). Then answer questions about your experience and about problems you might face in the classroom ("How would you handle [such and such] a discipline problem?"). Then have your partner look at your resume and generate tougher questions like, "What did you do in 1995; nothing is listed on your resume?" or, "What are your goals over the long run as a teacher?"

After some experience as the applicant/candidate, trade with your partner and play the role of employer/interviewer, an experience that gives you the opportunity of seeing the selection process with that functionary's perspective.

You will also find it helpful to discuss the interview and a job hunt with your college supervisor. Do that, also, with those who have been through it most recently, last year's seniors, who are now in teaching positions.

The Interview Itself

At last your interview day has come. Be on time! Dress as teachers do in that school district, preferably erring if at all on the conservative side. Be prepared to show important information about yourself and to seek information about the job that is not readily available elsewhere.

As a general rule, if you are relatively comfortable during the interview, your relaxed state will help the interviewer. Consciously or otherwise, this will tend to elevate the rating given you.

There are various ways to relax prior to the interview. One of them, a simple exercise that you can use unobtrusively while sitting in the waiting room, calls first for you to breathe in deeply through your nose, exhale slowly through your mouth. Then, after a few inhalations, and while continuing the breathing, think about relaxing the top of your head, inside your head, your eyes, your face, neck, and so on, downward until you reach your toes.

This is an exercise in relaxation worth using at other times as well. However, you may prefer simply to relax by unobtrusively rubbing your palms together and reminding yourself of the years of training you have had.

During the interview, be yourself. Answer the questions posed straightforwardly. Share your strengths. Show your enthusiasm, energy, and determination. Do not hesitate, when appropriate, to ask questions. Learn about the school's history, about the neighborhood it serves, and about plans for next year. While you convey who you are and what you seek, try at the same time to present yourself in ways that would make the interviewer or hiring committee "look good" if they choose you.

Another important factor to consider during job interviews is the kind of nonverbal messages you send. In one study, photographs of a male and a female (supposedly job seekers) were shown to 44 interviewers at an employment agency who were then asked to rate them (Amalfitano & Kalt, 1977). In some pictures the "job seekers" were looking straight ahead; in others they were looking down. Although the only difference between the photographs was where the subject was looking, those applicants making "eye contact" (by looking straight ahead) were more likely to be "hired" and were rated as being significantly more alert, assertive, dependable, confident, and responsible. They were also seen as having more incentive.

Other researchers have found that head movement and smiling are also important nonverbal communication factors during job interviews, although not as powerful as eye contact (Young & Beier, 1977). What is especially important about their experiment is that these researchers randomly chose half their subjects to display eye contact, smiling, and head movement, and half to minimize it. Those told to display it, whether it was their personal style or not, were rated as more "deserving of the job" than their counterparts in the other group.

When you return home from an interview, make notes in your journal about it and assess how it went. Use CONTROL-C to plan future interviews, especially if you left this one with any sense of disappointment.

If you have two successive experiences that left you feeling that things did not "click," it is vital that you take action. For although a first one might offhandedly be attributed to an outside factor—the personality or values of the interviewer (e.g., does not want a male teacher in a primary grade)—a succession of interviews that leave you with negative feelings raises questions about your part in those interviews.

We are not suggesting that repeated failure at obtaining a position is due to your inadequacy. People specializing in job searches, such as Kimeldorf (1993), suggest that the typical applicant experiences multiple rejections before being hired. Of course, job market conditions and your areas of specialty can be major factors. Our view is only that a critical appraisal of your interviews will help you better prepare for future interviews, now or at later stages in your career. They will also help you maintain a positive attitude.

The conclusions we draw from specialists in the field of employment counseling and from educational administrators about interviews are the following:

1. Consider in advance what is likely to occur during your job interview.

2. Work at developing self-confidence about upcoming interviews. Use any methods that help you relax and give you a positive outlook.

3. Think about the questions that are likely to be asked. Prepare responses that you can give comfortably, taking into account both your own beliefs and the realities of the position.

4. Decide what you wish to convey about yourself as a person and as a prospective teacher.

5. Plan appropriate ways to describe your experiences in college and at work. Highlight your activities with children and/or adolescents, and communicate your special academic, artistic, and athletic interests.

6. Be yourself during the interview.

7. Attend to your nonverbal communication. Look at the interviewer, engage in eye contact, and find occasions to smile.

8. Check whether you are communicating effectively by observing the nonverbal behavior of the interviewer. Is he or she attentive or distracted, responsive or bored? Modify your behavior as needed.

9. With the questions you ask, work at knowing better the interviewer and the school system he or she represents.

10. At the conclusion of each interview, review the flow of it from beginning to end, taking note of the affect as well as the content. Use CONTROL-C.

11. Soon after each interview, make a follow-up contact with the interviewer. In this letter (or telephone call if conditions require faster contact), remind the interviewer of your appointment and thank the interviewer for the time given you. Also use the opportunity to briefly refresh the interviewer, if appropriate, of your qualifications and strengths.

THE REJECTION LETTER

Unhappily, you may receive one or more letters notifying you that you were not selected for a position. If it happens, remind yourself that it is the norm to get "turn-downs." Don't put yourself down. Instead, use this as an occasion to mobilize yourself to further activity in the job hunt.

Nancy wrote about a not uncommon series of events. You, too, may find that the quest for a job is complexly interwoven into the rest of your activities. For example, you may find yourself competing with a friend or classmate for a position, or wondering if your philosophy of education will be acceptable in the school where a position is open:

1/10: Today I called the principal at the other junior high. There's a possibility that I may have a "real" job next quarter. I'm going to the junior high on Monday to observe, talk to the two English teachers, and be interviewed. I'm uptight about it. I really want this job, but I've never gone for an interview before.

1/11: Problem: One of the girls I teach with also wants the job. That's fine. But the principal told me about it first. That's not the right thing to do. Lynn was hurt, and I feel bad about it. If I get the job she'll be bitter. Worse yet, we're good friends. We've both said that we wouldn't let it mess up our friendship, but one of us will probably be hurt. Of course, maybe neither of us will get the job. That would hurt, too. She hasn't filled out her application yet. I'm going to tell her that I have an interview on Monday. I think it's important to be honest with her. She'll be full of questions that I won't want to answer. I sure wish there were two jobs open . . . !

1/15: Today I had my interview. They are very traditional at this school. I'm afraid that they're afraid. They don't want a liberal. They asked me about grammar and how valuable I thought Romeo and Juliet was for ninth-grade students. What can I say? As far as grammar goes, I said that I thought it was a tool to be used in communication. I felt better after I talked to the two English teachers. They are conservative, but not so subject-oriented that they lose their humanity. I think they are doing some good, human things.

1/26: I didn't get the teaching position. Neither did Lynn. He hired a woman with 3 years experience. I feel sort of bitter and I have no right to. No one owes me anything.

2/15: What can I say? Looking back at my journals I see a definite change in attitude and I know the cause. I wanted that job and I didn't get it. I felt bitter. Then I got depressed. What was I going to do after graduation? What about the future? Know what I decided? Nothing. But it doesn't bother me anymore. I'm going to enjoy the spring.

Nancy worked through her disappointment and readied herself to enjoy her final term at college. Soon after writing that journal entry, she returned to the business of planning the next steps in her career, and found a good position.

THE ACCEPTANCE LETTER

One day the mail carrier delivers the letter you have been waiting for. You have been selected, and after your acceptance and some necessary formalities, you will be officially appointed. Assuming that you are a June graduate, you will be fortunate to get that letter in the spring. But it may come in June or late in the summer, because some teachers resign or take leave at that late date for such reasons as another job, a spouse's transfer to another area, pregnancy, illness, or a late retirement decision.

Whenever you get your letter, enjoy! After your celebration, you can turn to the challenging task of preparing to teach your own class or classes.

GETTING CERTIFIED

Once you have successfully completed your state's academic requirements for certification as a teacher, you should submit a formal application to your state's department of education. Your college supervisor or other university personnel can advise you about the process. Typically, one official is designated as the institution's certification officer and serves as liaison with the appropriate person in the state department of education.

Candidates in two-thirds of the states and the District of Columbia must pass one or more of the tests of the National Teacher Examination (NTE) before being certified.

The Educational Testing Service (ETS), which designed the NTE more than 50 years ago, introduced a new version in 1995. There is good reason for change. For many years, teachers and educators have been asking, "How can a single paper-and-pencil test acknowledge these phases [of a person's development: subject specialty, pedagogy, and student teaching], be multiculturally sensitive, and assess the real-life classroom experiences of prospective teachers?" (Merina, 1991, p. 3).

The new tests are administered in three stages. The first, known as PRAXIS I, is taken early in a student's career to enable candidates to have plenty of time to get additional instruction, if they should fail the first time. The test at that stage is on basic skills (reading, writing, and mathematics). The tests are by appointment; candidates may use computers for the reading and math tests and to compose essays for the writing test.

The Stage 2 tests, PRAXIS II, which evaluate content area knowledge, include the three tests of the NTE Core Battery: General Knowledge, Communication Skills, and Professional Knowledge. PRAXIS II also includes subject assessment and general and content-specific teaching knowledge tests. These multiple choice and computer interactive tests are taken shortly before or after graduation.

The Stage 3 tests, PRAXIS III, include evaluations of classroom teaching and interviews with the candidates. These evaluations are made after candidates have had supervised teaching experience.

If the thought of these tests is stressful, remember that after 16 or more years of school and college, you are "test-wise." You know what information to obtain about an exam you are scheduled to take, and you know what and how to study. Prepare. Also remember that in planning your course of study your institution undoubtedly took into account the kinds of assessments required for certification.

Assistance in preparing for the PRAXIS tests is available from several sources. ETS publishes a variety of helpful materials, including *Tests at a Glance*, which offers you test descriptions, sample questions, and test-taking strategies. This booklet, and others, may be obtained, without cost, by phoning 1-800-772-9476.

A book by Levy & Levy (1994) provides useful material to help prepare you for PRAXIS II. It contains 3 full-length practice tests for the NTE Core Battery and 20 sample specialty area tests. Besides the correct answers, the authors give helpful explanations and advice on taking the tests.

GETTING TO KNOW RELEVANT EDUCATIONAL LAW AND LEGAL ISSUES

Some laws are so relevant to the teaching profession that teachers need to be acquainted with them. One is the Individuals with Disabilities Education Act (IDEA), which we introduced in chapter 7. This was first signed into law in 1975 under a different title (Education for All Handicapped Children Act). IDEA requires local and state educational authorities to ensure that children with disabilities are receiving a free and appropriate public education. They must be placed in the least restrictive environment, "tailored to the unique needs of the disabled child by means of an individualized education program (IEP). The IEP must be prepared (and reviewed at least annually) by school officials with participation by the child's parents or guardian and at least one of the teachers presently instructing the student" (*Deskbook Encyclopedia of American School Law*, 1995, p. 407). That means students with disabilities must be educated with other students (i.e., "mainstreamed" or "included") to the greatest extent possible.

Besides the Acts previously cited, related laws to supplement IDEA and court decisions since 1978 have specified additional requirements that school systems must meet. For example, the definition of "children with disabilities" has been expanded to include autism and traumatic brain injury; parents have been given the right to have an independent educational evaluation of their children at public expense.

In all probability, you will not be involved in these school matters. We introduce them to acquaint you with the fact that education law is extensive. Moreover, it is by no means limited to issues about children with disabilities and about special education.

For example, some legal issues are relevant to classroom management and discipline in general. Consider teachers who must contend with both verbal and physical forms of disruption in their classrooms. How may they respond to the following?

- Verbal disruption: The student screams and curses and refuses to leave the room, for example.
- Public or private property damage: The student smashes an electric globe of the world, for example.
- Personal threat: The student's behavior involves injury or the threat of injury to a student or a teacher, for example.

From a legal point of view, verbal control, the major form of restraint, is generally acceptable. So is forceful behavior in defense of self or others. However, forceful behavior under other than defense conditions and touch control are likely not to be acceptable in your state.

The overriding question with regard to force revolves around the definition of "reasonable force." Force may take the form of (a) verbal control such as the teacher's use of oral and body language; (b) touch control (or the laying on of hands) such as the use of a firm grip, leverage, or pain; and (c) defense, which is a teacher's forceful behavior to protect oneself or someone else from personal injury. If you do not have information about what is allowed in what circumstances, discuss this legal issue with your supervisor.

PREPARING FOR THE JOB

When you walk into your own classroom, the experience will be very different from that of walking into your student–teaching assignment. On one hand, you will now know better the feeling of being the teacher, preparing, presenting, and evaluating a lesson, witnessing conflict of one kind or another and having to deal with it, and being evaluated and evaluating yourself. On the other hand, something you never before experienced will happen. You will enter a class that is going to be your class. There will be no cooperating teacher who has the ultimate responsibility, and no university supervisor to consult. Their absence may arouse two different feelings in you-satisfaction commingled with mild anxiety.

The new experience confronting you has the inevitable and unavoidable components of all growth-potential challenges: opportunities and risks. It places new responsibility on you, as it encourages you to put to work your knowledge and your creative ideas. You will hardly have to start from scratch, because you will be given a curriculum guide to follow. If anything, you may complain that there are too many constraints. Yet, no guide replaces you—your style of conducting the class, your personality as you relate to students, and your style of leadership.

Susi wrote this letter to her college supervisor not many days after she took over a class of her own:

9/10: I've been a real live teacher for one week, and I've been bursting to write you since day one. I can't begin to tell you how appreciative I am to you for reminding me all semester that when I'm in my classroom things can be different. All summer that tempting challenge to try new things has been in the back of my mind, and now I'm having a fantastic time exploring the myriads of educative processes.

I am learning slowly the delicate blend of freedom and control that is essential to a happy productive classroom. I am disappointed that the school insists on a formalized workbook program in reading and math. It amazes me that people are still convinced children learn best circling and X-ing workbook frames. I had hoped I could have worked some total programs myself. As it is, with the constraints, I am forced to supplement as best I can with more active learning experiences.

Susi delighted in having her own classes and in experimenting with some of her ideas. Also, she was engaged very early in practicing the principle of teaching that, as we have said, is one of the truly preeminent ones. As she put it in her graceful prose, "I am learning slowly the delicate blend of freedom and control that is essential to a happy productive classroom."

Put Susi's words on two 3-by-5 cards. Keep one at home to read when you are preparing for the next day and another in your desk drawer to use as a reminder during the day. Do it whether you teach kindergarten, twelfth grade, or at the college level.

The combination of freedom and control is important not only in the teacher's work with students, but also in the teacher's professional role. For example, Susi experienced both the freedom that comes from leading her own class and also the constraints of a school-imposed workbook program. Rather than being devastated by it or wasting energy railing against it or going about moodily in silent anger, she went about her business of finding time and ways to incorporate the more active learning experiences that she valued.

Soon after you sign your teaching contract, you will be given the school district's curriculum guide or course of study for your class or courses. If you are fortunate and still have a number of weeks before the term begins, study the curriculum guide and, within the limits set by it, develop your lesson plans for at least several weeks into the term. Is that being over-prepared? We think not. If new teachers do what they can in advance, they will have more time in the fall to deal with what could not be entirely prepared for and to enjoy the "non-work" parts of their lives.

As you prepare your lessons remember the attention span of your students. We think you will do yourself a great service if you will also bear in mind the obvious fact that their enjoyment will make a world of difference in your students' attitude and attention. In all probability you can attest to the validity of the statement on the basis of your own recollections of college courses.

Considering the age, education, and cultural backgrounds of your students, ask yourself what modes of instruction and what student activities would make a topic most interesting. There are many, and you are probably familiar with some of them:

role playing; sociodrama; creative dramatics; small-group discussions; spelling bees; "Jeopardy" style quiz matches; walking field trips around the school block or bus field trips some distance from school; growing plants; using or writing computer programs; keeping animals; cooking foods; crafting models; making maps; studying national, regional, or local newspapers and various news magazines; carrying out experiments; sculpting; painting; interviewing guest "consultants" from the neighborhood; and on and on.

You can take several other steps in preparation for your new position. First, following advice in chapter 2, become acquainted with the school building and the neighborhood. Also, learn about the best form of transportation from your home to school, the parking arrangements, your schedule, the school calendar, the teacher organizations, the school secretary, the librarian, the nurse, and the custodian. You will find it helpful to get the names of other teachers at your grade level or in your department, especially other new teachers whom you will want to get to know early in the term.

THE FIRST DAY AS TEACHER

You know quite a bit about that initial day before you even walk into your classroom for the first time. You know, for instance, that both you and the students will be excited and a bit uncertain about what the year will hold. You know that right from the start you want to present yourself as the adult leader who will insist on maintaining a sane working environment. You know, too, that the students, fresh from a summer's vacation, will be bubbling over with news to share with friends.

How then will you show them that you will be a fair adult leader who will be working in their interest?

The first day of class is important. You start conveying to your students your expectations of them. You do this by word and deed and attitude. If you are positive in your reaction to a student's question, other students will take note and you will encourage questions in the classroom. If you are positive to student initiatives, you will be encouraging them, too. If you are negative to private conversations during a class-wide discussion, you will be discouraging that behavior. You will more likely discourage it constructively if you explain, like a rational authority, that such sideline discussions "disturb the rest of us and, furthermore, we want you to participate with the rest of us."

If you think much of the chatter in the classroom the first day is a carry-over of the long summer vacation, you might choose to organize small-group or whole-class discussions (or other activities) focusing on the vacation for two purposes: to get it out of their systems and to mine the very rich material of the vacation months. Whatever your method, you want to convey to the class from the outset that you require cooperation on the part of all students.

HUMOR

Humor is a great human resource. It can serve many useful purposes, including the function of anxiety reduction. Perhaps you have noticed that tension rises when a speaker and an audience first encounter each other, and that it speedily dissipates if the speaker begins with a relevant joke or humorous story. Both speaker and audience feel a great sense of relief at that point.

Humor will reduce your own anxiety and the students', and it will make class more interesting and appealing. Moreover, it pairs well with the firm class control that is a keystone to effective teaching. If you feel comfortable using humor, build it into your lesson plans. Patty felt that way, as she said in a retrospective report at the end of the term:

> 5/30: It was almost impossible to exist in my classrooms without a sense of humor. This is probably true in every classroom. Laughter is a great remedy too. Even days when I entered the classroom in not the best of moods, something would happen to lift me.

Be alert to cartoons, humorous news items, and appropriate anecdotes that you can use to leaven the serious business of learning with the lightness of humor. One of the authors tells this joke to his college class during the first minutes of the first day of class each term:

> Here we are. The vacation is over. Reminds me of a story a neighbor told me about what happened in her house on the first day of school a few years back.

> It was the first day of school and she heard her son's alarm clock ring, but after a few minutes he still wasn't down for breakfast. So what could she do? She went upstairs, knocked on the door and said, "Johnny, Johnny, get up. It's after seven! You'll be late for school."

> "Ok," he grunted. But as soon as his mother left the room he rolled over to snooze some more.

> A few minutes later the mother walked back upstairs, pounded a little harder on the door, walked in and said with more authority, "Johnny, you must get up right now. Breakfast is on the table."

> "I'll be right down," Johnny said assuredly. But as soon as his mother left the room he pulled the covers over his head.

> Five minutes later—still no Johnny and breakfast was getting cold. The mother trooped back upstairs, walked in the room and this time pulled the covers back and said, "Johnny, get up right this second. You are going to be late for school if you don't hurry."

> "I don't want to go to school," Johnny moaned.

> The mother replied: "But you have to go to school, Johnny. You are the principal."

Besides well worn jokes like this one, other forms of humor can help you establish a serious, yet comfortable, working atmosphere from the first day on. For example, many concepts you teach can be illuminated by examples that are themselves comical and that make learning a more lively and involving process for students. Further, humorous role playing can be used (e.g., Columbus coming ashore in America and finding a Wendy's; or Shakespeare completing a manuscript and not being able to find a photocopy machine or the zip code of his publisher).

The classroom situation itself gives rise to humor, although the kind that degrades or humiliates anyone should be strictly discouraged, with the reasons for that clearly spelled out: "We don't do things in our class to hurt anyone. We can learn, and enjoy ourselves, without that."

CATEGORIZING STUDENTS BY NEED

Another activity helpful to you on the first day is to begin to make mental notes about the students in your classes. To help you to direct your attention to individuals, begin to classify them in several functional categories:

1. The spontaneously active students who enjoy school and participate eagerly. They are as important as any others but need no special attention at this time, except the opportunity to be active in the learning opportunities that you arrange.

2. The interested but marginally active students. They are not high priority at this time; however, just as soon as possible you want to encourage them to participate before the first group of "activists" take over in a discussion.

3. The passive, withdrawn students who seem "out of it." Because such children and adolescents feel more like observers than participants, they will need your attention early. That could take the form of a warm hello, a friendly glance in their direction, a question to encourage involvement, or assistance in a project or assignment.

4. The turned-off students who seem, at first, to be passive but are not so at all. They are quiet because they have no wish to be in school, no interest in class activities, and are quietly angry in an environment which they experience as alien and hostile. You can begin the process of trying to identify them so that, as the weeks progress, you can try various ways of helping them.

5. The disruptive students who come to school on the first day of class with learned patterns of behavior that could soon alienate classmates and school personnel. Although their attitude is not personally directed at you, you must deal with it from the opening bell. Along with a warm offer to these students to join the class goes the unequivocal message that disruptive behavior will be dealt with instantly and at its first appearance.

6. The informal class leader, a student who has great influence over peers. The student may be in that position because of past achievement, physical presence, personal charisma, or other reasons. This influence, which can be used for good or bad purposes, should be valued by the teacher and brought into service to the class. For example, such a person can be a force in the classroom by being a model of good class citizenship.

To make positive use of the student and at the same time to make the class experience productive for him or her, you will need to see the student as very much other than a threat to your leadership. If you begin to react defensively, remind yourself that you are the responsible authority, and that your job is to use all resources to make the class a valuable experience for all your students.

7. Students with some physical or mental disabilities, some of whom were formerly assigned to special education classes but who now are mainstreamed. Such students will fit into the categories already described. The only special attention they might require is any that their disability might call for. Examples are placement in front of the room because of a visual or aural disability, additional time for writing because of a motor disability, and protection and support for special needs students because their differences may lead other students to tease them.

If you do not receive it, you should request the IEP and advice on all your special needs students from the principal, counselor, psychologist, school nurse, or other person assigned the responsibility of overseeing their welfare.

THE EVENINGS OF THE FIRST WEEKS

At the end of each day during your first weeks, it will be helpful to review and evaluate your experience, perhaps by making entries in your journal. In what ways did you meet the objectives you had set? In what ways not? What will you do about objectives you did not meet? Should they be a part of tomorrow's objectives?

Also, ask questions at another level. Review the day's events and ask, "What made me feel very good? Can I build more of that in my plans for tomorrow, later in the week, the next week? What about the events of the day that made me feel bad? Was it in my relationship with the students? Which ones? What do I feel about them? Why do I feel that way? What can I do tomorrow so that when that day ends I will not have the same bad feelings?"

Engaging in this type of thought session and making journal entries will probably seem like great chores when you come home tired and want to relax and go to bed. And there is, after all, a whole year to solve problems. However, experience has shown that if you struggle with your problems during the first days and weeks, the next ones will be easier.

Questions presented here, and others important in your personal situation, should be on your personal agenda every day after school until you feel at ease, self-confident, and in control. Then you can consider them weekly. By that time you will, in all probability, have made assessment an integral part of your professional way of life, an ingrained habit that separates the real professionals from the generally mediocre teachers.

Of course, as you think about each day's events, you might want to use CONTROL-C. Also, if the situation calls for it, make use of the good services of a colleague or a friend to obtain another perspective, especially if you have been unable to work out a problem.

THE REAL WORLD

In the world you enter when you start your first teaching job, you will not find perfection and you will be disappointed if you expect it. It is wise to set high standards, but not to expect the unachievable in an imperfect world. Yes, the real world has beauty, abundance, health, and compassion, but it also has unhappiness, ugliness, poverty, physical and mental illness, and brutality. Students in your classes will not have entirely escaped at least some of the awful experiences in the second set of conditions. They may not be free of those experiences when they come to class and, therefore, they may not be able to achieve what they might have under other circumstances.

If you take a position in a school where student performance falls below—perhaps considerably below—the national achievement norms, you must learn to live with that situation if you are to develop your effectiveness. If you set realistic goals, you will enable your students to get maximum benefit from your teaching and, in this way, help them raise their level of performance. Under these circumstances you will find satisfaction in witnessing a fifth-grade child attain the fourth-grade level in a given subject when that child entered your class performing at the 2½ grade level.

We teachers are often in a position not greatly different from physicians. They, too, serve people who for a variety of reasons are not up to national norms (in their case physically). They succeed in sustaining life in patients like that but often at a less than optimal level of health.

The medical profession has its roots in a great humanistic tradition. So does ours. Among other activities, the medical profession strives for ways to overcome health deficiencies from past neglect. The educational profession strives for ways to reverse our students' disadvantages in the past, if not in the present time. Our nation will be immeasurably stronger when it institutes major programs to prevent health deficiencies and economic and educational disadvantages. We hope that time will come soon.

Whatever challenges you face, remember that ours is a profession of worth. We serve humankind when we teach 20 or 200 students a year. We can do that best when our eyes are wide open to the realities of the world and of the school in which we work.

CRITICAL ISSUES
- In detail, what steps can I take to prepare myself for the job interviews?
- What must I do to ready myself for my first teaching position?
- What plans do I have to arrange a life that combines professional success as a teacher and a satisfying personal life?

References

Alvino, J., & Editors of *Gifted Children Monthly* (1985). *Parents' guide to raising gifted children: Recognizing and developing your child's potential.* Boston: Little, Brown.

Amalfitano, J., & Kalt, N. (1977). Effects of eye contact on the evaluation of job applicants. *Journal of Employment Counseling, 14,* 46–48.

Asch, A. (1989). Has the law made a difference? In D. K. Lipsky & A. Gartner (Eds.), *Beyond separate education: Quality education for all* (pp. 181–205). Baltimore: Brookes.

Balch, P. M., & Balch, P. E. (1987). *Cooperating teacher: A practice approach for the supervision of student teachers.* Lanham, MD: University Press of America.

Battistich, V., Solomon, D., Kim, D., Watson, M., & Schaps, E. (1995). Schools as communities, poverty levels of student populations, and students' attitudes, motives, and performance: A multilevel analysis. *American Educational Research Journal, 32*(3), 627–658.

Bloom, B. S. (Ed.). (1956). *Taxonomy of educational objectives: Cognitive domain.* New York: McKay.

Book, C. L., Duffy, G. G., Roehler, L. R., Meloth, M. S., & Vavrus, L. G. (1985). A study of the relationship between teacher explanation and student metacognitive awareness during reading instruction. *Communication Education, 34,* 29–36.

Bradley, R., & Teeter, T. (1977). Perceptions of control over social outcomes and student behavior. *Psychology In the Schools, 14,* 230–235.

Bushway, A., & Nash, W. (1977). School cheating behavior. *Review of Educational Research, 42,* 623–632.

Canter, L., & Canter, M. (1976). *Assertive discipline: A take-charge approach for today's educator.* Seal Beach, CA: Canter and Associates.

Carrasquillo, A. L., & London, C. B. G. (1993). *Parents and schools: A source book.* New York: Garland Publishing.

Center on Families, Communities, Schools, & Children's Learning. (1995). *Research and Development Report, 6,* 1–12.

Chess, S., & Thomas, A. (1987) *Know your child.* New York: Basic Books.

Chinn, P. C., Winn, J., & Walters, R. H. (1978). *Two-way talking with parents of special children.* St. Louis: C. V. Mosby.

Clandinin, D. J., & Connelly, F. M. (1992). Teacher as curriculum maker. In P. W. Jackson (Ed.), *Handbook of research on curriculum* (pp. 363–401). New York: Macmillan.

255

Clapp, B. (1989). The discipline challenge. *Instructor, 99*, 32–34.

Clark, R. W. (1988). Who decides? The basic policy issue. *Criticial issues in curriculum* (87th yearbook of the National Society for the Study of Education), 179–187.

Cogen, V. (1990). *Boosting the underachiever: How busy parents can unlock their child's potential.* New York: Plenum.

Cohen, M. W., Mirels, H. L., & Schwebel, A. I. (1972). Dimensions of elementary school student teacher concerns. *The Journal of Experimental Education, 41*, 6–11.

Coles, G. (1987). *The learning mystique: A critical look at "learning disabilities."* New York: Pantheon.

College Board (1983). *Academic preparation for college.* New York: Author.

College Board (1985). *Academic preparation in the arts.* New York: Author.

Copeland, W. D. (1978). Processes mediating the relationship between cooperating teacher behavior and student–teacher classroom performance. *Journal of Educational Psychology, 70*, 95–100.

Copeland, W. D. (1987). Classroom management and student teachers' cognitive abilities: A relationship. *American Educational Research Journal, 24*, 219–236.

Corcoran, T. B., Walker, L. J., & White, J. L. (1988). *Working in urban schools.* Washington: Institute for Educational Leadership.

Daher, J. (1994). School–parent partnerships: A guide. In C. I. Fagnano & B. Z. Werber (Eds.), *School, family and community interaction: A view from the firing lines.* Boulder, CO: Westview Press.

Danielson, L. C., & Malouf, D. B. (1995). Federal policy and educational reform: Achieving better outcomes for students with disabilities. *Special Services In the Schools, 9*(2), 11–19.

Davis, J. B. (1990). Stress among secondary school student teachers: Factors which contribute to it and ways of reducing it. *The High School Journal, 73*, 240–244.

Deskbook Encyclopedia of American School Law (1995). Rousemount, MN: Data Resource Inc.

Doyle, W. (1986). Classroom organization and management. In M. C. Whittrock (Ed.)., *Handbook of research on teaching* (3rd ed., pp. 392–431). *New York: Macmillan.*

Dweck, C. S. (1986). Motivational processes affecting learning. *American Psychologist, 41*, 1040–1048.

Eby, J. W., & Smutny, J. F. (1990). *A thoughtful overview of gifted education.* New York: Longman.

Eccles, J. S. (1987). Gender roles and women's achievement–related decisions. *Psychology of Women Quarterly, 11*, 135–172.

Eccles, J. S., Jacobs, J. E., & Harold, R. D. (1990). Gender role stereotypes, expectancy effects, and parents' socialization of gender differences. *Journal of Social Issues, 46*, 183–201.

Engerbretson, D. L. (1977, March). Diabetic in physical education, recreation, and athletics. *Journal of Physical Education and Recreation, 48*, 18–21.

Fant, H. E., Hill, C., Lee, A. E., & Landes, R. (1985). Evaluating student teachers: The national scene. *Teacher Educator, 21*(2), 2–8

Feuerstein, R. (1980). *Instrumental enrichment: An intervention program for cognitive modifiability.* Baltimore: University Park Press.

Feuerstein, R., & Hoffman, M. (1990). Mediating cognitive processes to the retarded performer—Rationale, goals, and nature of intervention. In M. Schwebel, C. M. Maher, & N. S. Fagley (Eds.), *Promoting cognitive growth over the life span* (pp. 115–136). Hillsdale, NJ: Lawrence Erlbaum Associates.

Finn, J. D., Pannozzo, G. M., & Voelkl, K. E. (1995). Disruptive and inattentive–withdrawn behavior and achievement among fourth graders. *The Elementary School Journal, 95*, 421–434.

Fracasso, M. P., & Busch-Rossnagel, N. A. (1992). Parents and children of Hispanic origin. In M. E. Procidano & C. B. Fisher (Eds.), *Contemporary families: A handbook for school professionals.* New York: Teachers College Press..

Friebus, R. J. (1977). Agents of socialization involved in student teaching. *Journal of Educational Research, 70*, 263–268.

Fromm, E. (1976). *Escape from freedom.* New York: Holt, Rinehart & Winston.

Fuller, F. F. (1969). Concerns of teachers: A developmental conceptualization. *American Education Research Journal, 6*, 207–226.

Gardner, H., & Boix–Mansilla, V. (1994). Teaching for understanding in the disciplines—and beyond. *Teacher's College Record, 96*(2), 198–218.

Garland, C., & Shippy, V. (1995). *Guiding clinical experiences: Effective supervision in teacher education.* Norwood, NJ: Ablex.

Glasser, W. (1969). *Schools without failure.* New York: Harper.

Goldenberg, I. I. (1969). Reading groups and some aspects of teacher behavior. In F. Kaplan & S. B. Sarason (Eds.), *The Psycho–educational Clinic papers and research studies* (Vol. 4, pp. 109–118). Boston: Massachusetts Department of Mental Health.

Gordon, T. (1974). *T.E.T.: Teacher effectiveness training.* New York: McKay.

Grant, L., & Rothenberg, J. (1986). The social enhancement of ability differences: Teacher–student interactions in first- and second-grade reading groups. *Elementary School Journal, 87,* 29–49.

Haller, E. P., Child, D. A., & Walberg, H. J. (1988). Can comprehension be taught? A quantitative synthesis of "metacognitive" studies. *Educational Researcher, 17,* 5–8.

Hanhan, S. F. (1988). A qualitative and qualitatively different format for the evaluation of student teachers. *Action in Teacher Education, 10*(2), 51–55.

Harty, H., & Mahan, J. M. (1977). Student teachers' expressed orientations toward education while preparing to teach minority and mainstream ethnic groups. *Journal of Experimental Education, 46,* 34–41.

Haywood, C., & Brooks, P. (1990). Theory and curriculum development in cognitive education. In M. Schwebel, C. A. Maher, & N. S. Fagley (Eds.), *Promoting cognitive growth over the life span* (pp. 165–192). Hillsdale, NJ: Lawrence Erlbaum Associates.

Hearn, J. C., & Moos, R. H. (1978). Subject matter and classroom climate: A test of Holland's environmental propositions. *American Educational Research Journal, 15,* 111–124.

Hoy, W. K., & Woolfolk, A. E. (1990). Socialization of student teachers. *American Educational Research Journal, 27,* 279–300.

Hule, B. (1989, October). Teaching students cultural mediation. *School Safety,* 20–22.

Jackson, P. W. (1990). *Life in classrooms.* New York: Teachers College Press.

Jansma, P. (1977, September). Get ready for mainstreaming! *Journal of Physical Education and Recreation, 48,* 15–16.

Johnson, D., & Johnson, R. (1989). *Cooperation and competition: Theory & research.* Edina, MN: Interaction Book Co.

Johnson, D., & Johnson, R. (1991). Teaching students to be peacemakers. Edina, MN: Interaction Book CO.

Jussim, L. (1990). Social reality and social problems: The role of expectancies. *Journal of Social Issues, 46,* 9–34.

Kainan, A. (1994). *The staffroom: Observing the professional culture of teachers.* Brookfield, VT: Ashgate Publishing.

Kavale, K. A. (1990). Effectiveness of differential programming in serving handicapped students. In M. C. Wang, M. C. Reynolds, & H. S. Walberg (Eds.), *Special education: Research and practice.* Oxford: Pergamon.

Kimeldorf, M. (1993). *Educator's job search: The ultimate guide to finding positions in education.* Washington: National Education Association.

Kolze, R. C. (1988). Finding first–rate teachers. *The American School Board Journal, 175*(7), 29, 41.

Krathwohl, D. R., Bloom, B. S., & Masia, B. (1964). *Taxonomy of educational objectives: Affective domain.* New York: McKay.

Lazarus, R., & Folkman, S. (1984). *Stress, appraisal and coping.* New York: Springer.

Levy, J., & Levy, N. (1994). *NTE: PRAXIS II.* New York: Prentice Hall.

Liben, L. S. (1995). Psychology meets geography: Exploring the gender gap on the National Geographic Bee. *Psychological Science Agenda, 8*(1), 8–9.

Lipsky, D. K., & Gartner, A. (1989). The current situation. In D. K. Lipsky & A. Gartner (Eds.), *Beyond separate education: Quality education for all.* Baltimore: Brookes.

Lloyd, M. A. (1994, November). Maintaining vitality in the classroom. *APS Observer, 7,* 11–13.

Lloyd, B., & Duveen, L. (1992). *Gender identities and education: The impact of starting school.* New York: St. Martin's Press.

Losey, K. M. (1995). Mexican American students and classroom interaction: An overview and critique. *Review of Educational Research, 65*, 283–318.

Madsen, C. H., Jr., Becker, W. C., Thomas, D. R., Kosen, L., & Plager, E. (1972). An analysis of the reinforcing function of "sit–down" commands. In M. H. Harris (Ed.), *Classroom uses of behavior modification* (pp. 169–182). Columbus, OH: Charles E. Merrill.

Madsen, C., & Madsen, C. (1974). *Teaching discipline: Behavioral principles toward a positive approach* (2nd ed.). Boston: Allyn & Bacon.

Maker, C. J. (1982). *Curriculum development for the gifted.* Aspen, MD: Aspen Publications.

Mau, W–C. (1995). Educational planning and academic achievement of middle school students: A racial and cultural comparison. *Journal of Counseling & Development, 73*, 518–526.

McGrew, K. S. (1995). National outcome data collection programs: How they can be used at the local level. *Special Services in the Schools, 9*(2), 51–62.

McLaughlin, R. D., & Ross, S. M. (1989). Student cheating in high school: A case of moral reasoning vs. "fuzzy logic." *High School Journal, 72*(3), 97–104.

Merina, A. (1991, March). National teacher exam takes a new twist. *NEA Today, 9*(7), 3.

Morris, D. O. (1992). African-American students and their families. In M. E. Procidano & C. B. Fisher (Eds.), *Contemporary families: A handbook for school professionals.* New York: Teachers College Press.

Murwin, S., & Matt, S. R. (1990, April). Fears prior to student teaching. *The Technology Teacher, 49*, 25–26.

Newman, C. J., & Licata, J. W. (1986–1987). Teacher leadership and the classroom climate as predictors of student brinkmanship. *The High School Journal, 70*(2), 102–110.

Packard, K. L., Schwebel, A. I., & Ganey, J. S. (1979). Concerns of last semester baccalaureate nursing students. *Nursing Research, 28*, 302–304.

Palanki, A., Burch, P., & Davies, D. (1995). *In our hands: A multi–site parent–teacher action research project.* Baltimore: Center on Families, Communities, Schools and Children's Learning.

Piaget, J., & Inhelder, B. (1969). *The psychology of the child.* New York: Basic Books.

Procidano, M. E., & Fisher, C. B. (1992). *Contemporary families: A handbook for school professionals.* New York: Teachers College Press.

Raths, J. (1982). Evaluation of teachers. In H. E. Mitzel (Ed.), *Encyclopedia of educational research* (5th ed., pp. 611–617). New York: Free Press.

Rosenthal, R. (1973, September). The Pygmalion effect lives. *Psychology Today, 7*, 56–63.

Rosenthal, R. (1985). From unconscious experimenter bias to teacher expectancy effects. In J. Dusek (Ed.), *Teacher expectancies* (pp. 37–65). Hillsdale, NJ: Lawrence Erlbaum Associates.

Rosenthal, R., & Jacobson, L. (1966). Teachers' expectancies: Determinants of pupils' IQ gains. *Psychological Reports, 19*, 115–118.

Rothman, H. R., & Cosden, M. (1995). The relationship between self-perception of a learning disability and achievement, self-concept and social support. *Learning Disability Quarterly, 18*, 203–212.

Salvia, J., & Ysseldyke, J. E. (1991). *Assessment in special and remedial education* (5th ed.). New York: Houghton Mifflin.

Sarason, S. B. (1982). *The culture of the school and the problem of change* (2nd ed.). Boston: Allyn & Bacon.

Sarason, S. B. (1990). *The predictable failure of educational reform.* San Franssiso: Jossey-Bass.

Schloss, P. J. (1992). Mainstreaming revisited. *The Elementary School Journal, 92*(3), 233–244.

Schwebel, A. I., & Cherlin, D. L. (1972). Physical and social distancing in teacher–pupil relationships. *Journal of Educational Psychology, 63*, 543–550.

Schwebel, M., Maher, C. A., & Fagley, N. S. (1990). *Promoting cognitive growth over the life span.* Hillsdale, NJ: Lawrence Erlbaum Associates.

Scott-Jones, D. (1994). African American families and schools: Toward mutually supportive relationships. In C. L. Fagnano & B. Z. Werber (Eds.), *School, family and community interaction: A view from the firing line.* Boulder, CO: Westview Press.

Scruggs, T. E., & Mastropieri, M. A. (1994). Successful mainstreaming in elementary science classes: A qualitative study of three reputational classes. *American Educational Research Journal, 31*(4), 785–811.

Seeman, H. (1988). *Preventing classroom discipline problems: A guide for educators.* Lancaster, PA: Technomic Publishing.

Seiler, W. J., Schuelke, L. D., & Lieb-Brilhart, B. (1984). *Communication for the contemporary classroom.* New York: Holt, Rinehart & Winston.

Seligman, M. E. P. (1991). *Learned optimism.* New York: Knopf.

Shavelson, R. J., & Stern, P. (1981). Research on teachers' pedagogical thoughts, judgments, decisions, and behavior. *Review of Educational Research, 51*(4), 455–498.

Skolnick, C. L. (1986). Why I'm sorry I don't teach English. *English Journal, 75*(7), 36–37.

Slavin, R. (1994). *Cooperative learning: Theory, research & practice.* Boston: Allyn & Bacon.

Slavin, R., & Shaw, A. (1992). *Success for all: A relentless approach to prevention and early intervention in elementary school.* Arlington, VA: Educational Research Section.

Southern, W. T., & Jones, E. D. (1991). *The academic acceleration of gifted children.* New York: Teachers College Press.

Starko, A. J., & Schack, G. D. (1989). Perceived need, teacher efficacy, and teaching strategies for the gifted and talented. *Gifted Child Quarterly, 33,* 118–122.

Stevens, R. J., & Slavin, R. E. (1995). Effects of a cooperative learning approach in reading and writing on academically handicapped and nonhandicapped students' achievement and attitudes. *The Elementary School Journal, 95*(3), 241–259.

Tanner, D., & Tanner, L. (1995). *Curriculum development: Theory into practice* (3rd ed.). Englewood Cliffs, NJ: Prentice Hall.

Tompkins, J. R., & Tompkins-McGill, P. L. (1993). *Surviving in schools in the 1990s: Strategic management of school environments.* Lanham, MD: University Press of America.

Treffinger, D. J. (1975). Teaching for self-directed learning: A priority for the gifted and talented. *The Gifted Child Quarterly, 19,* 46–59.

U.S. Bureau of the Census (1992). *Statistical abstract of the United States* (112th ed.). Washington, DC: Government Printing Office.

U.S. Department of Education (1994, Fall). *Office of Educational Research and Improvement Bulletin,* p. 3.

Walker, S. Y. (1991). *The survival guide for parents of gifted kids: How to understand, live with, and stick up for your gifted child.* Minneapolis: Free Spirit Publishing.

Wang, M. C. (1989). Adaptive instruction: An alternative for accommodating student diversity through the curriculum. In D. K. Lipsky & A. Gartner (Eds.), *Beyond separate education: Quality education for all* (pp. 99–119). Baltimore: Brookes.

Wang, M. C., & Baker, M. C. (1985–1986). Mainstreaming programs: Design features and effects. *Journal of Special Education, 19,* 503–521.

Weinstein, R. S., Madison, S. M., & Kuklinski, M. R. (1995). Raising expectations in schooling: Obstacles and opportunities for change. *American Educational Research Journal, 32*(1), 121–159.

Westling, D. L., & Koorland, M. A. (1988). *The special educator's handbook.* Boston: Allyn & Bacon.

Williams, J. L. (1995). *Differences between cooperating teachers and student teachers in their assessment of student teacher performance: Potential threats to a successful relationship.* Paper presented at the 75th annual meeting of the Association of Teacher Educators, Detroit.

Wilson, N. O. (1992). *Optimizing special education: How parents can make a difference.* New York: Plenum.

Yee, S. M-L. (1990). *Careers in the classroom: When teaching is more than a job.* New York: Teachers College Press.

Young, D., & Beier, E. (1977). The role of applicant non-verbal communication in the employment interview. *Journal of Employment Counseling, 14,* 154–165.

Ysseldyke, J. E., Thurlow, M. L., & Maher, C. A. (1995). Educational outcomes for students with disabilities. *Special Services in the Schools, 9*(2), 1–28.

Author Index

Subject Index